Faith
factor NT

Jackie Perseghetti

FaithKidz®

Equipping Kids for Life

COOK COMMUNICATIONS MINISTRIES
Colorado Springs, Colorado • Paris, Ontario
KINGSWAY COMMUNICATIONS LTD
Eastbourne, England

Faith Kidz® is an imprint of
Cook Communications Ministries, Colorado Springs, CO 80918
Cook Communications, Paris, Ontario
Kingsway Communications, Eastbourne, England

FAITH FACTOR NT
© 2007 by Jackie Perseghetti

Cover and interior design by BMB Design/Scott Johnson.

First Printing, 2007
Printed in the United States of Amerirca

1 2 3 4 5 6 7 8 9 10

The Web addresses (URLs) recommended throughout this book are solely offered as a resource to the reader. The citation of these Web sites does not in any way imply an endorsement on the part of the author or the publisher, nor does the author or publisher vouch for their content for the life of this book.

ISBN 9780781444590

For You, Lord

Contents

Acknowledgments

This single page out of the entire book is one I find most difficult to write for it cannot possibly contain the gratitude and thanks I owe to so many. You are all dear to me and deeply appreciated whether your name makes it to the confines of this page or not. You know who you are.

To the editors at Cook Communications Ministries, both past and present, thank you for believing in this project and helping to make it the best it can be. Special thanks to Jeannie Harmon for her wonderful work on the original *Caution: Dangerous Devotions*. Jeannie, who could have imagined that it would one day be translated into Portuguese! Also, special thanks to Mary McNeil whose vision helped make *Faith Factor* a reality. Mary, your passion, patience, hard work, and friendship won't be forgotten. Although every author cringes at editorial "red ink," I'd like to express my appreciation to Jennifer Lonas for her insightful comments and great suggestions. Lastly, a special thank you to Diane Gardner, a very patient supervising editor who worked with me to meet hefty deadlines. Diane, not only are you an awesome editor, but you are gracious as well. Thank you from the bottom of my heart.

To my friends and faithful prayer warriors who stood in the gap: Janis Wright, Marla Hartzell, Jeannie Roddy, Felice Gerwitz, Rebekah Fairchild, Darlene Jones, Cinda Hammond, Pam Bidwell, women in my BSF small group, and our Home Growth group—you will never know how much your prayers and encouragement have meant!

To my dear family, thank you for your encouragement and love:

Doug, not only are you the best husband in the world, but also my dearest friend. Thank you for all those evening walks to clear my head and wonderful foot rubs to revive my weary body! I love you and couldn't have done this without your support.

Ben, your interest and asking how the book was coming along was a source of encouragement to keep me chugging away when my fingers and brain were protesting. Thanks for helping to keep me focused. Of all the sons in the world, if I could choose just one … I'd choose you—all the time.

Bethany, not only were you helpful while home on breaks, but your encouragement continued across the miles. Thank you for all your help, suggestions, enthusiasm, and prayers. More than a daughter, you are a friend.

Dad and Mom, thank you for your faithful support through your many prayers and reminders to "take care of myself."

Finally, no words contrived by man could describe the debt of gratitude and love I owe to the One who has truly made all this possible. It is to Him alone I dedicate this book. I love you, Lord. May this book be used for Your glory and to point many towards You.

Your nearness is my good... (Psalm 73:28)

Introduction

Why Faith Factor?

A popular saying I once heard states, "Faith is walking to the edge of all the light that you have—and taking one more step." And that's exactly what God is calling you and me to do today. But it's not a blind leap of faith. God has given us all the light we need, and that light is found in His Word, the Bible. All we need to do is read, understand, and apply God's Word to our lives. That's the purpose of this book.

Some of you who are familiar with my former titles, *Caution: Dangerous Devotions* and *Caution: More Dangerous Devotions,* may be wondering, *Are Faith Factor, OT* and *Faith Factor, NT* different? To that I would say yes! While maintaining the same quality of retelling the biblical text, these two books have been updated and expanded to include more background information, cultural explanations, more sidebars, and, in the case of the companion to this book, the entire Old Testament (rather than just through the book of Psalms). You will also find comparative timeline tidbits that place biblical and secular history side by side, as well as online access to more devotional lessons we simply had no room to squeeze into the books. You can find those lessons online at *www.cookministries.com/FaithFactor* as well as a convenient topical index for both devotionals.

It's my prayer that *Faith Factor, OT* and *Faith Factor, NT* will ignite your heart and grow your faith—and may all the glory for that go to God alone.

Walk on!

> *The apostles said to the Lord, "Increase our faith!"*
> *He replied, "If you have faith as small as a mustard seed ..."*
> *(Luke 17:5–6)*

> *It's impossible to please God apart from faith. And why? Because anyone who wants to approach God must believe both that he exists and that he cares enough to respond to those who seek him.*
> *(Heb. 11:6 MSG)*

Matthew

Each book of the Bible was written with a special purpose in mind. Matthew focuses on the Jewish people in Jesus' day who were familiar with the Old Testament Scriptures and prophecies about a King who would someday come. Over and over Matthew shows how Jesus fulfilled the Old Testament prophecies. In fact, Matthew quotes the Old Testament frequently, and the words "so it was fulfilled" appear multiple times. I don't know what you think, but this tells me that Jesus was no ordinary person!

> *Prophecy is a message telling people what God will do in the future. The prophecies about Jesus were made more than four hundred years before He came!*

The first seventeen verses of Matthew may seem quite boring, but they actually show how Jesus came from a royal line. God had it all planned down through the ages to the very last detail. As you read through Matthew, notice how Jesus the King fulfilled prophecy, received God's stamp of approval, proved His strength of character, chose people to follow Him, set new standards with old rules, handed out royal invitations, and encourages us to examine and trust Him. Enjoy your walk through this book.

Said and Done
Taken from Matthew 1—2

Foundation

Just as you prepare yourself each morning before starting your day, so you need to prepare your heart before reading God's Word. The best way to do that is to spend a few minutes in prayer. It doesn't need to be a long prayer—a simple sentence expressing your heartfelt desire to God will do. Each time you read God's Word, ask Him to open your eyes and to teach you.

Focus

Have you ever been amazed when something you were told was going to happen really did happen? How about being told three hundred different things about a person that were going to happen and finding out that each of them came true exactly as foretold? Sound impossible? Not in this case!

Joseph wondered if his situation was a bad dream. *I love Mary. Mary loves me. And we're engaged to be married.* He rehearsed the words over and over in his mind. He knew that neither of them had done anything to be ashamed of. Yet Mary told him she was pregnant. It just didn't make sense! It didn't, at least, until God sent an angel to explain it to Joseph.

"Joseph, don't be alarmed." The angel reassured him. "Mary's baby is from the Holy Spirit and is one of a kind. You are to call Him Jesus, for through Him people will be saved from their sins."

The news stunned Joseph, and his mind raced to the words spoken hundreds of years earlier by the prophet Isaiah: "The virgin shall bear a Son, and they shall call His name Immanuel, meaning 'God with us.'"

"Can it be?" Joseph breathed with wild wonderment.

Many months later when Mary was close to giving birth, the Roman government called for a census of the entire empire (Luke 2:1–3). Since Joseph was a descendant of David, he and Mary were required to make the journey to Bethlehem, Joseph's ancestral home. In Joseph and Mary's eyes the timing couldn't have been worse, but in God's eyes the timing was perfect. A prophecy in Micah 5:2 said that the Savior would be born in Bethlehem, and that's exactly what happened.

That night, angels joyfully announced the Savior's birth to shepherds, telling them to look for specific signs that would prove the truth of their words. When the shepherds came to the stable, they fell to their knees in worship. Each and every sign the angels had given them about the baby had been fulfilled! (See Luke 2:8–20.)

Wise men from the East (advisers to kings) noticed an unusual star in the sky as well. Some who were familiar with the Scriptures knew what it meant and began their journey to find the newborn Savior. Upon arriving in Jerusalem several months later, they asked where they might find this newborn King. Hearing about their visit, King Herod became troubled and questioned the wise men about what they had seen. He lied, saying he too wanted to worship the baby and asked the wise men to report back once they had found the One whom they were seeking. The wise men never returned, for

It has been said that the odds of someone fulfilling only eight of the prophecies Jesus fulfilled are the same as blindfolding and asking someone to pick out, on the first try, one specially marked coin from a two-foot-deep pile of coins covering the entire state of Texas!

Herod the Great descended from Esau. To learn why this is so significant, read more about it in **Faith Factor OT** *or straight from the Bible in Genesis 27.*

God had warned them in a dream not to go back. This annoyed King Herod, who was jealous and fearful of the baby King the wise men had come to worship.

"All baby boys two years of age and younger are to be killed!" the king angrily decreed.

And so it was done. The great weeping and wailing that rang out in the land fulfilled an Old Testament prophecy from Jeremiah. (See Jeremiah 31:15.) And when Joseph took his family and fled to the neighboring land of Egypt after being warned in a dream, you guessed it, another prophecy was fulfilled—"Out of Egypt I called my son" (Hosea 11:1).

After Herod died, an angel again appeared to Joseph in a dream, telling him to return home—not to Bethlehem but to Nazareth. *Nazareth?* Joseph questioned in his heart, knowing the town housed the Roman garrison for all of northern Galilee. Jews who lived in Nazareth were often looked down upon as "compromisers" who interacted with their Roman enemies. Being called a Nazarene was not a nice thing! Was this the best place for a king to be raised? Obeying the Lord, however, Joseph settled his family in Nazareth—fulfilling more prophecy: "He will be called a Nazarene" (Hosea 11:1). God gave us more than three hundred prophecies in the Old Testament about a Savior who would come to save people from their sins, and each and every one was accomplished through the life of Jesus.

Clearly, Jesus was no ordinary person!

Footwork

Anything worth having usually requires a little effort. In this section you'll need to use a little energy. But don't panic! Your Bible is all you'll need. Just look up the Scripture verses and answer the questions that follow. Doing this will build your spiritual muscles and make you strong in the Lord. Really!

Now turn to Luke 22:67–71 in your Bible. This is one of Jesus' predictions about Himself as He stood before the religious rulers just before dying on the cross. What did He say? Do you believe it?

systems used in history, dates listed are

Fruit

If you could sit down with Jesus and ask Him questions concerning things you might not understand about Him, what would you ask? Write your questions on an index card and tape it to the back inside cover of this devotional. When you've finished your journey through the New Testament, reread your questions and discover how many you're able to answer!

Would You Believe It?
Taken from Matthew 3

Foundation

Take a few minutes to prepare your heart for today's lesson. Ask God to speak to you from His Word.

FOCUS

Have you ever seen or heard things that caught you totally by surprise?

"What's this all about?" one person probably whispered to another upon joining the outskirts of the crowd near the Jordan River.

"I'm not quite sure, but let's move in closer so we can hear what this strangely dressed man is saying!"

> **John the Baptist was the first true prophet sent by God to the Jewish people in four hundred years. His attire was similar to the prophet Elijah's from the Old Testament. (Check out 2 Kings 1:8!)**

"Repent! God's kingdom is at hand!" the raspy voice cried out. It belonged to a man named John, who would later be known as John the Baptist. Everything about John was unusual. Instead of living in a tidy little house on the edge of town, John lived in the wilderness. Instead of eating normal food, he ate locusts and wild honey. As for John's clothes of camel's hair and leather belt—well, they were practical, sturdy, and as plain looking as the wilderness around him.

John the Baptist claimed to be God's messenger,

Old Testament (OT) closes and a 400-year

yet he didn't live, talk, or look like a religious leader of his day. He was quite a different type of person!

People came from all over, gathering by the river to hear John's message: "Repent, for the kingdom of God is at hand!" Those words were as strange as John's appearance. *Repent* means to turn around, to stop doing or being one thing and to start doing or being another. John was telling the people to stop living a life that ignored the covenant, or agreement, God had made with them—a covenant that stated how they could live in a relationship with Him and one day worship before His throne in heaven.

Some of the listeners who gathered at the water's edge no doubt wondered if John the Baptist knew whom he was talking to. They were Jews—the very descendants of Abraham! Surely that qualified them to be included in heaven!

Others, though, listened to John's words, repented, and were baptized in the river as a symbol that their hearts had been made right with God.

More and more people came to hear what John had to say. Many recognized him as a prophet and were baptized. But others scoffed. Among the scoffers were some of the religious leaders.

"Why do we need to be baptized? We are already in good standing with God," they arrogantly argued.

From out of nowhere a man approached John as he was busy baptizing people in the river. Looking up, John recognized Jesus—the very One he had been proclaiming! John couldn't believe it when Jesus stepped into the water.

> *Locusts were insects eaten by poor people. They provided a nutritious source of protein.*
>
> ---
>
> *In the Old Testament, God challenged the Israelites to love and trust Him wholeheartedly as they stood before the Jordan River. (See Joshua 1—2.) Many generations later and on the banks of this very same river, John the Baptist challenged people with that message once again.*

"Lord," John said, "I need to be baptized by You, yet You come to me?"

Jesus looked into John's eyes and spoke reassuringly. "It must be this way for now to fulfill God's righteous requirements."

By allowing Himself to be baptized, Jesus identified with all sinners and gave His approval to John's message: "The kingdom of God is at hand … and He is now standing in your midst!"

As Jesus came up out of the water, the heavens split open and the Spirit of God came down in the form of a dove and landed on Him. In that instant, God's voice spoke from heaven: "This is My beloved Son, who pleases Me." God Himself spoke for the entire world to hear, and when He did, He set His seal of approval on His Son, Jesus.

Footwork

Read Matthew 3:1–17. (Go on, look it up!) Notice what verse 17 says. How did God feel about Jesus?

Fruit

People have many different opinions about Jesus. Some will scoff like the religious leaders; others will understand and believe in Him. Don't be thrown off track by scoffers. God gave His divine approval to Jesus as His Son and to no one else. No opinion could be greater or matter more than God's.

God does not send another prophet until

What If I Just . . . ?
Taken from Matthew 4:1–11

Foundation

Take a few minutes to prepare your heart for the lesson. Ask God to speak to you through His Word today.

Focus

Are you ever tempted to take shortcuts to get what you want (or have been promised) sooner?

At the baptism of Jesus, God spoke from a cloud, announcing to everyone that Jesus was His beloved Son. Soon after that Jesus went into the wilderness to spend time alone with God.

The wilderness wasn't beautiful; it was a barren wasteland. Between yellow sand and crumbling limestone, twisted ridges ran in all directions. Mounds of dust and jagged rocks created hills.

After forty days and forty nights of fasting and praying, Jesus felt worn out, weary, and hungry, setting the stage for a series of tests. Jesus was at His weakest, and Satan, the great Tempter, would attack at his strongest.

"Jesus," Satan said, "You look hungry. Obviously, God's not taking care of Your needs. If You're really God's Son, why don't You turn these rocks into bread?" How Jesus hungered! He could take Satan's challenge, prove He was God's Son, and satisfy His hunger all at once.

the New Testament (NT) time period.

"God has said," Jesus answered, "we live by His words, not just by the bread we eat." Jesus knew it was most important to have His needs met by God. He would not use His powers to selfishly meet His own needs.

Next, Satan took Jesus to the temple in Jerusalem, and they stood on its highest point. "You say You're the Son of God. Throw Yourself down from here, and when people see that You're unharmed, they will follow You!" Then he added, "Isn't it written that angels will hold You up in their hands and protect You from harm?"

Jesus knew He must call people to Himself in order to teach them about God, but He would not shock them into it. He wouldn't force God's hand to protect Him by doing something willful and foolish. Jesus answered, "God has said, 'Never test Me or dare Me to prove Myself.'"

Satan tried one last attack to get Jesus to compromise. Perhaps Jesus could be tempted to take a shortcut, to get the glory without suffering on the cross. Showing Jesus the people and kingdoms of the world, Satan whispered, "Bow down and worship me, and you can have it all—without cost!"

Jesus would not give in to temptation. He flatly stated, "God has said, 'You must worship and serve Me alone.'" Jesus would take no shortcuts. He had a mission and He would complete it, no matter what the personal cost.

When Jesus refused to give in to these temptations, Satan had no choice but to leave. When he did, angels ministered to Jesus. Perhaps they brought Him food; certainly, they worshipped Him. Jesus had been pushed to the deepest possible levels of testing, yet He didn't go through these tests for His *own* good. He endured them for *our* good to prove His character to us.

Did you know Satan tempted Adam and Eve the same way he tempted Jesus? He appealed to their hunger, to personal gain, and to power and glory (Genesis 3:1–5). What Adam and Eve failed to do in the perfect setting of the garden of Eden, Jesus was able to do in a wasteland.

Satan tempts you and me in the same areas today: physical needs and wants, possessions and power, and prideful independence from God.

Footwork

In your Bible, turn to Matthew 4:11. What two specific things happened after Jesus

endured the tests? Now look at verses 4, 7, and 10. What phrase did Jesus use every

time He responded to Satan's attacks?

Fruit

How would you have reacted to the temptations Jesus
experienced? How should you react to temptations in your life?
Is there a big difference between the two? Tell Jesus about it
right now.

Them?!

Taken from Matthew 4

--- *Foundation* ---

Don't skip this part! Stop and pray, asking the Lord to teach your heart. Checking in with God and giving Him permission to teach you is really important if you want to grow in your walk with the Lord and keep your faith exciting.

Focus

When people choose teams, does it seem like they always pick the most popular or talented first? That's not how Jesus chooses.

The flies were buzzing about while fish were being cleaned and nets were being hauled in. It seemed like any ordinary morning—that is, until something special happened.

Along the shoreline fishermen were cleaning and repairing their nets. Many spoke loudly and coarsely with one another, and some were just plain rude. Rough speech and crude treatment were common behaviors for these men. Hidden in this group, like the pieces of a puzzle, were two brothers named Peter and Andrew. Busy with the task at hand, they hardly noticed Jesus approaching. "Follow Me. You will be fishers of men," Jesus directly stated to them.

> **Abandoning a family business in Jesus' day often resulted in being dishonored in that community.**

The brothers looked at each other, speechless. Had they heard correctly? Was this Rabbi (Jewish teacher) asking *them* to follow *Him*? But they were synagogue dropouts! Yes, they had the required religious training all Jewish boys went through, but they hadn't been at the top of their class. Only after finishing formal synagogue training would a cream-of-the-crop student search out a rabbi and ask to be his disciple. The student would then closely follow the rabbi, practically living and breathing every moment of the day with him. He'd watch his teacher carefully, taking note of how he lived and what he said and didn't say—all with the goal of becoming exactly like his rabbi. That was called *discipleship*.

Since Peter and Andrew hadn't been shining synagogue students during the required religious training, they simply followed in their father's trade of fishing. But now a rabbi had approached *them!* And much to everyone's surprise, the two dropped their half-mended nets into the sand and followed Jesus.

Continuing on, Jesus saw two other fishermen sitting in a boat, mending nets with their father. They were James and John, the sons of Zebedee. Because of their hotheaded tempers, Jesus would later nickname them "Sons of Thunder." Their tempers, however, didn't seem to bother Jesus.

One by one Jesus chose His team. They weren't the most educated, nor were they necessarily the most talented or best liked. In fact, Jesus even chose a tax collector named Matthew as His disciple—definitely not a wise move if He wanted to impress others. Loudmouth Peter often said one thing and did another. Thomas had his own battles with unbelief, and Judas actually turned traitor! What was

> *Tax collectors were considered traitors in the eyes of their own people. They worked for the Roman government and often charged higher taxes than required so they could secretly pocket money for themselves.*

> *Jesus' choosing His disciples (instead of their approaching Him, a rabbi) was His way of telling them, "I believe in you, and I will give you what it takes to walk in My ways. Come, follow Me."*

Jesus thinking? Didn't He know who and what He was getting?

Jesus knew everything about these men, and yet He chose them anyway. Picking only the most promising disciples wasn't something Jesus needed to do. He was more interested in the character of these men than in what they could do for Him. He accepted them as they were, and He would help them become all they needed to be.

Footwork

Look up Mark 3:14 in your Bible. Jesus chose His disciples for two reasons. One was to send them out to share the good news of salvation with others. What was the other reason?

Fruit

Do you take time to "be with" Jesus? Find a quiet place and time where you can be alone for a few minutes. For the next seven days make this your meeting time and place with God. You might want to talk to Him about your troubles, spend time doing your devotions—or both! Whatever you decide to do, do it consistently for the next seven days. Make the time to simply be with Him.

for "heretical" teachings that supposed

Ouch!
Taken from Matthew 5—6

— Foundation

Be sure to pray before you read today's lesson, asking God to speak to your heart and help you understand His Word.

Focus

Have you ever noticed how people sometimes pretend to be something they're not or do things because they hope to be noticed? It wasn't much different in Jesus' day.

Jesus began traveling throughout Galilee, teaching in the synagogues and healing people. As news about Him spread, more people began following Him. Seeing the crowd one day, Jesus led His disciples up a hillside and sat down. The disciples knew this was serious. Often a teacher would teach standing or even pacing, but whenever he sat down it meant he was going to share something very important and close to his heart.

Jesus looked into the face of each of His disciples. "The pure in spirit—those who know they need God—are greatly blessed because they will be welcomed into God's kingdom. The pure in heart—those who are honest with themselves and God—are greatly blessed because they will see the face of God." Jesus continued on, naming character qualities of those

> *When a Jewish man prayed, he stood with arms stretched out, palms upward, and head bent down. It was a hard thing not to notice.*

insulted the Greek gods and corrupt-

who would truly follow Him. As He finished speaking to His disciples, Jesus noticed the crowds making their way up the hill, so He addressed them as well. He had much to say to such a group.

> The phrase "I tell you the truth" indicates a solemn statement that hearers should pay attention to. This phrase and similar wording occurs more than thirty-one times in the book of Matthew.
>
> Five times in this chapter alone, Jesus addressed the Pharisees' incorrect thinking by using the phrase, "You have heard it said ... but I tell you."

Jesus looked into the faces of the people. Some came with sincerity, others with desires of gaining personal favors or healing. Some were curious; others were proud religious leaders wanting to make an appearance. Whatever their reasons for coming, Jesus knew they had an underlying problem. None of them could live up to God's standards of righteousness. In fact, the religious leaders took it upon themselves to lower the standard of God's laws by adding their own easily kept rules. By obeying these added-on rules, they could look on the outside like they were keeping the Law, while on the inside their hearts were far from God.

Jesus addressed this problem: "You have heard from the Law of Moses that you shall not commit murder. However, if you look down on someone with contempt and call him a fool, you have committed murder in your heart, for you have set out to destroy that person." Jesus challenged the people to look at their inner heart attitudes instead of just keeping rules so they would look good on the outside. He gave new meaning to their familiar laws, which made some people quite uncomfortable. "Don't do things hoping to be noticed by others," Jesus added, "for if you do, you will have no reward in heaven. When you give, give secretly. When you pray, pray to God. Don't pray using big words and long sentences to impress others, and don't stand in places just to be noticed."

This was an issue for many people. Three times a day they were called to stop and pray no matter what they were doing or where they were going. As the hour of prayer drew near, some of them would purposefully walk down busy market streets, hoping that large crowds would notice how religious they were when they stood praying.

Giving money to the poor, praying, and fasting (going without food for the day to show God how serious they were) were all considered things a righteous person did. As a result some people did them only to be seen by others. Some who fasted messed up their hair and clothes and even painted their faces white to make themselves look pale! Those who gave money waited for a crowd to walk by, and then noisily and proudly tossed their money into the bin.

Jesus wasn't fooled by people pretending to be one thing on the outside while being something else on the inside. God's kingdom would not consist of those who were religious but of those who were right with God.

Footwork

Turn in your Bible to Matthew 5:20. What did Jesus say about a person's attempts at trying to be righteous? Where must your righteousness come from?

Fruit

In your life you'll be tempted to do things only for show. Even though some of these things may be good, it's your heart attitude that matters to God. Commit today to living truthfully, and avoid possibly being labeled a hypocrite by others!

ristotle is born, Alexander the

Believe It!
Taken from Matthew 11

--- *Foundation* -----------------------------

Take a few minutes to prepare your heart by asking God to help you understand what He wants you to learn.

Focus

Have you ever hoped for something and then become disappointed when things didn't turn out the way you had expected?

John the Baptist paced back and forth in the dark, damp, and almost pitlike tiny cell. He had been thrown there for speaking boldly to Herod Antipas, the governor of Galilee. After hearing John's challenge to repent of his wrong and evil deeds, angry Herod wanted to do away with John but knew he couldn't kill him outright. Since John was considered a prophet, killing him would cause an uprising. Instead, Herod had John thrown into the dungeon of an old fortress, planning to quietly execute him later.

It had been one year since that time—a slow and painful year during which John became a prisoner even to his own thoughts. John's only connection to the outside world was an occasional visit from those who had once followed him. But now they were following Jesus. When they came to see John, they brought short reports to encourage him. John listened, but the more he heard, the more confused he became. Pretty soon his confusion grew into nagging doubts.

I've based my entire life on the fact that Jesus is the One who is promised to come as Messiah. John rehearsed his thoughts over and over in his mind. Of that he was sure. After baptizing Jesus, John had seen the sky split open and the dove descend and rest on Jesus. He had heard God's voice from heaven proclaiming to all that Jesus was His Son. *But isn't the Messiah supposed to set up a new kingdom on earth? Isn't He going to judge people and put an end to evil?* John wondered.

In the darkness of his cell, John the Baptist quietly questioned. From all the reports he had heard, Jesus was not squashing the enemies of the Jewish people. He had done nothing to stop or overthrow the evil Roman Empire. Things were not going as John had expected. Could he have been mistaken about Jesus?

Needing an answer, John sent some of his followers to ask Jesus the question that burned in his heart: "Are you the Messiah, the One God promised to send, or should we look for someone else?"

When Jesus heard this question, He gave a simple and direct answer to comfort John. "Tell John everything you have seen and heard: The blind can see, the crippled can walk, the lepers have been cleansed, the deaf can hear, the dead are alive, and the poor have heard the good news."

These were all prophecies of what "the One who was to come" would do. These were all things Jesus was doing. Then Jesus added, "Blessed is the person who doesn't lose heart when things aren't going as expected and doesn't lose faith because of Me." Jesus knew what He had come to do, and He knew God's perfect plan and timing. Although John had expected everything to happen all at once, that wasn't God's plan.

> *"The One who is to come" is an Old Testament title for the promised Messiah that was based on Psalms 40:7 and 118:26.*

> *When answering John's question, Jesus specifically quoted a prophecy in Isaiah 35:5–6 about the coming Messiah — an exact description of Jesus' life and ministry!*

> *Check out Mark 6:14–29 for "the rest of the story" about Herod Antipas and John the Baptist!*

Instead, Jesus encouraged John to examine Jesus' very life and actions to see how He fulfilled the Old Testament prophecies.

John needed to see the evidence, be patient, trust God, and not doubt. Even though things weren't going as John had expected, God was in control and knew the full picture. These were the encouraging and understanding words that Jesus sent back to John—words that reached him just before Herod Antipas had him beheaded.

Footwork

Take a look at Matthew 11:6 in your Bible. What do you think Jesus meant by this statement? The Greek word in this verse for "fall away" literally means "to stumble." Do you sometimes "stumble" over issues involving Jesus and His claims?

Fruit

Take a few minutes right now and tell Jesus about an unmet expectation that burns deep within your heart. (Don't worry about offending Him. He already knows what you're struggling with!) Ask Him to help you walk through the tough times when you don't fully understand Him or what He's doing.

The next time life doesn't go the way you had hoped, will you remember Jesus' character and choose to trust Him, or will you doubt and lose all hope? The choice is yours.

Uh-Oh

Taken from Matthew 13

— Foundation

Spend some time preparing yourself for today's lesson. Ask God to search your heart and show you what He wants you to learn. He may ask you to change—be ready to follow His lead.

Focus

When you take a look around your church, what do you see? Christians, right? Not necessarily. An old saying goes, "Just 'cause you're in the cookie jar don't necessarily mean you're a cookie!"

Large numbers of people flooded the beach, desiring to hear what Jesus had to say. Seeing the growing crowd, Jesus climbed into a nearby boat—not to get away but enable everyone to hear Him since sound carried best over water. The crowd stood quietly on the shoreline, waiting for Him to speak.

"One day a farmer went to sow seed in his field," Jesus began, "and as he scattered the seed, some fell onto the path where birds swooped down and ate it. Other seed landed in rocky areas where the soil was shallow, causing plants to shoot up quickly and then die in the hot sun. Still other seed landed among weeds, which later grew tall and killed the plants. But the seed that fell on good soil yielded a great crop."

The crowd listened intently. Being farmers, they understood what Jesus was talking about. Paths between the gardens were hard and packed down. Any seed accidentally spilled there became an easy meal for birds.

They also knew that rocks might be buried just two or three inches below beautiful soil, and they could block a plant's roots from going down deep. If not rocks, then weeds or thorns threatened to steal nourishment from the plants and choke them out. Yes, the crowd well understood Jesus' story.

Jesus continued. He explained how the types of soil represented different heart attitudes people have toward God and His Word. Some people have hardened hearts (like the hardened path) and won't allow God's Word to sink into their lives. Others might have an interest in God, but when difficult times come (like the sun scorching the plants), they fall away and no longer follow Jesus or live for God. Another attitude is revealed in people who start out living for God but gradually allow the distractions and worries of life to crowd out their love for Him. The last type of soil is the good kind. It represents people who desire to live for God and listen to His Word. These people have the joy of experiencing God doing wonderful things in and through their lives.

Jesus didn't stop there. Looking around at the crowd, He told another parable comparing God's kingdom (made up of those who really believe and know Him) to a huge wheat field.

> *The tare plant was a weed called darnel and was very similar to a poisonous ryegrass.*
>
> *Knowing how upper-class society often ignored farmers and herders, Jesus chose these parables about farming to communicate the importance of these people in His eyes.*

"A farmer planted wheat in his field. Late at night an enemy came and secretly planted tares," Jesus began. The people listened eagerly. Tares were poisonous weeds that looked just like wheat plants. By the time the grains developed enough to tell the plants apart, the roots of the tares would be so entangled with the roots of the wheat plants, the farmer would have to wait until harvest to separate them. The wheat would be kept, and the tares would be destroyed.

Jesus told this parable to describe people who were real followers of His and those who were pretend followers. Although the two might grow together (just like the wheat and the tares), they wouldn't be together forever. One day they would be separated.

Jesus spoke these parables as a serious warning to all people so they would examine their lives. What was their heart attitude toward God? Were they wheat or were they tares?

Not all who claim to be Christians really are.

Footwork

Find Matthew 13:49 in your Bible and read it. What did Jesus say is going to happen? When? (Don't guess. Look it up!)

Fruit

Take a moment and think about Jesus' description of the soils. What type of soil describes your heart today? If it's a little weedy or has a layer of rock underneath, tell God about it right now. Go ahead. Give Him permission to change your heart. Tell Him where you stand, and ask Him to take you where you need to be.

ranslated into Greek for the Greek

I'm Not Wearing That!
Taken from Matthew 22

— Foundation —

Stop and pray, asking God to speak to your heart.

Focus

Do you know people who brag about being invited to parties, hinting they're better than you and deserve to be invited because they're cool (and you're not)?

Preparations had been made. Invitations had been sent out. Guests would arrive any minute. Although everything was ready, one slight problem emerged. The invited guests decided not to attend the great royal banquet. Some were busy with other things, while others simply ignored the invitation.

Seeing this response, the king hosting the party sent his messengers into the streets to invite anyone they could find, both good and bad, to the banquet. As these people accepted the invitation, the messengers handed them a clean robelike garment to wear to the party—a gift from the king.

> By providing robes for his guests to wear at the banquet, the king made sure all his guests were on the same level. No one could strut around claiming to be better than the others!

Guests soon arrived and began enjoying the wonderful food. The party was beyond what they had imagined!

When the king came out to greet his guests, he noticed everyone wearing the wedding clothes he had provided—everyone except one man. That man had insulted the king by entering the banquet in filthy clothes.

king over Egypt. The Septuagint ("seventy"

"Friend," the king said, "how is it that you came in here not wearing the clothes I provided for you?"

The man was speechless. He had been foolish to think it wouldn't matter. He looked at his own clothes. They looked like filthy rags compared to the glistening white robes the other guests were wearing. He could have been properly dressed if only he would have put on the robe he'd been given.

Instead, the man was thrown out of the banquet into the dark night. Not only that, he was tied hand and foot so he couldn't sneak back in! Having been an invited guest, the man was now rejected because he didn't make the right preparations for coming. He didn't wear what the king had provided.

When banquets were held, two invitations were expected. The first invited the guests to attend. The second announced that the time for the banquet had arrived and their presence was requested. The king in this story invited his guests a total of three times!

Jesus told this parable one day while in the temple courts in Jerusalem. Through it He targeted heart attitudes of people who thought they were better than others and deserved to go to heaven based on how they lived their lives. The king represents God, who invites and desires all people to enter His heavenly kingdom (the royal banquet). The invited guests represent you and me. God's only requirement is that we come dressed in the clean garments (the righteousness) He provides. Being clothed in anything else—no matter how acceptable we think it is—will only result in our being rejected and turned away from spending eternity with Him.

Footwork

Read this parable in Matthew 22:1–14. According to verse 12, what question did the king ask? What was the man's answer? Would God have reason to ask you this question?

Fruit

This is personal. It doesn't involve anyone but you and God. Get alone with your thoughts for a moment and search your heart as you ask yourself these questions: Are you wearing the clothes of righteousness Jesus provided for you? Do you have a personal relationship with Jesus? Do you even know what that means? (If you aren't sure, turn to the back of this book. There's a special message there just for you.)

200s BC — Archimedes, a great math—

ematician, scientist, and inventor,

Mark

As you read through the book of Mark, notice that it's the shortest of the four gospels.

Unlike Matthew, which shows Jesus as the promised Messiah-King who fulfilled all prophecy, Mark shows us how Jesus was the perfect Servant. He proved who He was by what He did.

While the book of Matthew was written with the Jewish reader in mind, Mark was written for a Roman audience and provided an action-packed overview of Jesus' life. The Romans would have been most interested in the actions of Jesus, so that's where Mark focused his attention, recording more miracles than any other gospel. In fact, twenty miracles of Jesus are given in detail in this book, and more than forty times the word *immediately* and variations of it appear within its pages. The book of Mark has been called the book of "action" with good reason.

In Mark you will see Jesus' authority and ability to control what you and I cannot. You will see His willingness to help people regardless of who they are, His knowledge of the future, and His power over death. As you read through this book, see what else you can learn from this action-filled presentation of Jesus' life. ————————————————

discovers the principles of density

Wow!

Taken from Mark 1:21–28

— *Foundation* —

Before you read through today's lesson, spend a few minutes talking with God. Ask Him to open your eyes and help you better understand His Word.

Focus

Ever notice how students running for class president at school try to convince others that they are the best, most qualified person for the job? Jesus didn't have to do that.

"Who *is* this person?" one man whispered to another. "I've never heard anyone teach quite like He does!"

The other man nodded in agreement and they both refocused their attention on the one speaking. It was their regular synagogue meeting, and a guest speaker had been invited to read the Scriptures. This in itself wasn't uncommon, for the synagogue leader would often call upon a qualified man for the task. Since scribes worked so closely with the Scriptures and had the duty of interpreting God's Law for the people, they were typically selected. However, the scribes sometimes included additional rules that reflected their own background and training. Since their knowledge came from scribal tradition, they would simply pass along sayings from those they had learned under. Each sentence spilling from their lips traditionally began with the words "There is a teaching that…" and ended with a quote from a famous rabbi.

What caught everyone's attention was that this guest didn't bother to quote

and buoyancy, invents the compound

other authorities. He spoke as if He *were* the authority! Such teaching sounded fresh and new, a wonderful change from what they were used to hearing.

The more Jesus read and taught from the Scriptures, the more curiously and intently those in the synagogue listened. Suddenly a disturbance arose at the back of the room.

"Jesus, what do You want with us?" a man who was possessed by an evil spirit cried out. "You haven't come to destroy us, have You?" The voice of a demon rasped through the man.

The demon spoke for itself and all the other demons who knew Jesus was the Messiah who had come to destroy Satan and his evil works.

I know You're the Holy One of God!" the demon spat out fearfully.

"Silence!" Jesus ordered. He would accept no testimony from the mouth of a demon. "Leave this man!" Jesus sternly commanded.

The demon had no power against Jesus. It let out a loud shriek and shook the man violently as it left him. The people who saw this were speechless. They had never seen anything like it before! Yes, they'd seen demon-possessed people, and yes, they'd seen demons cast out, but never by just a simple command. Usually a special formula of words had to be said and a ceremony performed—and even then it wasn't always successful. Jesus healed this man with just four words! His power and authority were amazing!

> *The temple and the synagogue had different uses in Jesus' day. The temple in Jerusalem was used for worship and animal sacrifices. There was only one temple, but there were many synagogues. A synagogue was used for teaching and instruction. Wherever at least ten Jewish families lived, by law there had to be a synagogue.*
>
> *Mark 3:11 tells us, "Whenever the evil spirits saw [Jesus], they fell down before him and cried out, 'You are the Son of God.'" The demons knew about Jesus—and trembled with fear.*

Not only did Jesus teach the Scriptures with authority, but He also had power and authority over demons. Because of this, people spread the news about Him throughout the entire region of Galilee.

Footwork

Look up Mark 1:24. What question did the demon ask Jesus? What fact did the demon state about Him? The demon knew who Jesus was but didn't trust in Him.

Fruit

What facts do you know about Jesus? Do they make a difference? Take a moment to think about Jesus' power and authority. In what area of your life could you believe and trust Jesus more? Pray and ask Him to help you in that area today.

I'm with Him!
Taken from Mark 1

— Foundation —

Prepare your heart before God, asking Him to teach you what He wants you to learn today.

Focus

Have you ever noticed how some people try to be the most popular? Not Jesus, although He had plenty of opportunities to do so.

Crowds came from near and far when they heard about Jesus' power and learned He was staying at the home of Peter and Andrew. Because of the Sabbath, they had been prohibited from carrying their sick to Jesus for healing until now. (Carrying the sick would have been considered work, and working on the Sabbath was against the law.) However, once the sun had set and three stars were shining, the Sabbath was considered officially over. As a result the whole town now gathered at the home where Jesus was staying. And one by one Jesus lovingly healed their diseases and cast out the demons that plagued them.

The next morning while it was still dark, Jesus quietly slipped out of the house and went to a secluded place to spend time with God in prayer. Noticing Jesus was gone, Peter and the disciples went looking for Him. Jesus was becoming very popular, and a large crowd was once again at their door asking for Him!

"People are looking for You everywhere!" Peter blurted out when they finally found Jesus. He felt quite proud to be associated with someone as popular as Jesus and wasn't ready for His reply.

"It's time for us to leave so that I can preach in other towns," the Lord stated.

Peter stood dumbfounded. He saw no reason to leave when things were going so well. He and the other disciples obeyed Jesus, however, and left Capernaum to travel throughout Galilee, where Jesus continued preaching in the synagogues and casting out demons.

While they were traveling, a man with leprosy approached Jesus. Leprosy was a terrible, incurable disease. At first people would get spots on their bodies. Soon those spots would turn into infected growths that began to smell. As the infection raged, body parts would rot, die, and eventually fall off the body. It was such a horrible disease that those with it were considered unfit to live in society and were cast out to live in a place by themselves. They also had to wear black clothes to hide their twisted bodies. Since the Law forbade lepers from coming near other people, they were required to shout, "Unclean! Unclean!" so that anyone who might come across their paths would be warned to stay far away.

The leprous man who approached Jesus was so lonely and desperate that he came right up to Jesus and fell to his knees. "If You are willing," the man begged, "You can make my leprosy go away and make me clean."

Jesus looked at the man with compassion and did something unheard of. He reached out and touched the leper! "I am willing to heal you," Jesus said tenderly. "You are clean!"

Immediately the leprosy left the man and he was cured! Jesus instructed him to

> *The Romans divided Israel into three separate regions: Judea, Samaria, and Galilee—with Galilee being a sixty-mile-long and thirty-mile-wide area in the north containing more than 250 towns. Galilee was an ideal place for Jesus to concentrate His ministry.*
>
> *The thriving town of Capernaum had great wealth and many pagan influences. It was also the headquarters for many Roman troops.*

war elephants over the Alps to invade Ital

tell no one but to show himself to the priest first. After the priest examined him, he was to offer the sacrifices commanded by the Law in order to be considered clean (without leprosy).

Unfortunately, the man in all his excitement disobeyed the Lord. Instead of doing what Jesus asked, he went out and told everyone what had happened. Jesus had a reason for not wanting the leper to tell. He knew that it would attract crowds for the wrong reasons and motives. Attracting crowds wasn't something Jesus came to do.

As a result of this man's disobedience, Jesus could no longer walk around a town openly, but had to stay in the "lonely places." Even then, crowds still came to Him from all over.

Footwork

In your Bible, turn to the first chapter of Mark. Read verse 35. How did Jesus start His day? Where did He go? What did He do? Do you think that made a difference in the choices He made?

Fruit

Times will come in your life when you'll have to choose between a good opportunity and the best one. Watch the choices you make. Be sure to spend time talking to God in prayer to make sure you're on the right track. It has been said that a crowd of people doesn't always mean success, and it is far better to be alone with God than in a crowd without Him!

Now What?

Taken from Mark 4

— *Foundation* —

Stop and pray, asking God to speak to your heart.

Focus

> Have you ever had one of those days when nothing goes right for you and it seems nobody cares? Where is God when you really need Him, anyway?

The wind picked up and white caps formed on the usually calm lake. The disciples scanned the sky. It didn't look like a storm was brewing, but then looks could be deceiving on the Sea of Galilee. On this lake bordered by mountains, storms often popped up out of nowhere. As the wind squeezed down through the mountains and whipped across the lake with a sudden burst, the once smooth water would churn into violent waves, slapping and tossing boats around as if they were mere toys.

The winds were increasing now, and so were the worries of the disciples.

"Let's cross over to the other shore," Jesus had stated before climbing into the boat. He didn't say, "Let's *try* to go to the other side," but simply, "Let's go." There was something definite and final about the way He had said it.

The disciples grabbed at the oars of the boat and struggled against the mounting walls of water. As their boat was tossed from side to side and water poured in, they looked back and noticed Jesus sleeping. He was riding in the seat of honor, a little seat in the back of the boat where a carpet and a cushion were arranged for distinguished guests.

The disciples couldn't believe Jesus was sleeping through this howling storm. They continued to struggle with the oars until they could no longer control the boat. Frustrated and fearful, they shook Jesus awake.

> *When Jesus calmed the storm, He demonstrated the authority that only God Himself exercised in the Old Testament. (See Psalms 89:8–9 and 106:8–9.) The disciples would have taken note of that!*

"Rabbi," they said, panicking, "we're about to drown. Don't You care?"

Jesus stood up in the boat. He had been waiting for them to come to Him and ask for help. Stretching out His hand, He spoke three simple words: "Peace! Be still!"

Immediately the wind stopped and the water became calm. The disciples couldn't believe their eyes.

"Why are you so filled with fear?" Jesus asked them. "Do you still not understand who I am? Do you still lack faith?"

It was true that the disciples had seen Jesus do many wonderful miracles. All of those pointed to His authority and power—and the fact that He was no ordinary person. If they had truly understood who was with them in the boat, they wouldn't have worried. But they were amazed and asked one another who this Jesus really was. Not only did demons obey him but the wind and waves did as well. They knew the only One who could control nature was the very One who made it. The disciples looked at one another, terrified. Was it possible?

Footwork

According to Mark 4:35, what were Jesus' exact words to His disciples? (Go on, look it up.) Notice Jesus didn't say, "Let's *try* to go to the other side," or "Let's go *halfway* and sink." What Jesus told the disciples to do, He would help them accomplish. Not only did Jesus have the power to help the disciples when they asked, but He had been with them in the storm even before they asked. The disciples were learning that they needed to trust Jesus' character.

Fruit

Are you facing a difficult storm in your life (things not going as well as you had hoped, friends turning against you, tough times at school, work, or home)? Take a moment right now and talk to Jesus about it. Invite Him into your boat to help you through your particular storm. Then thank Him in advance for His help.

You're Too Late
Taken from Mark 5

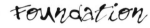

Take a few minutes to quiet your thoughts. Tell God what's on your heart. Ask Him to help you understand what's on His.

Focus

Does it frustrate you when you need help and people take their time getting to you?

Jairus quickened his pace. By now he was practically running. *This is bad. This is really bad,* he whispered to himself. His only child, a precious twelve-year-old daughter, was very ill. In fact, she lay dying in her bed at home. There was no time to lose.

As ruler of the synagogue, Jairus was well respected in the community. He had a place of honor in society and had servants working for him. But none of that was important compared to the life of his daughter. Instead of sending servants, Jairus would go and find Jesus himself. *Perhaps Jesus can heal her,* he hoped above all else.

Coming over the hill, Jairus saw a large crowd gathering around Jesus by the Sea of Galilee. "I found Him!" Jairus exclaimed with relief. Working his way through the crowd, he fell at Jesus' feet and began pleading. "Please help me! My daughter is dying. If you'll just come and touch

> **Mourners were often hired to weep and wail. Their loud wailing was an announcement that someone had died.**

her, she'll be healed. Please, I beg you!"

To Jairus's delight, Jesus followed him. Jairus's heart pounded with worry and excitement as if it were a clock registering seconds and minutes that couldn't be wasted. Would they get there in time?

The large number of people surrounding Jesus followed along. They were all crowding around Him, pushing and shoving to get close. Everybody wanted something.

As they moved along, a woman slipped into the crowd. She had a bleeding problem that made her sick and "unclean" according to the Law. She was lonely and desperate. Having tried all the doctors' remedies, she was now without money and feeling worse than ever. Jesus was her only hope.

Working her way through the masses of people, the woman reached out and touched the corner of Jesus' cloak. Suddenly she felt her body being healed! And just as suddenly Jesus stopped and asked who had touched Him in such a faith-filled way.

Jairus's heart sank. If they delayed any longer, his daughter would be dead, and it would be too late! Jairus grew impatient. Finally, from out of the crowd, a woman stepped forward and admitted the truth to Jesus.

Jesus selected Peter, James, and John to be with Him on two other occasions. One was at His transfiguration (Mark 9:2), and the other was in the garden of Gethsemane (Mark 14:32–33).

Aramaic was a Jewish language. Many people in that day spoke and understood Aramaic as well as Greek.

"You have been healed because you believed. Go home now in peace," Jesus told her.

The woman went on her way rejoicing. As she left, however, messengers came with news for Jairus.

"Jairus, don't trouble the Teacher any longer," they said. "Your daughter is dead." Jairus' sad eyes looked at Jesus.

Jesus ignored the messengers' report and spoke to Jairus. "There's nothing to be afraid of, Jairus; have faith in Me."

Jesus told the crowd to stay behind but allowed Peter, James, and John to follow.

When they arrived at Jairus' house, they saw mourners with torn clothes weeping and wailing loudly. Flute players were playing the common death-and-despair notes that blended with the mourners' cries.

"Why all this mourning and wailing?" Jesus asked them. "The little girl isn't dead; she's sleeping." (Jesus said the child was asleep because her death at this time would not be permanent. He was going to raise her from the dead.)

The mourners laughed and scoffed at Jesus. After putting them all out of the house, Jesus led the child's father and mother and the three disciples into the child's room. Taking the little girl by the hand, He tenderly commanded, "Talitha Koum!" (which in Aramaic means, "Little girl, stand up!")

Immediately she stood up and began walking around the room. The color had returned to her face, and life had come back into her body. The small group in the bedroom stood speechless. Jesus instructed them to give the girl something to eat, and warned them not to tell anyone what had happened.

Footwork

What did Jesus tell the synagogue official in Mark 5:36? (Look it up in your Bible.) With Jesus, nothing is ever too late or beyond His ability to change. That was something Jairus learned firsthand.

Fruit

Today, when something doesn't happen according to your timetable or when things don't go the way you'd like them to, stop and take a deep breath. Ask yourself, "Who is really in charge here?" God is not unaware of your situation. Thank Him for that, and then tell Him you trust Him. He knows what He's doing—even if it doesn't make sense to you at the time.

and his five sons lead a revolt.

Even So . . .

Taken from Mark 7

--- ƒoundation ---

Take a few minutes to prepare your heart. Ask God to quiet your thoughts and help you learn from His Word today.

Focus

Have you ever been left out of an activity or felt like you didn't belong?

Wherever Jesus went, crowds gathered around Him and pressed in from all sides to hear what He had to say. Word about Him kept spreading, making the religious leaders both jealous and nervous. On several occasions Jesus freely spoke out against their traditions and man-made rules. He was winning the hearts of the people and, for the religious leaders, that was not good.

One day Jesus decided to get away from the crowds and the angry Jewish leaders. He and His disciples left Capernaum and went to the region of Phoenicia, a land of Gentiles (non-Jewish people). Since Jews never associated with Gentiles, no one would consider looking for them there. This would not only be the perfect place to rest, but also would allow Jesus opportunity to give His disciples some important instruction. Not wanting anyone to know where they were, they made arrangements to stay in a house, but it wasn't long before someone knocked on the door.

The ancient region of Phoenicia is today's country of Lebanon.

"Oh, Jesus," the woman begged, "my daughter has an evil spirit. Could you please drive it out of her?"

Jesus looked at the Gentile woman. Although the focus of His ministry was first to the Jew, He knew they would reject His message, which was for all people, regardless of who or what they were. Looking at the woman with kindness, Jesus tested her faith with a statement.

"The children's dogs aren't entitled to what the children eat. No one has a right to take the bread out of the children's mouths and give it to the dogs."

Usually the word *dog* was an insulting word for a Gentile, but Jesus used it differently. He was referring to puppies kept in a home as pets. The woman understood Jesus' meaning. She didn't want to take His time away from teaching His disciples and didn't consider herself deserving of His attention as a Jewish person might be. After all, she was a Gentile.

"I know, Lord, but don't even the dogs get to eat whatever falls from the children's table?"

In those days it wasn't the custom to eat with forks, knives, and napkins. Instead, people ate with their hands. When their hands became soiled, they wiped them on a chunk of bread and then gave the bread to the house dogs to eat. By saying this, the woman was asking only for scraps of Jesus' favor, not a place of honor at the table.

Because of her humble and faith-filled response, Jesus granted her request. He could have turned her away, but didn't. Instead, He made Himself available to her and her needs.

"You have given an excellent answer. Go now. Your daughter has been healed."

The woman left and returned home to find the demon gone and her daughter resting peacefully.

The healing of this Gentile woman's daughter is the only miracle recorded in Mark that Jesus performed at a distance and without a vocal command.

The woman was born in Phoenicia, which was part of the province of Syria. According to Matthew 15:22, she was a "Canaanite woman." Check out Faith Factor OT for the full story on that people group!

Footwork

Read Mark 7:24 in your Bible. What did Jesus desire? What happened? Now skip down to verses 29 and 30. Notice what Jesus said and did. He didn't show special favor to some people above others; instead, He made Himself available to everyone who turned to Him—regardless. There is no such thing as an unimportant person in Jesus' eyes.

Fruit

This week when someone outside your circle of friends (or your comfort zone) needs help, make it a point to be there for him or her. It might just turn into an opportunity for you to tell that person about Jesus' loving care. Be His hands and feet.

What's Prayer Got to Do with It?

Taken from Mark 9

Foundation

Spend some time preparing your heart for today's lesson. Ask God to search your heart and show you what He wants you to learn.

Focus

Have you ever been able to do something perfectly well in the past, but suddenly you couldn't do it when it counted most? The disciples experienced that same kind of failure...

"I just don't understand it," one of the disciples said to the other.

"Yes, didn't Jesus give us power and authority to cast out demons?" whispered the other under his breath. The nine disciples stood embarrassed and defeated. The religious leaders, who had come to keep track of Jesus, were now arguing with the disciples.

"Perhaps Jesus doesn't really have that kind of power to give," they challenged. "Perhaps He isn't who He says He is."

The crowd standing around didn't know what to think. Then Jesus, Peter, James, and John arrived on the scene. The religious leaders, who had thought Jesus was off traveling, were surprised to see Him. The crowd ran to greet Jesus.

day's worth of oil. (Hanukkah cele-

Prayer ignites our faith and involves both an attitude and an action. The attitude it ignites is humble dependence on God; the action is turning to Him and inviting Him to work His power in our lives and circumstances. (This is the opposite of doing something in our own strength and asking God to add His blessing.)

When I pray, it brings ...
P—Perspective on my situation
R—Relief from carrying the burden myself
A—Assurance that God can handle whatever concerns me
Y—Yearning to know Him better

"What are you arguing about?" Jesus asked the nine disciples.

Before they could answer, a man from the back of the crowd pushed his way forward. "Rabbi," he said in despair, "I sought help from Your disciples because my son has an evil spirit in him. Whenever it takes control, my son falls to the ground, and his body becomes stiff while foam pours out of his mouth and his teeth grind. Your disciples were not able to cast out the spirit."

Jesus glanced at His disciples, who lowered their heads in defeat. These were the very men Jesus was trying to teach and train, the very men who would carry on after He left them and returned to His Father. Did they still not understand?

"How long can I put up with such unbelief?" Jesus sighed. "Go get the boy and bring him to Me."

The disciples said nothing. They just watched as the man brought his son to Jesus. "Has he been this way for a long time?" Jesus asked the father.

"Yes, ever since childhood. The demon often tries to kill him by throwing him into the fire or drowning him. Please have mercy and help us if you can," he begged.

Jesus looked into the man's eyes. He could see his faith had been weakened because the disciples couldn't do what they had promised. "If I *can* help you?" Jesus asked. "All things are possible—if only you believe," He stated, half to the man and half to His disciples.

With these words the boy's father started to regain his faith. "Teacher, I do have faith, but please take away my unbelief!"

Noticing a large crowd quickly approaching to see what was going on, Jesus turned to the boy and said to the evil spirit, "I order you to leave this child and never return!"

The spirit let out a piercing cry, shook the boy violently, and came out of him. The boy lay on the ground looking lifeless. "The demon killed him!" someone observed, but Jesus took the boy by the hand and helped him to his feet. The boy stood in front of them all, completely well.

After this, Jesus' disciples spoke to Him privately, "Why couldn't we drive this demon out? We've driven out demons before with no problem!"

Jesus gently answered, "Only prayer can drive out demons like this."

The disciples grew silent. Jesus had made His point.

Footwork

Read Mark 9:29 in your Bible. What did Jesus tell the disciples? Do you think they forgot to do something? (What?)

Fruit

God gives you talents and abilities to use for His glory and to accomplish His work. Whenever you take them for granted or think they originated with you, you're on dangerous ground and set for failure. At times in your life, you'll be tempted to handle things on your own without God. Don't.

emperor of Rome is born (Julius

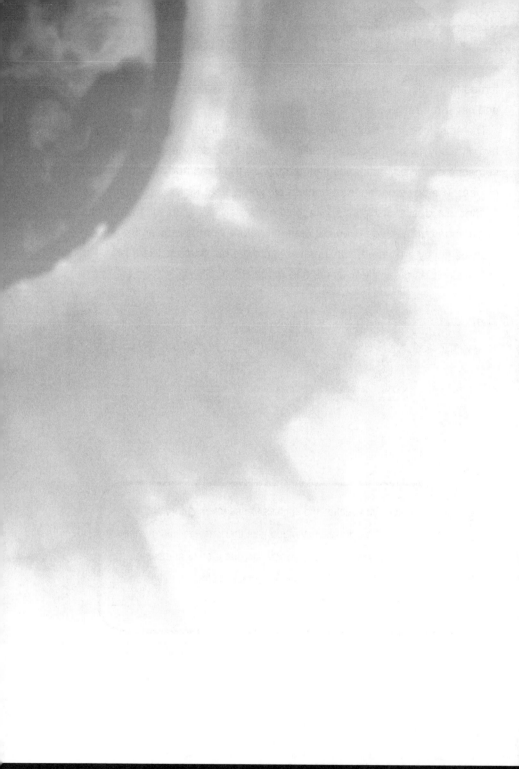

Caesar); Pharisees and Sadducees come

Luke

The book of Luke was written with the Greek person in mind. The Greeks were well educated and loved the arts, beauty, and talking about the meaning of life. They strove to be "perfect" and admired anything or anyone who even came close. To be impressed with Jesus, they would need to see Him as the "perfect" Man—exactly how Luke portrays Jesus. Being Greek himself, Luke allows us to see the beauty of Jesus' love in becoming a man to save sinners.

As you read through this gospel book, notice how Jesus willingly limited Himself as a man. Watch Him praying and weeping. See how He reached out to those others hated. Take note of His tenderness and care as well as the power that belonged to Him. Allow yourself to walk beside Him and see the beauty of His love. Luke is packed with great stuff—enjoy your journey!

And Stay Out!

Taken from Luke 8

Foundation

Take a few moments to pray. Simply ask God to challenge you today and give Him permission to speak to your heart. Thank Him for the power He has over evil.

Focus

Have you ever been around something that was evil?

Jesus stepped out of the boat and onto the sandy shore. He and His disciples had just crossed the Sea of Galilee into a different region when they heard a loud voice shrieking, "Why are you bothering me? What do You want, Son of God Most High? Please don't make me suffer!"

The voice came from a naked, dirty man with broken chains dangling from his arms and legs. A wild, almost savage look filled his eyes, and judging by the broken chains, he also had superhuman strength. The townspeople had tried to shackle this demon-possessed man, but he broke the chains as if they were only string. Instead of living in a house, the man lived among the tombs in a graveyard. Now he was on his knees before Jesus, not in worship, but to beg for mercy.

"Son of God Most High" were words the demon had spoken through the man. These were not words

> *A legion was the largest unit in a Roman army and had between three thousand and six thousand soldiers. This man had an army of demons living inside him!*

of respect, but rather general words used to describe deity without having to give worship or respect.

Jesus looked into the wild eyes of the man. "Tell me your name!"

The demons spoke through the man. "Legion," they answered, "for there are many of us."

Jesus wasn't afraid. He had power over these demons—something both He and they knew. Although the demons' goal was to kill life, Jesus was the Giver of Life, and He wouldn't let them continue destroying the man.

Knowing they were sentenced to the Abyss (their place of eternal punishment) but uncertain when they would be cast there, the demons begged for mercy. Seeing a large herd of pigs on a nearby hillside, they pleaded with Jesus. "Please, don't send us to our punishment, but let us enter that nearby herd of swine."

Jesus looked at the pigs. It wasn't God's timing to send the demons into the Abyss, so He allowed them to do what they asked. In an explosive scream, the demons left the man and rushed into the pigs. The herd went wild. Confused, they charged full speed over a steep bank, plunged into the lake, and drowned. The farmers tending the pigs saw this happen and ran off to tell people all over the countryside and in the town.

As people came to check out this unusual event for themselves, they found the once-naked man in his right mind and fully clothed. They also saw the dead pigs and were afraid, uncertain what to make of it all.

Because the Gentile (nonJewish) people weren't expecting a Messiah (and wouldn't try to crown Jesus as a king), Jesus allowed the man to tell everyone about his miraculous healing. This man became the first witness to the Gentile people.

Jesus' ministry east of the Jordan River was mainly to the Gentile people. The Jews disliked the Gentiles because of the way the Gentiles had treated them when they were captives in Babylon. (Check out Faith Factor OT for the interesting story about that!)

"Jesus cured this demon-possessed man!" came the happy report from those who had seen it.

The response was anything but enthusiastic. Many of the townspeople thought only of the loss of the swine that could no longer be sold in the market. "If this is what Jesus does," they stated, "maybe He'd better leave before we have any more losses." Sadly, they cared more about making money and living comfortable lives than they cared about the man Jesus healed. Being selfishly afraid, they wanted no part of Jesus and asked Him to leave their land. Jesus did.

As Jesus was climbing into the boat, the man who had been set free from the demons asked if he could come along. Jesus tenderly responded, "I need you to stay here and tell everyone what God has done for you." The man agreed and went away, fearlessly telling the whole town how Jesus had set him free.

Footwork

In your Bible, read Luke 8:31–32. What does it say? What were the demons doing? Who seems to be in control here?

Fruit

Demons are very real. They are Satan's army whose job is to try to destroy people and keep them from knowing God. They're powerful but don't have absolute power. Their end is final, certain, and coming soon—a fact they know well.

So, what do you fear? Right now, spend a few minutes telling Jesus about some scary thoughts you keep having or a fear you have been struggling with. Thank Jesus for His power over evil and ask Him to protect you and calm your heart. He will.

Oh, I Know!

Taken from Luke 9

Foundation

Take a few minutes to quiet your thoughts. Ask God to search your heart and teach you what He wants you to learn from today's lesson.

Focus

Have you ever given the right answer to a question but didn't understand what your answer really meant?

Jesus' face was set toward Jerusalem as He prayed. He knew it wouldn't be long before He would go there to die on the cross. Looking at His disciples, Jesus knew His time was running out. He needed to help them define and understand who He was, then train and lead them onward from there.

"What do people say about Me? Who do they say I am?" Jesus asked, turning to His disciples. He began with a question they could easily answer.

"Some say You are John the Baptist," replied one disciple.

"Others say You are Elijah," answered another.

The rest of the disciples added, "We have heard people say that You must be one of the ancient prophets come back to life."

Jesus looked directly into their eyes. It was time for them to understand this for themselves. "But what do you say about Me?" Jesus asked, challenging them.

The Roman commander Pompey attacks

> *The Jews believed a great prophet would come before the Messiah, and some mistakenly thought Jesus was that prophet. They expected the Messiah to be a political king who would lead them into great victories as a nation.*
>
> *This is the first time Jesus told the disciples about His death, burial, and resurrection—a shocking blow to their idea of the Messiah!*

Silence fell over the disciples. Some of them weren't quite sure what they thought. They had seen Jesus do many wonderful miracles of healing the blind, casting out demons, calming storms, and teaching with authority. They knew Jesus wasn't a mere man, and yet …

A voice suddenly broke the silence. "You are the Messiah sent from God!" Peter answered.

All the other disciples turned to look at Peter. His eyes shone with delight as he thought about how the Messiah would squash all the Jews' enemies. From childhood he had been taught about the coming Messiah. Now, living under the rule of the Romans, Peter thought it was the perfect time for the Messiah to come. *At last the Jews would be free!* he thought to himself.

Jesus knew Peter's thoughts. Peter had the right answer but didn't quite understand what that answer really meant. So He strictly warned Peter and the other disciples not to tell anyone. He would first have to teach them God's plan for the Messiah.

"I will suffer many things, and the religious leaders will reject me," Jesus told them. "After that, I will be killed, but I will rise to life three days later."

Jesus' words confused them all, and Peter stood stunned. Although he had given the right answer there were so many things he didn't understand about the answer he gave! Peter looked at Jesus and determined in his heart that he would come to know this Jesus better...

Footwork

Look up Luke 9:20 in your Bible and read it aloud. Now, read it again, substituting your name for "you" and the verb "does" for "do." Was this a group question or a personal one?

Jerusalem. Jews close the city gates and

Fruit

It's so easy to repeat the knowledge we've gained and yet have little or no understanding of the true meaning of what we're saying. If Jesus asked you the question in verse 20, how would you answer? What about the way you live your life? If words were forbidden, would the way you live your life reflect the answer you would normally give with your mouth? Take a moment to pray about it. Ask Jesus to pinpoint areas of weakness or wrong thinking in your life. Based on what He has shown you, make a commitment from this point on to live differently. Be sure to turn to Jesus daily for His help in doing so, because if you rely on your own strength, the changes you make won't last.

Hey! It's a Party!
Taken from Luke 9

Foundation

Stop and pray before you read today's lesson. Ask God to help you see anew the greatness and glory surrounding Jesus.

Focus

Have you ever been so excited about a great idea you had that you spoke without really thinking first?

Peter rubbed his eyes and looked up. Could this be a dream? Only moments ago he and two other disciples had come up the mountain with Jesus to pray. Perhaps they had dozed off for a few minutes, but they weren't sleeping now. They were fully awake and amazed at what was happening before their very eyes!

This event has commonly been called the transfiguration. *To be transfigured means "to change in appearance"—almost like a metamorphosis, a word used to describe the changing of a caterpillar into a butterfly.*

While Jesus was praying, His face began to look different, and His clothes became unusually white. The gleaming light from Jesus' clothes—bright like lightning—almost hurt Peter's eyes, much like looking directly into the sun. Jesus was not alone but stood talking with two men who had appeared. Peter strained and shielded his eyes to see better. Could it be? One man looked like Moses and the other like Elijah!

Long ago God had given the Ten Commandments to Moses. Elijah was a great prophet God used to call the Israelites to repentance and warn them of coming judgment. Many Jews believe Elijah was connected with the end times and the coming of the Messiah. While Moses reminded the Jews of the past; Elijah reminded them of the future. Both men left the world in a strange way. The Lord buried Moses (Deuteronomy 34:5–6), and a whirlwind took Elijah to heaven (2 Kings 2:11). Now they stood together talking with Jesus.

Peter couldn't believe his eyes. Here, talking with Jesus, were the two greatest Jewish heroes who had ever lived! Wondering what they were talking about, Peter scooted closer to listen. He sat breathless as he heard Jesus discussing with them the things He would accomplish in Jerusalem and His departure from earth. Peter gasped in wonder and delight. As a child he had learned about Moses and Elijah, and now they stood right in front of him! He could hardly contain himself.

Jesus took Peter, James, and John with Him so they could see He wasn't just a great prophet but was God's own Son.

True faith was built on three things—the Law, the Prophets, and Jesus—all three of which were represented on the Mount of Transfiguration! Peter would later write how Jesus was the highest authority—the "chosen and precious cornerstone." (1 Peter 2:6)

"Lord, it's good that we're here!" Peter exclaimed. The words exploded from his mouth, along with a sudden idea. "I know, let's make three huts—one for You, one for Moses, and one for Elijah!" Peter said, not really knowing what he was saying.

Suddenly, a huge cloud surrounded them, and Peter and the other disciples became afraid. A loud voice boomed, "This is My Son, My Chosen One. Listen to what He has to say."

When the cloud lifted, the disciples were left standing face-to-face with Jesus. Moses and Elijah were gone.

Peter didn't understand that his idea of three shelters implied that Jesus was only equal to Moses and Elijah, when in fact He was so much greater. God had just made that point very clear! Peter also didn't realize that by suggesting they build the shelters, he was assuming Jesus could just stay there and not go anywhere—even to Jerusalem to die on the cross! Peter began to realize his mistake. Just a few days earlier he had declared Jesus to be the Messiah; today he had forgotten. Peter and the other two disciples were quiet. They would treasure in their hearts the wonderful thing they had just seen and experienced.

Footwork

Turn to Luke 9:35 in your Bible and read it. What does it say? What three specific things did God say about Jesus?

Fruit

When you get excited about opportunities in front of you, whose plans will you consider first: God's or your own?

Look What I Did!
Taken from Luke 10

Foundation

Before you read the lesson today, ask God to speak to your heart through His Word and point out the things He wants you to learn or change.

Focus

Have you noticed how some people brag about what they can do, comparing themselves to others and assuming they are better? That's a danger Jesus addressed.

Jesus had a busy schedule. Knowing His time on earth was running out, He instructed seventy-two men to go out in pairs to tell others of God's coming kingdom.

"You will be like lambs in the midst of wolves," Jesus stated, warning them of possible danger and their own helplessness. Not wanting them to be distracted by belongings, He gave some basic instructions. "Don't carry a bag full of belongings or take along any extra shoes. And when you see people on the road, don't stop to exchange greetings."

Traveling prophets (both good and bad) became so common that rules were made concerning them. One rule stated that a prophet staying in a house longer than three days without working was to be considered a false prophet.

the last independent Egyptian ruler;

The customs for greeting people in that day were very long and involved and could distract the disciples from the importance of their task.

> *The "seventy-two" were men (other than the twelve disciples) who followed Jesus. They were sent out to prepare the way so that when Jesus entered a town, it would be ready to receive His message.*
>
> *It was considered offensive not to greet someone on the street, and pious people tried to be first in greeting an approaching person. However, it was also commonly understood that religious duties (such as prayer) were not to be interrupted for social greetings.*

Jesus also told the disciples to stay at the first home they came to. If a town wouldn't accept their message, they were to shake the dust off their feet—a customary sign of rejection. Those people would not be part of God's kingdom.

When the seventy-two had done exactly as Jesus instructed, they returned from their journeys with wonderful reports. "Jesus," one of the disciples reported, "we were able to do amazing things!"

"Yes," added another breathlessly, "we even had power over demons—in Your name, of course!" Their faces radiated with confidence.

Jesus could see they were caught up in their own excitement and successes. Perhaps some even compared their adventures and accomplishments to those of others who had gone out. They would be tempted to measure what they had done and then become prideful, thinking they were better than others.

Knowing this, Jesus said to them, "I watched Satan fall from heaven like lightning." Jesus recalled how Satan was once an important angel in heaven. Because of Satan's pride and desire to take God's throne for himself, Satan was cast out of heaven. (See Isaiah 14:12–15!)

"I gave you power and authority over serpents and scorpions, and over all the Enemy's power," Jesus told them. "But don't let what you've been able to accomplish be the reason for your joy. Instead, be joyful because God has recorded your names in heaven."

Jesus didn't want them to get sidetracked by all the things they could do but rather to remember they were working for God. They needed to keep their hearts focused on Him and the things that would really last. They needed to recall the things *God* did in and through them rather than what they did in their own efforts.

Footwork

In your Bible, look up Luke 10:20. What does the last part of that verse say?

Fruit

Do you base your feelings about yourself (good or bad) on what others say or do, or on the fact that you know and are known by Jesus? (If you aren't sure about your relationship with Jesus, turn to the back of this book. There's a special message there just for you.)

Let Me Think about It . . .
Taken from Luke 14

— *Foundation* —

Find a quiet place where you can be alone and pray. Ask God to speak to your heart. Ask Him to help you understand the importance of being committed wholeheartedly to Jesus.

Focus

Do you know friends who are quick to go along with something but soon drop out when they see it might cost them time or effort?

People came from near and far just to see and hear Jesus. Some decided to follow Him no matter what. Others tagged along halfheartedly. To the second group, Jesus turned and gave an eye-opening challenge.

"You can't be My disciple unless you love me more than your father, mother, wife, children, brothers, and sisters—and even your own life!"

To get His point across, Jesus explained further, using the word *hate*. A person's love for others should look almost like hate when compared to his love for Jesus. This statement wiped a few smiles off the faces of some in the crowd—especially those who loved others more than they loved Him.

Jesus continued. "And you cannot be My disciple unless you follow Me and carry your cross."

In Jesus' day, it was not uncommon to see a man carrying a cross through the

literature—including writers such as

heart of the city. When the Roman Empire punished a criminal by crucifixion, the criminal was forced to carry his own cross part of the way. Cross carrying declared to all bystanders that the Roman Empire was right and its ways were just. Jesus applied this example to discipleship. Jesus' ways are right, and those who follow Him must have their eyes set on a one-way road. They must each carry their own cross and follow Him always.

When Jesus said this, a few in the crowd grew uncomfortable. They weren't sure they were willing to do that. They had things to do, places to go, and people to see. Perhaps after they had lived a life of pleasure they would return and follow Jesus.

Some in the crowd looked at Jesus with eager eyes. They were willing to do anything, and why not? It all sounded like such an adventure! To these people Jesus gave another illustration.

"Let's say that you want to build a tower," Jesus began. "You would sit down and determine the cost before beginning to build. Otherwise, if you started the tower and weren't able to finish it, you would be laughed at."

The people understood what Jesus was saying. Towers were commonly built in vineyards where a man could keep watch to make sure thieves didn't steal the harvest. A half-built tower was not only laughed at; it was useless.

Jesus continued, "It's the same with discipleship. You must count the cost and commitment before you follow Me."

The crowd grew restless. Some on the edge slipped away unnoticed. They knew their hearts weren't right with God. Others listened closely; they had never heard such words. Being a follower of Jesus wasn't something you did because others were doing it. It was

> *Jesus also compared discipleship to salt (Luke 14:34–35). When salt gets wet and then dries, only a tasteless residue remains, which is useful for nothing. When followers of Christ blend into the world, they lose their saltiness. The now-tasteless residue of their lives can't season, preserve, or change the lives and environment around them.*

not something you took lightly or did halfheartedly. There was a personal cost and commitment involved. Although being a follower of Jesus might mean giving up earthly things, the blessings gained would far outweigh any losses!

Footwork

In your Bible, look up Luke 14:27. (Go on, look it up!) Read it aloud a few times and think about it. Jesus expects commitment from us. Sometimes the road may be hard, but Jesus has traveled it before us. He's already been there and knows what He is asking us to do.

Fruit

Tell Jesus what's going through your mind right now. Don't be afraid; He already knows what you're thinking. Be honest and tell Him all the reasons why it's difficult for you to follow Him. Ask Him to change your heart and desires and to make you a true disciple of His.

40s BC — Julius Caesar rules Rome. Th

He's Your Friend?
Taken from Luke 19

Foundation

Spend a few moments in prayer. Be honest and real before God. Ask Him to forgive you for any wrong attitudes or actions in your life.

Focus

Ever notice how some people strive to be included with the popular or cool group, trying to make themselves look good by who their friends are? Jesus did the opposite.

"Hey, I heard Jesus is passing through Jericho!" shouted one person to another. Soon a group of people had gathered along the road where Jesus would soon pass. Those who arrived late craned their necks and stood on tiptoes to catch a glimpse of Him. Zacchaeus was one of those people.

Zacchaeus was not a well-liked man. As a chief tax collector working for the Roman Empire (the enemy of the Jews), he was hated by almost everyone. Tax collectors collected money from every household and turned it over to the Roman Empire. Any extra money a tax collector collected (above what was required) he was allowed to keep for himself.

It was Zacchaeus' practice to charge especially high rates and pocket the extra money. Because he worked for the Romans, people had no choice but to pay him, often giving their money in fear of punishment. This stirred up their hatred for Zacchaeus all the more.

Julian calendar comes into use. ◆

Zacchaeus heard that Jesus was a friend of tax collectors. Oh, how he needed such a friend! Although his heart ached with loneliness, money held him in too tight a grip for him to give up his job.

As Zacchaeus approached the back of the growing crowd, a strange thing happened. The people bunched together in order to keep Zacchaeus out. The townspeople's snickers caused hot anger to rise in his cheeks. *So, this is their game*, he thought.

Fearing he would miss the only One who might accept him, Zacchaeus ran ahead of the crowd and climbed a tree with low-hanging branches, hoping to see Jesus as He walked past. Zacchaeus wasn't ready for what happened next.

Passing under the tree, Jesus stopped and looked up. "Zacchaeus," He said, "come down from that tree for I'm going to be your guest today!"

The crowd who saw this began to murmur. "Jesus is going to eat at the house of a sinner!" they gasped in disapproval. They couldn't believe Jesus would choose to be seen with a person like Zacchaeus!

Zacchaeus was overcome with joy. He saw the love and acceptance in Jesus' eyes and immediately became a changed man. He would serve and love Jesus with his whole heart from that moment on. Having become a new person on the inside, Zacchaeus then proved it by his outward actions.

"Jesus, right now I'm going to give half of everything I own to the poor," Zacchaeus stated. "And I will repay those I've cheated by giving them four times what I took." What Zacchaeus offered was above what the Law required for even thieves to repay!

"Today salvation has come to this house," Jesus responded, knowing

---

Jericho, the City of Palms, had a great palm forest and balsam groves that gave off fragrances for miles around. The Romans carried its dates and balsam to worldwide trade routes.

"Short" by Mediterranean standards meant Zacchaeus was most likely less than five feet tall!

As chief tax collector, Zacchaeus had others working under him. He didn't have to cheat to gain extra money—but had chosen to do so anyway.

Zacchaeus's heart. Then as if to finalize what had taken place, Jesus added, "The Son of Man has come to find the lost and save them."

Zacchaeus's life changed because Jesus cared enough to seek him out.

Footwork

Look up Luke 19:7 in your Bible and read what it says. Then skip down and read verse 10. What do you think is most important to Jesus? Do you think anyone is ever too sinful for Him to forgive and love?

Fruit

How will you respond to this message of God's love? Will you choose to stand back with your friends and look cool, or will you talk to someone no one else will talk to?

Ask God to give you an opportunity this week to share the message of His love with a "Zacchaeus"—and be ready. He will provide one.

by Brutus and Cassius—a day termed

"The Ides of March." • 37 BC — Antony

John

Each gospel gives us yet another view of Jesus. As we put them all together, we gain a better picture of who Jesus is. Let's take a minute and quickly review what we've learned so far. Matthew shows Jesus as a King fulfilling prophecies. Mark shows Jesus as a Servant and describes many of His miracles. Luke shows us Jesus as the perfect Man and the beauty of His love. The last sketch in our portrait of Jesus is the book of John. John opens our eyes to understand and see Jesus as He is and always will be: God.

Our journey through John will begin with the first miracle Jesus did. As you read through this book, notice the lives Jesus touched and how He touched them. See by what authority He did these things and listen to the claims He made about Himself.

appoints Herod the Great, a descendant

Who'd Have Thought It?
Taken from John 2

Foundation

Prepare your heart for today's lesson by spending a few minutes in prayer. Ask God to show you special things from His Word today.

FOCUS

Have you ever been asked to do something that didn't make sense, and you felt it was a waste of your time?

"Do what?" the servants asked.

The wedding celebration had run out of wine, and it was considered an insult for the host not to have enough food and drink for his guests. Something must be done, but what?

Because Jesus' mother, Mary, was helping with the wedding celebration, she instructed the servants to find Jesus and do whatever He told them to do. She knew if anyone could help, Jesus could.

"Fill these pots with water," Jesus instructed them, pointing to six large stone jars. Each jar held almost thirty gallons of water—enough to fill a small bathtub! It would take quite a while to fill all of them.

"What does this have to do with being out of wine?" one servant whispered privately to another servant as they worked at filling the pots.

"I don't know. Maybe Jesus didn't understand what we meant," the other replied.

It was a slow job. Little by little the water levels rose in the stone pots. When they were completely full, the servants reported back to Jesus for His next instructions.

of Esau, as King of Judea. During his

Perhaps now He'll tell us where we can get some wine, they thought.

"Go to the pots you just filled with water," Jesus told them, "draw some out with a dipper, and present it to the headwaiter."

The servants were shocked. By doing such a thing they could get fired! But recalling Mary's words, they obeyed Jesus and did exactly as He said.

The servants looked at the dipper as they plunged it into the cool water and drew it up full of crystal-clear liquid. It didn't look like wine. With trembling hands they brought the dipper of water to the headwaiter and closed their eyes, expecting the worst as he lifted the dipper to his lips.

"Where did this come from?" the headwaiter demanded. "It's the best wine yet!"

The servants were amazed. Only moments ago it had been water. How could this be? They turned and looked at Jesus with both awe and wonder.

This was just the beginning of the miracles Jesus did that showed His power and glory.

> *These large ceremonial stone jars weren't meant to be drunk from but were used for special ritual washings.*
>
> *Wedding ceremonies lasted a full seven days! It was common practice to serve the best wine first and then offer poorer quality wine after people's senses were dulled and they could no longer tell the difference.*

Footwork

Turn to John 2:5 in your Bible. What does it say? One of the interesting things about Jesus' first miracle was not what He did, but that He chose to use people to do it. Jesus used those who were willing to simply do as He asked.

Fruit

God doesn't need people who are able to do things well. He needs people who are willing to do as He asks. He'll take care of the rest. If you desire to be like the servants and be used by God, take a moment right now and tell Him that.

the temple into a larger and grander one.

It's No Secret . . . Anymore

Taken from John 3

Foundation

Take some time to talk with God before you begin today's lesson.
Ask Him to speak to your heart and help you to see how He can
change lives from the inside out.

Focus

*Have you ever watched someone you know begin to change
and do unexpected things?*

"Rabbi, everyone knows God speaks through You. No one could do the
miracles You do if God were not with him," the man stated. He was a
Pharisee and a member of the Sanhedrin, the Jewish ruling council.

Many members of the Sanhedrin considered Jesus an uneducated and
self-made rabbi. "Jesus didn't go through the years of schooling we went
through!" they muttered under their breath. "Yet so many people follow Him
and listen to His teachings!" others added in a jealous tone of voice. The
religious leaders had a growing dislike for Jesus and watched Him carefully.

Nicodemus and Joseph of Arimathea, also members of the Sanhedrin,
took an interest in Jesus too, but for different reasons. They had heard

reports about His teachings and the wonderful miracles He performed. *No self-made rabbi could do these things*, they thought. *Jesus must be a teacher from God!*

Nicodemus needed to find out for himself, so he slipped out in the dark of night to see Jesus. A night visit would ensure secrecy and give Nicodemus an opportunity to catch Jesus alone, away from the crowds.

Nicodemus looked over his shoulder. Seeing Jesus could be risky and might cause trouble if the other Pharisees found out.

"The truth is," Jesus said to Nicodemus when they met, "you cannot enter God's kingdom unless you have been born again."

These words hit Nicodemus like a bomb. He was from a good family, held a high religious position, and was wealthy. Why wouldn't he see the kingdom of God? The words Jesus spoke seemed strange.

"Born again?" Nicodemus asked, "I've already been born and now I'm old! I can't crawl back into my mother's womb—no one can!"

"You're a teacher of the Jewish people," Jesus replied gently, "and yet you don't understand this?" Jesus continued, explaining to Nicodemus that being born again meant being born again spiritually. He told Nicodemus how the Son of Man must die on a cross to pay the penalty for people's wickedness and sins.

Jesus then told Nicodemus about God's tender love and compassion. "Because of God's great love, He sent His only Son into the world. Anyone who believes in the Son will never die but will live forever."

Nicodemus looked thoughtful. He wanted what Jesus talked about but needed time to think.

The Sanhedrin was made up of seventy religious leaders and functioned like a supreme court for the Jews.

Nicodemus thought God's kingdom meant the deliverance of the entire nation of Israel from her enemies. Jesus corrected him, stating that God's kingdom is personal—not national. Some Jews today still look for a coming Messiah who will deliver them nationally. They miss the point.

Footwork

We don't know exactly what Nicodemus decided, but we do begin to see a change
mysteriously taking place in his heart. Look up John 3:2 in your Bible. What does
this verse tell you? Now skip ahead to John 7:50–51. What was Nicodemus doing
here? Do you notice a difference in him? Fearful Nicodemus found the courage to
speak up for Jesus. Lastly, turn to John 19:39–40. What was Nicodemus doing publicly? Notice how many spices he brought! He would almost need a wheelbarrow to
carry them through town—it would have been hard to be secretive about that!

Fruit

Take a moment and evaluate your life. By your actions, can
others tell that you love Jesus, or are you still trying to follow
Jesus secretly—in the dark? If you're hiding your faith, ask God to
take away your fear of what others think. Take steps to be more
open about what you believe. Don't be ashamed to be associated
with Jesus. He's not ashamed to be associated with you.

uicide.   •   27 BC — Octavian

89

I Pledge Allegiance
Taken from John 9

— Foundation —

Get alone with God for a few minutes. Tell Him about the things that matter to you. Ask Him to search your heart and help you be the person He wants you to be.

Focus

Have you ever stood for something you knew was true, even though no one stood with you?

One day as Jesus and the disciples were leaving the temple and walking down the street, they saw a man who had been blind since birth. "Teacher," the disciples asked curiously, "was this man born blind because he sinned or because his parents sinned?"

"Neither," Jesus replied. "He was born this way so that people would see God's power at work in his life."

With that, Jesus bent down, spat on the ground to make mud, and gently spread some on the man's eyes. "Now wash yourself in the Pool of Siloam," He instructed.

The man left to do exactly as Jesus said.

As cool water dripped down the man's face, he began to see something. "What is that?" he breathed excitedly. Slowly the black shadows began to melt into shapes and color. *Could that be a bird?* he wondered. "And those must be flowers!" he exclaimed with great joy. "Hey! I can see! I can see!"

(Augustus Caesar) becomes first emperor

Quickly he ran back home. Those who had seen him begging on the streets couldn't believe it was him. "It can't be," they whispered to one another. "It must be someone who just looks like that blind beggar!"

The healed man insisted he was in fact the blind beggar, and the people looked at him suspiciously. "Tell us how your eyes were opened!" they demanded.

The beggar told them exactly what Jesus had done.

The one who healed you can't be from God," they protested, "because He broke the Sabbath! Where is this man?"

"I don't know," answered the healed man.

Unable to find Jesus to ask him questions, the people took the man to the Pharisees who weren't so excited about the healing. Not long ago Jesus had healed someone on the Sabbath and then claimed to be God! Because of that, the religious leaders made a law warning that if anyone even said Jesus was the Christ, they would be kicked out of the synagogue forever.

The Pharisees weren't convinced of what the blind man said, so they sent for his parents to identify him.

"Yes, this is our son," they nodded. When asked why he was able to see, the parents knew that if they said it was because Jesus miraculously healed him, they would risk being thrown out of the synagogue! "Why don't you ask him? He's old enough to speak for himself!" they safely replied.

So the Pharisees summoned the healed man again. "Give the glory for your healing to God alone. We know Jesus is a sinner because He

> *The water that was poured over the animal sacrifice at the Feast of Tabernacles came from the Pool of Siloam. That water reminded the Jewish people of how God provided water for the Israelites in the wilderness. (See* **Faith Factor OT** *for details, or read about it for yourself in the Old Testament—Genesis 17 and Numbers 20.) Jesus possibly pointed to this very pool when He said, "If anyone is thirsty, let him come to me and drink" (John 7:37).*

healed on the Sabbath. He isn't from God," they flatly stated.

The blind man looked at them. It was wonderful to see things he had only heard or imagined before. This was truly a miracle. "I don't know if this man is a sinner, but I'm sure of one thing. I once was a blind beggar—but now I can see!"

Not liking that answer, the Pharisees demanded, "What did Jesus do to open your eyes?"

"I've already told you once and you refused to listen," the man replied. "Do you want me to tell you again so that you can become His disciples too?" he challenged.

The Pharisees grew angry. "You're a follower of Jesus! We're followers of Moses! We know for a fact that God appeared to Moses and spoke to him, but as for this Jesus who healed you, we don't know anything about Him or where He's from!" they shouted.

"I find that amazing," the healed man answered. "You have no idea where He comes from, and yet He healed me. Everyone knows that God listens only to those who do His will, not to sinners. Opening the eyes of a man born blind is no small thing. This man couldn't have done what He did unless He was from God."

The religious leaders began to hurl insults at the healed man and viciously accuse him. "You were born blind because you were unworthy," they attacked him with their words. "How dare you talk to us in such a way!" They then threw him out of the synagogue and forbade him to come back.

When Jesus heard about this, He came looking for the man. "Do you believe in God's special Son?" Jesus asked.

"Yes, I do, Sir, but who is He?" the man replied.

Jesus tenderly answered, "You are looking at Him; He is speaking to you right now."

"I believe in You, Lord," the man cried out and fell to his knees in worship.

Footwork

Look up John 9:25 in your Bible. How did the man respond to the angry accusations of the religious leaders? Look at the words carefully. The man had experienced something for himself—something no one could deny or take away from him.

Fruit

If you make a stand for Jesus, you may face being called names (such as "intolerant"), being threatened by others, or being pushed out of your group of friends. As Jesus came looking for the man who honored Him, He will come looking for you and will stand by your side. Don't let our society of "tolerance and diversity" silence you. Instead, be courageous and stand firmly on what you know and have personally experienced. Jesus will stand with you.

I Know That Voice!
Taken from John 10

— Foundation —

As you prepare for today's lesson, ask Jesus to help you trust in His tender care for you.

Focus

Have you ever had someone who cared for you no matter what you did, was always there for you, and was willing to fight to protect you?

"Just as a good shepherd lays his life on the line for his sheep, I also give My life for My sheep," Jesus began. His words were simple yet packed with meaning. The crowd listened contentedly. They were familiar with sheep and shepherds, yet somehow Jesus added new meaning to this everyday topic.

Everyone knew the lives of sheep depended heavily upon their shepherd. In the evening, wild animals such as lions, bears, and wolves, were a constant danger. It wasn't uncommon for hired workers, who were concerned only about making money, to run in fear and leave the flock behind. They didn't care, because the sheep didn't belong to them.

Jesus explained that He was the Good Shepherd; He would lay down His life to protect and defend even the littlest of sheep.

Part of a shepherd's job was to continually move his sheep to greener pastures to graze. If he didn't, the sheep would graze too much in one spot and ruin the land. Ruined land meant disease and no food for the sheep. While moving the sheep around, sometimes the shepherd would sense his flock getting frightened and would walk among them—perhaps making clicking sounds to let them know of his presence to comfort and calm them.

Shepherds also protected and rescued their sheep from danger. A simple drink from a fast-moving stream would often result in disaster for unsuspecting sheep. Some might get carried downstream, and others would drown because their wool soaked up water and weighed them down. When it was necessary for the sheep to cross a stream, they knew that the safest spot was right next to the shepherd, who would protect them.

It was a common fact that a good shepherd knew his sheep and gave each one a name. In the morning hours the shepherd went to a walled sheep pen where the sheep were often kept together for safety at night. Each shepherd called his flock out from among the others and led them to pasture. The sheep knew their shepherd's voice and came willingly when he spoke, but if a stranger called them, they wouldn't respond.

If night fell before the shepherd could lead his sheep safely back to the pen, the shepherd would look for an area closed in on three sides by rocks or other barriers. He would then lie down and close off the fourth side with his own body. He became the door or gate to the pen.

In chapter 34 of the Old Testament book of Ezekiel, the prophet predicted the coming of the Messiah, calling Him a shepherd.

For more information on the Good Shepherd, check out Psalm 23 in the Old Testament. David, who wrote that psalm, was a shepherd himself.

Not only is Jesus the Good Shepherd, but He's also called the Great Shepherd (Hebrews 13:20) and the Chief Shepherd (1 Peter 5:4).

"I am the Gate for My sheep," Jesus said to His listeners. All those who enter the sheep pen through Me will be safe. No thief will be able to harm them. The reason I came was so that My sheep would have life."

Jesus' words rang true as the crowd realized they were like sheep in need of a shepherd—not just any shepherd, but Jesus the Good Shepherd. They understood that Jesus would watch over those who followed Him and would always be there to lead them.

Jesus the Good Shepherd not only cares for His sheep but also backs up His words with His very life.

Footwork

In your Bible, turn to John 10:14 and read it. What does it say? In what way is this true (or not true) of you?

Fruit

Just as Jesus talked about thieves and robbers trying to steal His sheep, there will be false shepherds who will try to get you to follow them. They may promise you special privileges or abilities. They may promise you greener pastures. Don't be fooled. Know and follow Jesus' voice only. He has proven His worthiness. He's the Good Shepherd who laid down His life for you.

Now This Is Serious Stuff

Taken from John 11—12

Foundation

Stop and pray. Ask God to give you wisdom to understand His Word and an open heart to examine your life.

Focus

Have you ever wanted to be important, to know that your life really counts for something?

"But Lord," the disciples pleaded, "you can't go back to Judea! Remember the Jews tried to stone you there?" The disciples couldn't believe what Jesus wanted to do.

It had been two days since He had gotten word that His dear friend Lazarus was sick. He dearly loved Lazarus and his sisters, Martha and Mary, yet He purposefully waited before going to see them, knowing certain things must first happen for God to be glorified.

Jesus told His disciples that Lazarus was sleeping, but they thought that Jesus meant he was resting and would recover.

"Lazarus has died," Jesus told His disciples plainly. "And I'm glad I wasn't there, so that you might see what I'm about to do and believe. Let's return to Judea."

Thomas couldn't believe what was happening. Almost certain that Jesus would be killed, Thomas said, "Let's all go with Him so we will die together."

As Jesus approached the village of Bethany, Martha ran to meet him. "Lord," she panted, out of breath, "if only you had come earlier, my brother would have lived. But I know nothing is impossible with You and that if You ask God, He will give You anything You ask for."

Jesus responded, "Lazarus will rise from the dead."

Martha knew Lazarus would rise in the great resurrection at the end of time, but Jesus was talking about at that moment.

> *Being a witness and giving a testimony mean presenting the facts and evidence of something you know or have experienced personally.*

"I hold in My hands the power of resurrection life," Jesus said. "Everyone who trusts in Me will live forever—even if they experience death. They will never die if they believe in Me. Do you understand and believe what I'm telling you?"

"I do believe You, Lord," she replied. "I know you're God's Son, the Christ He promised to send to us."

With that, Martha ran off to get Mary, who was still at home. Hearing that Jesus had asked for her, Mary jumped up and ran out the door. The mourners followed her, thinking she wanted to go to the tomb to weep.

When Mary reached the place where Jesus was, she fell at His feet in grief. "Lord, my brother would still be alive today if only You had come earlier."

When Jesus saw her weeping along with all the others who had come, He was deeply moved. "Where has his body been laid?" He asked tenderly.

"We'll show you," they said.

Jesus wept because of His love for Lazarus and his sisters, and some in the crowd said, "Look! Jesus obviously loved him very much!"

But others questioned, "If He could open the eyes of a blind man, why couldn't He have kept Lazarus from dying?"

They didn't know God's plan.

Arriving at the tomb, Jesus ordered them to roll the stone away from the entrance.

"But he's been dead for over four days," they protested. "The smell will be horrible!"

"Didn't I say you would see God's power and glory if you believed?" Jesus asked.

So they rolled away the stone.

Then Jesus looked up to heaven and prayed so those standing around could hear. "Thank You, Father, for always hearing My prayers. I say this so these people will see that You hear Me and have sent Me."

Then Jesus called out loudly, "Get up, Lazarus and come out!"

The dead man suddenly appeared at the entrance of the tomb, fully alive! Jesus instructed the people to remove Lazarus's grave clothes.

When the crowd saw this, they were stunned. Many put their faith in Jesus because of this, but some reported Jesus to the Pharisees.

The Pharisees and chief priests called a meeting of the Sanhedrin. "Look what's happening here! This man is doing many wondrous signs and miracles. If we let Him continue, soon everyone will believe in Him!"

From that day on the religious leaders plotted to kill Jesus.

Time passed, and it was now six days before the Passover celebration. The raising of Lazarus had created such a stir that when Jesus ate dinner at Mary, Martha, and Lazarus's home, large crowds would stop by. They came not only to see Jesus but also Lazarus, whom Jesus had brought back to life. When word about this reached the chief priests, they desired to kill Lazarus, too, because they saw him as a threat. It was on account of Lazarus that many of the Jews were putting their faith in Jesus.

Footwork

Look up John 12:11 in your Bible. Read it once to yourself, then read it aloud, substituting *your name* for "him" and the word *people* where it says "many of the Jews." Think about what you've just read.

= made "Pontifex Maximus" — head of

Fruit

Does your life speak of the greatness of God? On a piece of paper, write down a few sentences about what your life was like before you came to know Jesus. (For example, were you fearful, lonely, selfish, unable to break a bad habit?) Now write a sentence about how God is changing you or about what He means to you. You have just written down your testimony! Don't worry if you couldn't come up with something spectacular. God often works in small and quiet ways. Pray about one person you can share your testimony with this week—and do it! If you're uncertain that you even have a personal relationship with Jesus, turn to the back of this book and prayerfully read the special message that's there for you.

Don't Worry about It
Taken from John 13—17

Foundation

Before you read through today's lesson, ask God to help you learn more about His unconditional love.

Focus

Have you ever been around someone who knows your weaknesses but loves you in spite of the hurtful things you might say or do to them?

Jesus looked at His disciples. He knew the strengths and weaknesses of each, yet He loved them beyond measure. He also knew he had very little time left with them. Although there were many things to tell them, He sought to encourage their hearts, knowing the days ahead would present one of the toughest tests they'd ever face.

"I'm going to tell you something now before it happens so that when it does, you'll believe all the more that I am who I say I am," Jesus began. His disciples listened curiously as He continued. "One of you will betray Me."

The disciples looked at one another. *Who could it be?*

"Who is it, Lord?" John asked.

Jesus answered, "The one who takes this bread from my hand is the man."

As Jesus dipped the bread and handed it to Judas, Satan entered the soon-to-be betrayer. "What you have in your heart to do, do it without

ne year after the apostle Peter is

delay," Jesus told Judas who quickly slipped away into the night.

Jesus continued, "I am going to be with you for just a little while longer. You'll search everywhere for Me, but you can't come where I'm going. Someday you'll be able to follow Me, but not now."

"But Lord," Simon Peter blurted out, "I want to go with you now! I'll even give my very life for you!"

Knowing Peter's weaknesses, Jesus patiently answered, "Are you really prepared to die for Me, Peter? This very night, before the rooster crows you'll say you never knew Me—not one time, but three separate times."

Jesus turned to His disciples. "Don't worry about what will happen. Put your faith not only in God but also in Me. I'm going back to My Father in heaven to get things ready for you. And just as I go, I promise to come back for you—for I am the Way to heaven; I am Truth; and I am Life. There is no other way to God apart from Me."

> *Jesus tells His disciples in John 14:27 that He will give them His peace. His peace is different than the temporary kind the world offers.*

Jesus went on to explain how the Father would send the Holy Spirit to comfort them. "I am giving you My peace, so don't be troubled or worried," He comforted.

Jesus then talked about how He was like a vine and they were the branches. They would have all they needed if they stayed attached to Him.

The disciples listened, but their minds wandered back to something Jesus had said earlier. *What does He mean by, "In just a short time, you won't see Me. But one day you'll see Me again?"* they wondered.

Knowing His disciples didn't understand, Jesus added, "I came into the world from My Father, and now it's time for Me to return to My Father."

"Now we understand what You're saying," they exclaimed. "We know that You came from God, and we believe in You!"

Although He was glad that they finally understood, Jesus knew that in His hour of need the disciples would turn their backs on Him and run in fear for their own lives. He could have been disappointed in the disciples or tried to make them feel bad for what they were about to do, but he didn't. No matter what their actions,

born, Virgil, a Roman poet, finishes

Jesus would always love His disciples and keep their best interest in mind. By telling them in advance what was going to happen to Him, He was lovingly preparing them for what they were about to face. And they would need His encouragement in the hours ahead.

Jesus' eyes were full of love and concern. "I have shared all of this with you so that you will find peace in Me," Jesus said. "You will experience many trials and troubles in this life. But be encouraged! I have conquered the world."

Footwork

Read John 16:33 in your Bible. Jesus tells His disciples three different facts. What does He say?

Fruit

What worries you? What takes away your peace? Jesus made you special, and He's concerned about the things that concern you. Take an index card or a piece of paper and write down three things you're most worried about. Next, write John 16:33 across the top. Spend a few minutes thanking Jesus that He is bigger than any problem you could ever face. Ask Him to give you His peace and strength to deal with your problems.

riting the Aeneid, a 12-book epic

Yeah? Prove It!

Taken from John 18

Foundation

Pray before you read through today's lesson. Ask God to speak to your heart through His Word and to help you better appreciate Jesus' determination to accomplish what He came to do.

Focus

If you knew you were going to be tortured because people didn't understand you, would you try to explain or defend yourself?

It was evening. Knowing His hour had come, Jesus took His disciples to an olive grove to pray. "Please, Father," Jesus agonized, "if there is any way possible that people can be saved without My dying on the cross, let this pass from Me. But most important, let Your will be done, not Mine."

Jesus finished praying and returned to the disciples, who were just a stone's throw away. Heavy in heart, Jesus had asked them to keep watch and pray, too, but they had fallen asleep. They had no clue what was about to happen.

Suddenly, torches lit up the olive grove. A detachment of soldiers led by Judas Iscariot came toward Jesus. The religious leaders stood in front, wearing a smug look on their faces. They laughed inwardly at their cleverness in paying one of Jesus' disciples a small amount of money to betray Him.

"Who do you want?" Jesus asked, knowing they had come for Him.

"Jesus of Nazareth," they stated.

"I am the One you seek," Jesus replied.

The authority and power of His words made them shrink back and fall to the ground, so Jesus asked them again, "Who do you want?"

When they gave Him the same reply, Jesus answered, "I already told you that I am He." Then He added, pointing to His disciples, "Since I'm the One you're looking for, let these other men leave."

Peter couldn't believe what was happening. "No! You can't take Jesus away!" he shouted as he grabbed a sword and cut off the ear of the high priest's servant.

Jesus put a stop to it immediately. "Shouldn't I do what I came to do?"

He then healed the man's ear and allowed Himself to be bound and taken away.

Just as Jesus had said, the disciples scattered in fear. Although Peter ran with the others at first, he changed his mind and secretly followed the religious leaders, keeping a safe distance. They had led Jesus through a courtyard on their way to the high priest for an illegal secret trial.

According to Jewish law, it was illegal to strike a captive.

Caiaphas, leader of the Sadducees (an elite group of Jewish religious leaders), was in good standing with Rome. He served as high priest for eighteen years and later helped to persecute the Christians.

Peter entered the courtyard and stood by the fire where others were warming their hands. Hoping to mix with the group unnoticed, he kept one eye in the direction they had taken Jesus.

"Hey," a girl remarked as she saw the flickering light fall upon Peter's face, "aren't you one of Jesus' disciples?"

"I am not," Peter shot back nervously. His body trembled with fear; surely he would be in danger if they discovered the truth. The questions came two more times as others recognized him.

"No!" Peter lied, "I don't know Him!"

Suddenly a rooster crowed three times and Peter remembered Jesus' words. He had denied Jesus just as Jesus had predicted. Peter fled, his heart torn with grief.

Behind closed doors, the high priest was still questioning Jesus concerning His disciples and His teachings. "I always spoke openly and said nothing in secret," Jesus replied. "If you ask anyone who has heard Me, they will plainly tell you what I have said."

A sharp sting shot across Jesus' face as one of the officials standing nearby slapped Him. "How dare You answer Caiaphas in such a way!" he threatened between clenched teeth. "No one of such unimportance should speak to the high priest in such a manner!"

Jesus could have proven He was far greater than any high priest but didn't. Instead, He patiently answered, "If I have said something wrong, tell Me. But if the words I have spoken are true, then why did you hit Me?"

At dawn, Jesus was taken to the palace of the Roman governor. The Jews wouldn't enter the building but remained outside for fear of becoming ceremonially unclean and not being able to celebrate the Passover. Pilate came out onto the steps and talked with them there.

"What charges do you have against this man?" he asked.

"He's a criminal!" they shouted.

Pilate told them to try Jesus in their own Jewish courts.

"We don't have the authority to execute Him!" they responded. They wanted to be certain Jesus would be put to death.

Pilate stepped back inside the palace and questioned Jesus again. "Are You really King of the Jews?" he asked. "What have You done?"

"I rule over another kingdom that is not of this world. If I were king over this world, all of My servants would have risen up to keep the Jews from arresting Me," Jesus calmly answered.

"So You admit You're a king!" Pilate replied.

Jesus stated, "What you say is true. I was born into this world to be a witness to the truth, and all those who seek truth listen to Me."

Footwork

Read John 18:11 in your Bible. What did Jesus say? Notice how He set His mind to do what He needed to do out of love for us.

Fruit

From what you've learned so far, see if you can point to five things Jesus either said or did that helped prove He was no ordinary man. (Hint: Do a quick review of the other gospel books if you need to.) Add these things to your ongoing list of what you are learning (or remembering) about Jesus.

This Was No Accident
Taken from John 18—19

Foundation

Before you begin today's lesson, spend a few minutes in prayer. Search your heart and ask God to help you see how Jesus' death was no accident.

Focus

Would you ever willingly be punished for something you didn't do?

Pilate didn't know what to do with Jesus. "As far as I'm concerned, He's done nothing wrong," Pilate told the crowd. "Since it's the Passover custom for me to release one prisoner to you, should I set the 'King of the Jews' free?" he asked, fearful of making an unpopular decision.

"No!" the mob shouted. "Don't release Him! We want Barabbas!"

Now Barabbas was a criminal worthy of punishment, but the Jews were asking for his release because they wanted Pilate to kill an innocent man!

Granting the crowd their desire, Pilate ordered Jesus to be taken away, where He was stripped of His clothes and severely beaten. One by one, each stinging blow from a whip with clawlike metal pieces landed across His back, ripping open His skin.

"All praise to the Jewish king!" the soldiers mocked, bowing down before Jesus and laughing. They placed a purple robe on Him and shoved a crown of thorns on His head, which dug into His scalp and caused a flow of blood to trickle down. The soldiers then hit Jesus and spit in His face.

AD 4 — Herod the Great dies, and accordir

Wanting to give the crowd one last chance to do the right thing, Pilate brought Jesus out before them again. "Here is Jesus," Pilate said.

"Crucify Him! Crucify Him!" the angry mob shouted.

"Take Him and crucify Him yourself!" Pilate said. "I see nothing wrong with which to charge Him."

"Our law says that He must die for claiming to be the Son of God," they shouted.

When Pilate heard this, he grew afraid and pulled Jesus to the side. "Tell me where You're from," he said in a panicked voice. When Jesus gave no answer, Pilate demanded, "Why don't You speak to me? Don't You know that I have the power to set You free or to crucify You?"

Jesus replied, "The only power you have is that which God has allowed."

Pilate was torn. "This Man claims to be your king," he said to the enraged mob. "Do you really want me to crucify Him?"

"Caesar is our only king!" they yelled.

Pilate then turned Jesus over to be crucified. Soldiers led Jesus through the streets, forcing Him to carry the crossbeam of His own cross. Reaching Golgotha, the soldiers drove metal spikes into Jesus' hands and feet and hung Him between two criminals who were also being crucified that day. They then divided up Jesus' clothes, casting lots for His tunic. This act fulfilled an Old Testament prophecy: "They divide my garments amng them and cast lots for my clothing" (Psalm 22:18).

As Jesus hung on the cross, some mocked Him. Others challenged Him to come off the cross and prove His power to save Himself. "He saved others, but he can't save himself!" they laughed. (See Matthew 27:39–42.)

Jesus could have proven His power but would not. He knew everything

> *When Jesus said, "It is finished," He used the Greek word* tetélestai, *a business term meaning "paid in full."*

> *The veil in the temple was several feet thick and prevented people from coming into the presence of God. With Jesus' death on the cross, it was torn open by God's own hand, now providing access for all.*

that was taking place had to be completed so the Scriptures would be fulfilled.

Looking to heaven He cried out, "Father, into your hands I commit my Spirit. It is finished."

At that instant, the veil in the temple was miraculously torn in two from top to bottom.

Since the next day was Passover, the Jews asked the soldiers to break the legs of those being crucified so they could die more quickly and be buried before the Sabbath began. After breaking the legs of the two criminals, the soldiers came to Jesus and noticed He was already dead, so they left His legs unbroken. Wanting be sure Jesus was really dead, one soldier thrust a spear into Jesus' side, causing blood and water to flow out.

Even in dying, Jesus was in control and fulfilling details of prophecy: "Not one of [his bones] will be broken" (Psalm 34:20) and "They will look on...the one they have pierced" (Zechariah 12:10).

Jesus' death was no accident; it was an event planned by God for a very special purpose.

Footwork

In your Bible, read John 19:30. What were Jesus' words? Do you think He was talking about His life or the payment for man's sins?

Fruit

If someone said to you, "It's a shame. Jesus was just a good man who happened to be in the wrong place at the wrong time and got killed," what would you say in response?

four parts. His son, Antipas inherits

Seeing Is Believing?
Taken from John 20

- *Foundation*

Take a few minutes to quiet your heart . Thank Jesus for what He has done for you, and ask God to strengthen your faith in Him.

Focus

Have you ever doubted your faith? Have you ever asked in the back of your mind, "How can I know for sure I'm right?

"No! It can't be!" Mary Magdalene panicked. She had come to the tomb during the last watches of the night. Even in the early morning light, Mary could plainly see something was not right. Although a large stone sealed the tomb's entrance to prevent anyone from entering the cave and stealing Jesus' body, the stone had been rolled away! Unable to bear this bad news alone, Mary ran to tell Peter and John.

"They have taken the Lord out of the tomb," she panted, trying to catch her breath, "and we don't know where they have put him!" Despair filled her voice.

Peter and John immediately began running to the tomb. Mary followed behind, unable to keep up.

Being first to reach the tomb, John peered in and saw the strips of linen Jesus had been wrapped in. *No one would steal a body and take the linen off,* he thought.

Peter came down the path, pushed past John, and went inside the tomb. He was out of breath and wheezing. Looking over at the linens, Peter noticed they were intact—as if the body had just evaporated right out of them! Seeing Peter in the tomb, John cautiously stepped inside, saw the linens, and believed along with Peter that Jesus had risen from the dead—although neither understood how. Puzzled by what they had seen, the disciples went back home.

The "last watches of the night" was usually between 3:00 and 6:00 a.m. in the morning. It was customary to visit the tomb of someone you loved for three days after the burial. Since traveling wasn't permitted on the Sabbath, this was the soonest Mary could come.

Finally Mary arrived and was alone at the tomb—or so she thought. Her eyes were puffy and swollen with tears.

"Woman," a voice spoke from behind her, "why are you crying? Who is it you are looking for?"

Mary, who thought the gardener was speaking to her, didn't turn from the empty tomb. "Sir, if you have taken Him away," she managed between sobs, "please tell me where you have put Him, so I can get Him."

Jesus finally said to her, "Mary."

The sound of that voice was strangely wonderful—so full of love and tenderness! She turned toward the voice and looked right into the eyes of Jesus. "Rabboni!" she cried as she reached out to Him.

"Don't cling to Me, Mary; I haven't yet returned to heaven. But go and tell the others that I'm alive, for they will want to see Me, too."

Mary took off running. She had never felt so light and full of speed! Finding the disciples, she burst out, "The Lord is alive! I've seen Him!" and began to tell them what Jesus told her.

Later that day the disciples were secretly meeting in an upper room of a house. The same Jewish authorities who had put Jesus to death would no doubt be looking for them, too! They held their breath at the sound of footsteps and every knock at the door. All the disciples were there except Thomas, who wanted to be alone in his grief.

"Be at peace!" Jesus said, suddenly appearing before their eyes.

At first the disciples wondered if He was a ghost, but after Jesus showed them His hands and His side, they were overcome with joy. So it *was* true! Jesus *did* rise from the dead! They must tell Thomas!

Thomas was always cautious and slow to believe, but when he did believe something, he believed it with all his heart. "You saw His hands and side, but unless I place my finger in the nail marks on His hands and my hand in the wound on His side, I will not believe," Thomas replied.

A week had gone by and the disciples were meeting behind locked doors in the upper room again. Thomas joined them this time, and Jesus appeared just as He had before. "Thomas," Jesus said lovingly, "feel the nail marks and stick your hand into my side. No longer doubt, but believe!"

Thomas did as Jesus invited him to do. "You are my Lord and my God!" he breathed in an almost whisperlike voice filled with love and awe.

"You believe, Thomas, because you've seen Me and touched Me. But the ones who are truly blessed are those who haven't seen Me and yet believe," Jesus tenderly replied.

Footwork

Read John 20:29 in your Bible. The second sentence is talking about us! What does it say?

Fruit

Have you ever wondered why the stone was rolled away? God rolled it away not for His own benefit, but for ours. He invites people to see the proof of the empty tomb and believe. Jesus' death and resurrection are historical facts that have been documented by both Christians and nonChristians. We have these facts written down for us in the Scriptures so we might know what happened and believe.

Turn to John 20:31 in your Bible and mark it with a highlighter. Read it aloud several times, emphasizing a different word each time you read it. Think about what you are reading, and memorize the verse. Remember that your doubts and fears never alarm God. Tell Him about the things you struggle with, and ask Him to help you grow in your faith.

twelve, amazing the religious lead-

But What About . . .?

Taken from John 21

Foundation

Spend a few moments talking to God. Ask Him to examine your heart and help you to love and follow Jesus all the more.

FOCUS

Do you find it hard to do what you're supposed to do because you're distracted by what other people are or aren't doing?

"Nothing! Plain old nothing!" Peter grunted as they pulled in the nets. They had been fishing all night. Now it was morning, and they had nothing to show for all their work. Not one fish! It was embarrassing.

"Friends," a voice called from the shore, "try throwing your nets on the other side of the boat!"

The disciples looked at one another. It wasn't uncommon for people standing onshore to see fish in the clear water. Oftentimes fishermen would have a helper who stood onshore and called out directions for where to throw the net. The disciples were so discouraged, they were willing to listen to any advice and did as the stranger suggested.

Suddenly something tugged at the net, and the boat tilted. The net was full of fish! John looked up at the stranger on the shore and exclaimed, "It's Jesus!"

Peter jerked his head up and looked with excitement. He wanted to be the first to greet the Lord, so he quickly put on his outer garment, jumped into the water, and started swimming. The others followed along in the boat, dragging the fish behind them.

ers with His knowledge and understanding.

Arriving on shore they smelled the sweet aroma of fish cooking and saw fresh loaves of bread. "Come and join Me for breakfast," Jesus invited.

After the meal, Jesus turned to Peter and asked, "Peter, do you love Me more than they do?"

Peter looked at the other disciples. He remembered how he had bragged about loving Jesus more than they did. He also remembered boldly insisting that he was willing to die for Jesus even if everyone else denied Him.

"Yes, Lord," Peter said uncomfortably. "You know I do!"

"Peter," Jesus said a second time, "do you really love Me?"

Peter closed his eyes for a moment. He wanted to blot out the terrible memory of hearing the rooster crow after he had denied his Lord. Again, he answered, "Yes, Lord, You know I love You!"

According to Jewish law, it was considered a religious act to offer someone a greeting. Since no religious act could be done unless a person was fully clothed, Peter quickly put on his outer tunic before jumping into the water.

Jesus then looked deep into Peter's eyes and lovingly asked for the third time, "Do you truly love Me, Peter?"

Peter felt very hurt, but he met Jesus' gaze. "Lord, you know all things," he said longingly. "You know that I love you."

"Then take care of my sheep and feed them," Jesus replied tenderly.

Not only did Jesus forgive Peter for denying Him, but he also trusted Peter with a job to do! Peter was to take care of other believers who were Jesus' flock of sheep. Jesus explained to Peter how God would use him and how he would eventually die. Then Jesus said, "Follow Me!" Those words were familiar to Peter because they were the same words Jesus had used when He first called Peter to be one of His disciples.

Peter's heart leapt within him, then a quick, panicky feeling struck. Noticing that John was following behind them, Peter asked, "Lord, what about him?"

"What difference does it make to you what John does or doesn't do?" Jesus questioned. "You must decide to follow Me for yourself, Peter, regardless of what other people think or do."

Footwork

Read John 21:21 in your Bible. Read it again, substituting your name for Peter's and the name of someone who distracts you after the words: "Lord, and what about ...?" Now skip down to verse 22 and read Jesus' reply to you.

Fruit

You'll be tempted at times to look at others and measure yourself by what they do or don't do. Don't! Your walk and relationship with God depends on no one else but you. With your eyes on the Lord and your Bible as your guide, walk with Him. Don't worry if others follow.

over Rome and reigns for twenty-two year

He was bitter and ill-tempered, ter—

rorizing people toward the end of his reign

Acts

Acts is an exciting book full of history about the beginning of the church and the first Christians. It helps us see exactly what happened after Jesus rose from the dead and returned to heaven. In Acts we see the beginning of the Christian church, the missionary journeys of Paul and Peter, and other exciting events.

Acts was written by Luke, the same person who wrote the gospel of Luke. The first verse of Acts opens where the last verse in the gospel of Luke ends—almost like part 2 of the story. In the Gospels we see Jesus dying for our sins. In Acts we see Him very much alive and being glorified in heaven. In the Gospels we learn about Jesus' teachings, and in Acts we see the results of those teachings and what He continues to do in and through the lives of His followers.

As you read through Acts, keep your eyes open for events that took place during Paul's three missionary journeys and the names of the different places he visited. You'll see those names again as you continue your journey through the New Testament. Above all, enjoy your journey through this wonderful book. You'll find that it's like a giant puzzle board into which all the other pieces of the New Testament fit. ———————

When he died, everyone rejoiced.

Do What?!

Taken from Acts 1

Foundation

As you prepare your heart for today's lesson, ask the Lord to point out what needs to change in your life.

Focus

Have you ever been told to do something, but you didn't know how to begin?

The disciples looked at one another in awkward silence. In the forty days since Jesus had been raised from the dead, He had talked with them, eaten with them, and even let them see and touch His scars so they would know that He really was alive. He also continued teaching about the kingdom of God so they could be sure it was Him and not an imposter. For forty days He had come and gone, but today something was very different.

"Stay in Jerusalem," Jesus instructed His disciples. "Wait here to receive the gift I told you about that My Father promised to send you."

The disciples weren't sure what this meant. "Are You going to bring the kingdom back to Israel now?" they asked.

Jesus corrected them and gave them a challenge: "My Father has planned the exact time of My return, but this isn't something for you to know. But He will send you the Holy Spirit, who will give you power to testify about Me in Jerusalem, Judea, Samaria, and throughout the entire world."

When Jesus finished speaking those words, He was taken up to heaven.

AD 21 — Rome begins to manufacture pens and

Speechless and amazed, the disciples stood watching until they could no longer see Jesus in the clouds. *Jesus wants us to go and tell others about what we know and have experienced,* they thought among themselves. *But first we have to wait? Wait for how long? And how will we know when we receive this gift? Will we recognize it when it comes?* All these questions raced through their minds as they looked up into the sky.

Suddenly two men dressed in white appeared. "Why are you standing here looking to the heavens?" they asked the disciples. "Don't you know that this Jesus, who has gone into heaven on a cloud, will come back exactly the same way—just as He said?"

With that the disciples left the Mount of Olives and returned to Jerusalem. When they arrived, they went to the upper room where they had been staying and meeting together. All eleven of the disciples were there, as well as Jesus' brothers, His mother, and other women who were His followers. At first there was uncertainty about what to do next. While they waited for God to send His promised gift, should they make special plans for spreading the news about Jesus around the world? Should they divide themselves into teams and map out the areas surrounding them? Should they all stay together as one group? How would they go about this task Jesus gave them to do?

But rather than worry about how they would carry out Jesus' instructions to be His witnesses, the disciples decided they would do God's work in

Houses in the disciples' time were built with smaller rooms on the main floor to support big rooms on the top level. These upper rooms were places where large groups would commonly meet.

Jesus will one day return in the clouds to the Mount of Olives (Zechariah 14:4)—the same place and the same way He left this earth. He will return in the same resurrected body He had when He appeared to His disciples, and everyone on earth will see Him (Revelation 1:7). Although we know where and how this will take place, we don't know when (Acts 1:7).

God's way. Before doing anything else, they prayed together and then waited for the Holy Spirit Jesus had promised to send.

Footwork

Look up Acts 1:8 in your Bible. What two things did Jesus say would happen to the disciples?

Skip down to verse 14. What did the disciples and those with them do?

Fruit

This week you may be faced with a big task which seems hard to begin. What will your first move be? Will you jump right in and try tackling it in your own enthusiasm until you run out of steam or motivation? Will you seek the counsel of many friends until the waters are muddied with all the choices and opinions you've gotten? Or will you simply try to gut things out in your own strength? Take a moment to evaluate your usual response in situations like this. In the Old Testament God states, "'Not by might nor by power, but by my Spirit,' says the Lord Almighty" (Zechariah 4:6). Memorize this verse, then look for other verses in the Bible that talk about living life in God's strength and power instead of your own.

Special Delivery
Taken from Acts 2

Foundation

Before you read today's lesson, spend some time talking with God. Ask Him to help you understand the strength He offers you and how it can take you beyond your own abilities.

Focus

Does it ever make you curious when your friends suddenly do something they wouldn't or couldn't do before?

It was the celebration of Pentecost—one of three festivals that every Jewish male living within twenty miles of Jerusalem had to attend. The streets were full of people and buzzing with activity.

During this celebration the disciples continued praying and waiting for the gift Jesus had promised to give them. Before going back to heaven, Jesus had told them to wait for this gift in Jerusalem. He said that they would receive power when the Holy Spirit came upon them, but so far nothing had happened. The disciples had been meeting constantly to pray, and they had even selected another apostle named Matthias to take the place of Judas, the one who betrayed Jesus. The number of Jesus' disciples had now grown to 120 (Acts 1:15), and on the day of Pentecost, they were all together in one place. That's when it happened.

A loud rush of wind burst down from heaven and swirled about them, and what looked like individual flames of fire hovered above the head of each person in the room. The apostles couldn't help but think back to Moses and the way God had used a pillar of fire to guide the Israelites through the desert and show them His presence—just as He was now showing His presence to all those in that room. (See Exodus 13:21–22.)

> **Disciple** *was the general name for any believer and follower of Jesus Christ.* **Apostle** *(or "sent one") was the term given to the twelve disciples Jesus sent out to tell the world about Him. They had been trained by Him and were eyewitness of His life, death, and resurrection.*

As the Spirit of God rested on each believer, he or she began to speak in different languages. They were all baptized into with the Holy Spirit, who would comfort, guide, and enable them to do God's will. This was the gift Jesus had promised them when He said, "John baptized with water, but in a few days you will be baptized with the Holy Spirit" (Acts 1:5).

What joy! What power! What a surprise!

People on the street heard this noise and stopped in front of the house to listen. Many understood what was being said because the language they heard was their own native tongue.

Amazed, they asked, "What's the meaning of all this?"

Some, however, made fun of the disciples. Laughing, they answered, "They've simply had too much wine to drink!"

Hearing this, Peter spoke to the crowd. He was no longer a coward, afraid to stand up for Jesus.

"Pay careful attention to me," Peter fearlessly proclaimed. "The men who are speaking aren't drunk. Who would be at this time of day? But you're witnessing what the prophet Joel foretold long ago. It's only nine in the morning! No, this is what was spoken by the prophet Joel."

The crowd listened as Peter continued to boldly tell them that Jesus was the Messiah—the only One approved by God—and that He was able to back up His words with His actions. Peter explained how Jesus fulfilled the Old Testament prophecies, how His dying on the cross was no accident, and how His resurrection from the dead proved His claims about Himself. "Let everyone be sure of this," Peter said as a final challenge to them. "You may have crucified Jesus, but God raised Him from the dead and made Him to be both Lord and Christ."

His words pierced the people's hearts. "Tell us what we should do!" they said.

Peter answered simply but powerfully: "Turn away from your sins, seek God's forgiveness, and be baptized in the name of Jesus Christ."

Those who heard and received Peter's powerful message were baptized, and about three thousand people became followers of Jesus that day!

Footwork

Acts 2:47 says, "The Lord added to their number daily those who were being saved." Think about this for a few minutes, then read the verse aloud, emphasizing the word *Lord*. How does saying it this way change your thoughts?

Fruit

Think about your life. Do you count more on your strength, or do you rely on God's strength? Which do you think is more dependable and gets better results? If you said God's strength, you're absolutely right! Take a moment right now and ask God's forgiveness for the times you've tried to live life in your own strength and haven't given His power a chance to be lived out in your life. Then make a commitment to walk with Him through the power of His Holy Spirit in you. You'll experience a peace and joy you've never had before.

He's Changed

Taken from Acts 4

— Foundation —

Before you begin today's lesson, spend a few minutes talking to God. Ask Him to help you understand the power He has to change lives.

FOCUS

Do you know anyone who has changed so much that it makes others stand back and say, "Wow! What happened?"

"We're telling you that if you continue to preach and teach about Jesus, you'll regret the day you were ever born!" the religious leaders said with a sneer.

"Yes," threatened one of the members of the Sanhedrin. "Don't you remember that we have the power to deliver you over to the Romans to be put to death, or have you already forgotten the death of Jesus?"

> *The name Sanhedrin, the Jewish ruling council in Jerusalem, comes from two words meaning "together" and "seat." The Pharisees (who relied heavily on the prophets) and the Sadducees (who relied mainly on the Law of Moses) made up this political body.*

Peter stood there, unflinching. He could feel the hot, heavy breath of the one threatening him. Peter and John had been arrested by the Sanhedrin for preaching about Jesus and for a wonderful miracle that God performed through them—healing a crippled man in Jesus' name.

As Peter listened to what would happen if they didn't stop preaching about Jesus, he thought about his Lord. It seemed only

crucified, buried, and rises from the

yesterday that Jesus Himself had stood trial before these very men. Peter's mind raced back to Jesus' loving response to his once prideful boasting.

"I'll never deny You, Lord," Peter had announced, "even if everyone else falls away!" (See Matthew 26:33.)

Peter closed his eyes as he recalled the rooster crowing when he denied Jesus the third time. What a coward he had been to deny the One who loved him so very much. But all that was past now. Jesus had personally forgiven Peter and had given him a special job to do. Not only that, but the power of the Holy Spirit was present for him and all the disciples to rely on. Peter had changed. He now had a boldness and power that amazed even him!

"Have we made ourselves clear?" the voice demanded, snapping Peter back to the present.

Peter looked over at John, who was also being threatened, and he spoke for them both. "Can't you see that we must obey God instead of man? We can't keep quiet about all the incredible things we've witnessed."

The Sadducees were wealthy religious rulers who came from the line of priests. They didn't believe in angels or in the resurrection of the dead. It has been said, "That's why they were SAD, YOU SEE!

The Sadducees tolerated the Pharisee's talk of life after death, dismissing it only as a theory. But Peter and John's message of Jesus rising from the dead threatened them because it was based on reality.

This infuriated the Sanhedrin, but they realized there was nothing more they could do, so they released Peter and John.

Rejoining the other believers, the two reported what had happened to them and the threats made against them if they should choose to continue spreading their message about Jesus. After hearing this, the believers united in prayer. They didn't ask God to take away their problems. Instead, they thanked Him that He was in control.

"Lord, you know about these threats against us. Help us to continue speaking out boldly in your name," they prayed.

When they had finished praying, the place where they were meeting began to shake, and all of them were filled with the Holy Spirit's power and boldly declared the Word of God.

Footwork

In your Bible, read Acts 4:29. What specifically did the believers ask God to do for them? Would you have asked that?

Fruit

Peter and John's experiences with Jesus and the empowering of God's Spirit completely transformed their lives. They knew what and in whom they believed, and they were willing to stand on that fact. Look up Acts 4:12 in your Bible and read it, emphasizing the word *no* each time you see it. Then read the verse several more times until you've memorized it. This is solid ground on which to stand, and it's the very fact Peter and John stood upon.

Crime Doesn't Pay
Taken from Acts 4—5

Foundation

Take a few minutes to quiet your thoughts before you begin today's lesson. Tell God what's on your heart and ask Him to help you understand what's on His.

Focus

Do you have a friend who acts one way at church to impress others but acts a totally different way the rest of the week?

Great things were happening in the group of believers. Even though they heard the warnings and threats about what would happen if they continued to speak out about Jesus, they stood firm. And God stood with them, blessing them beyond measure. Such a spirit of love and unity filled the believers that they willingly shared what little they had with those in need. The new believers thought of one another as brothers and sisters. Barnabas was one such example. Although his real name was Joseph, the apostles renamed him Barnabas ("Son of Encouragement") because he had a way of encouraging others.

One day Barnabas sold some land he owned and presented the money to the group. "This is for the needs of others," he said, laying it at the apostles' feet. No one had asked him to do this; he did it out of his love for Jesus and a willingness to help other believers.

When Ananias and his wife, Sapphira, saw Barnabas's example and the

to capture and persecute Christians.

Barnabas, a Levite from the island of Cyprus, was an early disciple of Jesus. It was he who later introduced the newly converted Paul to the apostles in Jerusalem (Acts 9:27) and accompanied him on his first missionary journey.

Striking Ananias and Sapphira dead seems like a harsh judgment, but God used it to make a point and set an example. In the Old Testament, God commanded the Israelites to stone Achan to death for hiding stolen goods in his tent (Joshua 7:25–26).

praise he received, they went out and sold some of their land, hoping to gain a little attention and glory for themselves.

"Wait a minute," Ananias said. "Why should we give all the money we earned when we can keep some for ourselves and let everyone think we brought it all?"

"That's a great idea!" Sapphira agreed. "No one will ever know."

The two planned what they would tell the others and how much money they would keep back for themselves. Ananias rose early the next morning, taking extra time to look his best so that he would make a big impression on the others. *Wait until they see what I have to share with the group*, he thought proudly, feeling smug about his and Sapphira's little secret.

Just as Barnabas had done, Ananias came and laid his money from the sale at the apostles' feet, announcing, "The Lord directed me to sell my field and bring in the money to help other believers in need." He waited for a response of appreciation, but he didn't get the one he expected.

"Ananias," Peter replied, "you have given Satan a foothold in your life. You could have kept a part of the money from the sale for yourself, but instead, you sought to deceive. You thought you could get away with lying to us, but in fact you lied to God."

When those words struck Ananias's heart, God struck Ananias dead. After he was taken away to be buried, the group who had seen what happened fell silent in great fear and awe of God. God demanded that they have pure hearts before Him, and He wouldn't tolerate dishonesty.

Three hours later Sapphira came in, unaware of what had happened to her husband. Expecting a grand welcome for the wonderfully generous thing she and Ananias had done, she was startled when she didn't get the reaction she had expected.

"Tell me," Peter said, "is this the full price you received for selling your land?"

Sapphira didn't even bat an eye. "Of course! That's all of it!"

"Have you agreed to lie," Peter asked, challenging her, "testing God's Holy Spirit to see how much you can get away with before He judges you? Look over there! The very men who buried your husband are coming to carry your body out as well."

With that, Sapphira fell dead at Peter's feet, and the men carried her body out, burying her next to her husband.

Footwork

In your Bible, read Acts 5:4. Then read the last sentence again. Lying to God is pretty serious stuff!

Fruit

God already knows your thoughts, so don't even think about lying to Him. The consequences can be deadly serious! Instead, love and serve Him with your whole heart. Don't pretend to give Him everything if you're holding something back.

We're Baaack!

Taken from Acts 5

Foundation

Stop and pray before you read today's lesson. Ask God to help you understand the importance of obeying Him.

Focus

Laws are for us to obey, but should we obey man's laws if it means disobeying God's laws?

Solomon's Colonnade was a large porch on the east side of the temple where all the believers of Jesus met. Since word of Ananias and Sapphira's fate had spread, people were more cautious about joining the believers. They didn't want their halfheartedness toward the things of God to cause the same thing to happen to them. As a result, the believers (now called the church) were protected from hypocrites and pretenders, and God increased the number of true believers daily.

Miracles occurred often, and because the believers met at a public place on the temple grounds, the crowds that gathered there stood in awe as they witnessed the incredible things God was doing through these followers of Jesus. Peter and the apostles were also regarded with great respect in the people's eyes.

When the members of the Sanhedrin saw the believers' popularity, they became jealous and fearful. Such a large following could cause an uprising, and the Roman government would step in and no longer let the Sanhedrin govern the people. To keep this from happening, they arrested the apostles and put them in jail.

But God sent an angel in the middle of the night to open the doors and set the apostles free. "Go to the temple and continue preaching about Jesus," the angel told them.

So the apostles set out to do just that. At dawn they entered the temple area and began teaching the people about Jesus, just as the angel had instructed them.

Meanwhile, the high priest and his assistants called together the Sanhedrin, and they sent officers to the jail to get the apostles.

Moments later the officers returned and fearfully reported what they had discovered: "We found the jail locked and undisturbed. Even the guards were standing there. But when we opened the doors, the apostles were gone!"

This puzzled the captain of the temple guard and the chief priests. What had happened to the apostles? Suddenly a messenger burst into the room. "You won't believe this," he panted, trying to catch his breath, "but the same men you threw in jail yesterday are back in the temple courts teaching!"

The chief priests and members of the Sanhedrin were speechless. *So*, they thought, *our guards are standing guard in front of empty jail cells, and we're here ready to judge prisoners we don't even have! And if that isn't bad enough, they're outside at this very moment preaching in the temple courts under our very noses!*

> *Gamaliel, a highly respected Pharisee, was an expert in Jewish law and a member of the Sanhedrin. The apostle Paul had studied under him (Acts 22:3).*

> *Flogging was a cruel form of beating using a whip with tiny pieces of metal or bone tied to its tips to dig and tear at the skin. Jewish law limited this punishment to forty strokes and those who did the flogging rarely went over thirty-nine strokes to prevent accidentally breaking the law through a miscount. Jesus was flogged the maximum thirty-nine times.*

The temple captain left with a few of the officers and quickly returned with the apostles. The high priest fired out one question after another. So great was his distaste for the apostles and Jesus that he refused to say Jesus' name. "We warned you not to teach in, in … *that* name!" he bellowed.

Peter and the others simply replied, "God is the One we must obey!" Then Peter continued. "You killed Jesus, but God raised Him from the dead."

With those words Peter began to explain to the religious leaders how their sins would be forgiven if they repented and put their faith in Jesus.

When they heard this, the leaders were furious and were ready to have the apostles killed on the spot. But then a Pharisee named Gamaliel stood and spoke. His words calmed the enraged Sanhedrin. "Think carefully about what you do with these men," he said. "If what they're doing is purely an act of men, then it will die out in its own in time. But if what they're doing is of God and you try to stop it, you'll be fighting with God Himself."

Persuaded by his counsel, the Sanhedrin had the apostles flogged and ordered them again not to speak of Jesus.

The apostles left the Sanhedrin praising God because He had considered them worthy to suffer for Jesus. Day after day in the temple courts and from house to house the apostles continued declaring to everyone the good news about Jesus.

Footwork

In your Bible, look up Acts 5:29. What did Peter saying about obeying God? Does it sound to you as if he thought this was an option?

Fruit

If forced to choose today, would you stand with Jesus or against Him? Take a moment and think about the condition of your heart and how you live your life (or don't live your life) for Him. If you need to ask God's forgiveness, do it now. If you need to step out and be bolder about sharing your faith, ask Him to give you the courage as well as the opportunities. He'll do both.

end of his reign. He was murdered by his

Nothing Personal
Taken from Acts 6—8

- *Foundation*

Spend a few moments in prayer. Thank God for the freedoms you have and offer them back to Him so that He can do as He pleases with them.

Have you ever been picked on because you're a Christian?

Five thousand believers now followed Jesus, and the church continued to grow daily. The church was made up of people from many different backgrounds. Some of the Jews who had always lived in Palestine were called *Hebrews* and spoke Aramaic. They began looking down on the Greek-speaking Jews (called *Hellenists*) who had lived outside Palestine. When it came time to share with one another, they neglected the people in this group.

Seeing the problem, Peter and the apostles appointed seven men to take charge of handing out the shares of money and food. With the help of these seven, the apostles could then devote their time to prayer and preaching about Jesus. They apostles instructed the believers to choose men who were full of wisdom and controlled by the Holy Spirit's power. The first two men they selected were Stephen and Philip.

Stephen was well loved by many. He was not only kind and wise, but he also had a great ability to speak out for the Lord. God performed amazing miracles through Stephen.

Check out Acts 6:5–6 to see the list of the seven leaders chosen to distribute the shared food and money to the believers. They were all Grecian (Hellenist) Jews.

Stoning was a common form of capital punishment. After two hearings to determine someone's guilt, the person was taken to a cliff and pushed off by those who had testified against him or her. If the person lived, big boulders and stones would then be thrown down on top of him or her.

One day a group of men, who didn't like Stephen's message, began to argue with him. When they realized they were no match for his wisdom or the power of the Holy Spirit in his message, they became angry.

"We heard Stephen speaking against Moses and God!" they said, lying. They also convinced others to spread these lies about Stephen so that in no time he was brought before the Sanhedrin for questioning.

"This man doesn't stop speaking against the temple and against the Law," they said, falsely accusing him. "He has been telling the people that Jesus will tear down the temple and make changes in the Law Moses gave us!"

Hate-filled eyes turned toward Stephen. The temple was sacred, and because it held such a high place in the religious leaders' hearts, they often made the mistake of worshipping it.

Jesus never claimed to destroy the temple. He had said, "Destroy this temple [My body], and I will raise it again in three days" (John 2:19). As for Moses' laws, Jesus came to fulfill them, not destroy or change them (Matthew 5:17), and that would bring a new law into effect. What Stephen said was correct and true. The fault wasn't with him but with those who heard and twisted his message.

"Is what they're saying true?" the high priest asked angrily. He and the other members of the council couldn't help but notice that Stephen's face looked almost like that of an angel.

Instead of defending himself, Stephen gave the religious leaders a history lesson. He reminded them that God called Abraham to a foreign land, and then He called Moses to lead His people out of slavery in Egypt. He also told how Israel rebelled against God and made a calf out of gold. He even spoke about how David's son Solomon built the temple, proclaiming it as a symbol of God's presence but not His home.

Then Stephen passionately concluded, "You are a stubborn and rebellious people, just like those who came before you! Just like them, you fight against the Holy Spirit and persecute those God sends to you. Your fathers killed the prophets, who prophesied about the Righteous One and His coming, and then you followed in their steps by betraying and killing Him."

The men of the Sanhedrin seethed with anger after hearing these words. Hatred filled their eyes, but Stephen didn't notice. Looking beyond them, he saw Jesus standing next to God as if to welcome him into heaven. "Do you see? There's the Son of Man standing on the right side of God in heaven!"

The Sanhedrin refused to listen anymore. Covering their ears, they attacked Stephen, dragged him out of the city, and stoned him. As Stephen was dying, he looked toward heaven and repeated the words of His Savior, "Father, forgive them please ..." With those words on his lips, Stephen died.

As all this was happening, a religious leader named Saul watched with approval while guarding the cloaks of those stoning Stephen. Little did he know the impact that event would make on his life in the near future.

Footwork

In your Bible, turn to Acts 8:1–4 and read the rest of the story. What happened as a result of Stephen's death? Although people who opposed God's plan were attacking Stephen, he knew God was still in control.

Can I Join You?

Taken from Acts 8

Foundation

Stop and pray before you read today's lesson. Thank the Lord that He is in control of the circumstances in your life and that nothing happens just by chance.

Focus

Have you ever seen something happen that you knew wasn't just by chance or coincidence?

After Stephen's stoning, a great persecution broke out against the believers in Jerusalem, and everyone except the apostles fled throughout Judea and Samaria, taking the message of Jesus wherever they went. One such person was Philip.

While traveling in Samaria and proclaiming Jesus, an angel sent from God appeared to Philip. "Travel to the south on the desert road that goes from Jerusalem to Gaza," the angel instructed him.

Even though this seemed like an unusual request, Philip obeyed the angel and headed for the desert road.

Looking down the road, Philip saw a chariot kicking up dust. It was a royal chariot belonging to an Ethiopian queen. A man in charge of all the queen's riches was on his way home to Africa after worshipping in Jerusalem. Weary of trying to please the many gods of the Ethiopians, he desired to know more about the one and only God of the Jews.

"See that chariot ahead? Run up to it and walk beside it," the Holy Spirit directed Philip.

Philip didn't hesitate. As he ran up to the chariot, he heard the man reading aloud from the Old Testament book of Isaiah.

"I can't help but hear that you're reading from the prophet Isaiah. Do you understand the words?" Philip asked.

The man looked down from his chariot and studied Philip for a moment. The word *help* was written all over the man's face. "I want to, but I need someone to explain them," he said and invited Philip to join him in the chariot.

The man was reading a passage that said, "Like a sheep being led to the slaughterhouse and a lamb who doesn't utter a sound when it's being sheared, He never said a word, but was denied justice in His suffering."

With a puzzled look on his face, the man asked Philip, "Can you tell me whether the prophet is referring to himself or another?"

Philip not only answered the man's question but also used that very passage of Scripture to explain the good news of Jesus who had fulfilled those prophecies.

As they passed by some water, the man said, "Here's some water. What is there to keep me from being baptized?"

Because it was customary to read aloud in Philip's day, he could easily hear what the Ethiopian man was reading. Want to read that same passage for yourself? Check out Isaiah 53:7–8 in the Old Testament.

Baptism is an outward action proclaiming your loyalty to Jesus and showing others that you choose to identify with Him alone.

Philip saw the sincerity in the man's eyes. It would be very unusual to baptize this man who was neither Jew nor Samaritan. Yet it was obvious to Philip that God was at work; the chances of traveling on a road in the middle of a desert and meeting a nonJewish man who happened to be reading the Scriptures and wanted an explanation were slim to none.

The Ethiopian halted the chariot, and both he and Philip climbed out. Then right there by the side of the road, Philip baptized this new believer in Jesus. What joy surrounded the event!

After the men had waded out of the water, Philip suddenly disappeared; the Holy Spirit miraculously transported him to another place so that he could continue on with the things God had prepared for him to do. The man he baptized returned to his homeland praising God for all that had happened.

Footwork

Read Acts 8:35 in your Bible. What did Philip do? How did he do it? It's interesting to note that Philip began where the man was—right at the man's level of interest. With love, gentleness, and dependence on the Holy Spirit, Philip was able to explain things and lead the man into a relationship with Christ.

Fruit

This week, look for opportunities to humbly lead someone to Christ. Simply ask God to use you in this person's life and to give you wisdom to know how to talk on that person's spiritual level. Then be ready, obedient, and sensitive to His leading. (It might also be helpful to review the salvation verses at the end of this book.)

mushrooms by his wife who wanted her so

Presto Change-O!
Taken from Acts 9

Foundation

Spend some time preparing your heart for today's lesson. Examine your life—where you've been and where you're headed. Ask God to help you see how His love for you isn't based on your performance.

Focus

Have you ever heard someone say, "I've done too many bad things for God to ever love me or forgive me"?

"So, they think they've gotten away, do they?" Saul muttered to himself as he went to the high priest for legal papers. He was a Pharisee who would have nothing to do with this Jesus nonsense. Having gleefully watched the stoning of a believer named Stephen, Saul thought the punishment only proper for making such blasphemous claims about Jesus being God!

Saul quickened his step. Some believers had escaped to Damascus, and he was determined to go there and drag them back to Jerusalem so they could be tried and put to death. The papers from the high priest ordered the synagogue rulers in Damascus to help him find these people. The officers of the Sanhedrin—policemen of sorts—would accompany him on the six-to-eight-day journey to Damascus. Because Saul was a Pharisee, he couldn't associate with these men so he walked alone, with lots of time to think. He thought of the Christians he had killed—and had to admit that they had all died with bravery. Stephen's last words asking forgiveness for his enemies haunted Saul's memory.

Saul violently shook his head with anger. He was a Pharisee, a protector of the Jewish law. If true, the message Stephen had spoken put that beloved law in danger. "No!" Saul breathed with hatred. He would fight to the end of his strength to stop these Christians!

The last stretch of the road to Damascus went up Mount Hermon. Damascus was nestled in the green valley below. Saul smiled to himself. Soon he would have those Christians who had escaped. "They'll get what's rightfully coming to them," he sneered, his hatred driving him onward.

Suddenly, out of nowhere, a blinding flash came down from heaven—and Saul went blind and fell to his knees.

"Saul, Saul," a voice said, "Why are you persecuting Me?"

The voice was loud and clear to Saul, but the travelers with him heard only a loud noise.

"Tell me, Lord, who You are."

"I'm the One you're persecuting—Jesus," replied the voice.

Jesus instructed him to go into the city and wait for someone to tell him what to do next.

> Ananias was the first person to call Saul a Christian "brother." (He wasn't the same Ananias mentioned in Acts 5.)
>
> Tarsus was the Greek capital of the Cilicia region. It was also Saul's hometown.

When Saul picked himself up off the ground, he realized that he couldn't see. Instead of marching triumphantly into Damascus to carry out his murderous plans, Saul would be led humbly into the city like a young child. For three days he couldn't see a thing and refused to eat or drink.

The Lord told Ananias, a disciple living in Damascus, to visit a certain house and ask for Saul. When Ananias heard Saul's name, he replied, "But Lord, this man has done terrible things to your followers! And the reason he's here in Damascus is to arrest and kill more!"

But the Lord answered Ananias, "Go to him! I've chosen Saul to be My witness to the Gentiles, their kings, and the Jews."

Ananias did as God instructed and went to the house. Finding Saul, he placed his hands on him and called him "brother." As Ananias explained how Jesus had sent him there, a scalelike substance dropped off Saul's eyes, and he rose up a changed man.

After this, Saul stayed with Jesus' disciples in Damascus and began preaching in the synagogues the very message he had sought to destroy. But the rapid change in Saul confused the nonbelieving Jews living in Damascus. "Isn't this the same man who came here to arrest those followers of Jesus? And now he's proving that Jesus is the Christ by his very own changed life!" they worried. That fear made them plot to kill Saul. Guards were posted at every gate to keep him from leaving, but he learned of their plans and escaped over the city wall in a basket with the help of believers.

Returning to Jerusalem Saul tried to join the disciples there, but they would have nothing to do with him. "Perhaps this is one of his tricks," they said, eyeing him suspiciously.

It wasn't until Barnabas came forward and defended Saul that they listened and finally accepted him.

Saul boldly proclaimed Christ in Jerusalem and went to the very group Stephen had been trying to reach before he was stoned to death. Being a skilled debater himself, Saul left these hostile Jews speechless, and in their anger they made plans to kill him as they had Stephen. When the believers in Jerusalem heard this, they took Saul to Caesarea and sent him off by ship to Tarsus.

Footwork

Open your Bible to Acts 9 and read verses 21–22. Notice anything special? Jesus was able to turn the bad in Saul's life into proof—proof of who Jesus is and what He can do.

Fruit

Throughout your life, you'll run into people who will make excuses for not accepting God's gift of salvation, saying they've done too many bad things for God to love them or forgive them. Don't believe it; God doesn't.

throughout the empire, but he prohibits

It Can't Be—Can It?
Taken from Acts 12

- *Foundation*

Stop and think before you pray today. Prayer isn't getting God to bless what we want to do; it's how we get our hearts in line with what God is doing and the blessings that follow! Ask God to realign your heart by helping you grow in your personal prayer life.

Focus

Have you ever prayed for something that seemed impossible and were surprised when your prayers were answered?

In the darkness metal handcuffs cut into Peter's wrists. On either side of Peter slept two guards who were chained to him. More guards stood watch at the door. King Herod, who had just beheaded James, ordered Peter to be locked in prison to await the same fate. James was the first apostle to be killed. Peter, it seemed, would soon be the second.

He sat quietly in the prison, deep in thought. Hatred toward the church in Jerusalem was growing among the Jews who had chosen not to believe in Jesus. They despised any Jew who became a follower of Jesus and were elated when Herod had James put to death. Since this had pleased the rebellious Jews so much, and since Herod wanted to gain favor with them, he sought to

> *Prayer is simply talking with God (not at Him) and leaving things in His capable hands.*

them from trying to convert others

Who's who? *Herod the Great reigned during the time Jesus was born. He met the wise men and later had the Jewish baby boys killed. Herod Antipas—great grandson of Herod the Great—murdered John the Baptist and was the ruler who questioned Jesus. Herod Agrippa—Herod Antipas's nephew—ruled during this time in Acts. He's the one who beheaded James.*

When you pray, it produces a ...
P—*a peaceful heart*
R—*a readiness to do things God's way*
A—*an attitude change*
Y—*a yearning to grow closer to God*

have Peter killed as well. Herod figured it would only increase his popularity.

Peter looked over at the guards chained to him, then he slowly drifted off to sleep. He knew God was in control and he could trust God with his life as well as his death.

Then, in the darkness of the cell an angel suddenly appeared, and Peter's handcuffs fell off. He wasn't sure whether this was a dream or if it was really happening! The angel motioned for Peter to follow, and they quietly slipped past the guards and out the door.

The night air shocked Peter into reality. *I'm really not dreaming! God sent an angel to rescue me!* he thought. He rushed to the house where many believers were inside praying for him.

Peter quietly knocked on the door and waited.

"Who is it?" a servant girl named Rhoda asked through the door.

Trying to stay hidden in the shadows, Peter announced who he was in a hushed voice.

When Rhoda recognized Peter's voice, she became so excited that she left him standing outside while she ran to tell the others. "Peter! It's Peter! He's at the door!" she squealed.

The believers gave Rhoda a pitiful look. "That's impossible, Rhoda. You're just overly tired and are imagining things," said one.

Another sighed, "Poor Peter. It's probably his angel!"

But Rhoda kept insisting that she was telling the truth, and Peter kept knocking at the door. When they finally opened the door and saw Peter, they were amazed and everyone began talking at once. What an unexpected answer to their prayers!

Motioning for his friends to quiet down, Peter described how the Lord had miraculously rescued him from prison.

When Herod discovered that Peter had escaped, he was stunned and furious. His plans to silence Peter from proclaiming the gospel had miserably failed.

Footwork

Look up Acts 12:14–16 in your Bible and read it. Now reread verse 16. How does it describe the reaction of the believers who had been praying for Peter's release from prison?

Fruit

God does answer prayer, and He invites us to talk with Him about what concerns us. Although our hearts may feel heavy at times, God knows how He'll work things out, for He has a perfect plan for our lives. One way to see God's faithfulness in our lives is to keep track of how He has answered our prayers. This is easy to do. Simply write down your prayer requests in a notebook. Then as the Lord answers your prayers, write down the date they were answered and include a brief sentence describing how they were answered. Remember, God doesn't always say yes to our requests. Sometimes He answers with a no, or sometimes we have to wait.

rules over Judea, the Romans conquer

It's Not That Bad
Taken from Acts 15

— Ғₒᵤₙₐₐₜᵢₒₙ ————

Before you read today's lesson, thank God for who He is, and ask Him to help you see how only He can make good come out of a bad situation.

Focus

Have you ever seen or heard how God used something bad (or negative) to bring about something good?

When Paul and Barnabas returned from their first missionary journey, they brought wonderful news to the Gentile believers at Antioch. Everyone there rejoiced to hear what God had done through them.

But some believers came from Jerusalem to Antioch with news that wasn't so good. In fact, it was insulting to the believers in Antioch. "You can't possibly be true believers like us unless you live by the Law of Moses and become circumcised," they stated. They looked down on the Antioch believers and tried to place harsh religious requirements on them. These rules came from Jewish religious traditions, not from Jesus.

When Paul heard about this, he became angry, and a sharp argument arose. God had proven once that He had accepted these believers by giving them His Holy Spirit (Acts 10:44–47). Wasn't that enough proof? Were the Jewish believers in Jerusalem now going to reject those whom God had accepted? *May it never be!* thought Paul as he set off with Barnabas to see the apostles and elders in Jerusalem to discuss the matter.

Upon their arrival in Jerusalem, the church welcomed Paul, and he eagerly reported to them how God had worked among the Gentiles (nonJewish people). Some of the Pharisees who were believers replied, "But the Gentile believers must obey the Law of Moses, and all the men must be circumcised; otherwise they aren't really true believers!" So the elders and apostles all discussed this question.

Peter was at the meeting too. Standing to speak on behalf of the Gentiles, he told the church leaders, "My brothers, we know that we have been saved through the grace of our Lord Jesus and not by keeping our own laws. The Gentiles have been saved the same way as well!"

Next, the assembly listened as Paul described the wonders and signs God had done among the Gentiles. As a result, the members of the council decided not to make the Gentile Christians obey all the laws of the Jews. Instead, they came up with a few simple rules for these believers to follow. Writing a letter to the Antioch believers, the council apologized on behalf of those who had caused such grief and gave the believers the guidelines the council had approved. The matter had been settled, and the Gentile Christians didn't have to become Jews.

Want more details about this story? You can read the exciting account of Paul and Barnabas's first missionary journey in Acts 13—14.

Mark abandoned Paul and Barnabas when they reached the second stop of their first missionary journey. When Barnabas and Paul parted, Barnabas took Mark back to the first stop of that former journey— Cyprus—building up both Mark and the new believers there.

Not long after that, Paul turned to Barnabas with an idea: "Let's travel back through Galatia and see how the believers there are doing."

Barnabas agreed and wanted to take his cousin Mark (also called John Mark) along, but Paul disagreed. "He deserted us on our first missionary trip!" Paul reminded Barnabas, feeling anger and disappointment surface at the memory of it all. A feeling of disgust stuck in his throat. "Mark has no part in this ministry and won't be coming along!"

Since Paul and Barnabas couldn't agree, they went their separate ways. Paul took Silas (one of the Jerusalem messengers) with him and set off for Galatia, encouraging the churches and proclaiming God's Word along the way. Barnabas took Mark and set sail for Barnabas's homeland of Cyprus.

Footwork

In your Bible, read Acts 15:39. Notice that Barnabas took Mark along with him to Cyprus. What do you think happened to them? Do you think that Barnabas's encouragement may have helped Mark overcome his earlier failure in ministry and become useful again? Now turn to 2 Timothy 4:11 and see what Paul later said about him.

Fruit

Don't be discouraged by what appear to be hopeless circumstances. God is still in control. For instance: Because of the Jerusalem council, Gentile believers were freed from the bonds of the Jewish law and were able to worship God and become the true early Christian church. And because of the split between Paul and Barnabas, two missionary teams were available to preach the good news about Jesus instead of just one!

Sometimes God uses difficulties in our lives to bring about greater results. Trust Him. He knows what He's doing.

I Demand an Apology!
Taken from Acts 16

Foundation

Spend a few moments in prayer talking to God. Ask Him to examine
your life and help you take your eyes off your own problems and
place them back on Him.

FOCUS

*Have you ever been unfairly blamed for something you
didn't do?*

"Go where?" Silas and Timothy asked as they looked at Paul in disbelief.

"Macedonia," Paul answered. "I had a vision of a man standing and
calling out, 'Come over to Macedonia and help us,'" Paul replied. "I
believe God wants us to go there."

Since Barnabas and Paul had parted company, there were now two
missionary teams. Barnabas and Mark went back to Cyprus, and Paul
and Silas returned to Derbe and Lystra— where Paul had been stoned
on his first missionary trip. While there, Paul met a young believer
named Timothy who was strong in his faith. Because they needed help,
Paul invited Timothy to join them while he and Silas delivered the
decisions from the Jerusalem council to the rapidly growing Gentile
churches.

"Macedonia," Paul repeated, and soon the three set sail for a place
farther west than they had ever been before. After many days they arrived

at the Roman colony and military outpost of Philippi, which was on the Roman highway. Philippi was the leading city in the region of Macedonia, and its citizens had rights as Romans. They were treated as if they actually lived in Italy.

The region of Macedonia was part of what is now modern Europe.

Since there was no synagogue, Paul and his companions ventured outside the city gate and walked to the river, where they expected to find an official place of prayer. As they rounded a corner and cleared the bushes, Paul noticed a group of women who had gathered to pray on the Sabbath. One of them was a very wealthy woman named Lydia, who made fine purple fabric. After Paul had finished talking to the women about Jesus, God opened Lydia's heart, and she and her whole family believed and were baptized.

One day as Paul and his companions walked down to the river to pray, they met a slave girl who was controlled by an evil spirit. The demon gave her the ability to predict people's futures. Her owners gleefully pocketed all the money people paid for her services. For many days the girl followed Paul around, loudly proclaiming, "The men you see are showing you the way of salvation. They serve God Most High." Even though this statement was true, Paul refused to accept testimony from demons. Turning to the girl, he commanded the evil spirit to come out of her in the name of Jesus. Immediately the demon left—and the girl lost her ability to predict the future. Her owners were furious because their source of easy money was gone. Clenching their teeth and making threats, they grabbed Paul and Silas and dragged them before the authorities.

"These Jewish men are causing great trouble in our city!" they seethed. "And they push customs that are against the law for Romans citizens to practice!" they lied. The owners had to think up some accusation that would be punishable so they could get even with Paul and Silas.

Given no chance to defend themselves, Paul and Silas were flogged and thrown into a prison cell with their feet fastened in stocks. Orders were also given to guard them carefully.

Paul and Silas knew that they had done nothing wrong. But rather than becoming bitter or resentful, they prayed and sang worship songs to the Lord.

Prisoners in nearby cells listened with amazement as songs of praise echoed in the damp darkness.

Then around midnight, without warning the ground shook and fear rippled through the prisoner's minds. Would they be buried alive? Cell doors flew open and chains came loose. The jailer had been asleep, but when he woke up and saw what had happened, he drew his sword. If his prisoners had escaped, he knew he would be killed in their place. *Better to kill myself now than be executed later,* he thought.

"Stop!" Paul shouted before the jailer could harm himself, "Everyone is here!"

The jailer couldn't believe his ears. He dropped his sword on the ground and fell before Paul and Silas, trembling. "How can I be saved? Tell me what to do!"

"If you want to be saved," Paul replied, "put your trust in the Lord Jesus Christ."

Then Paul and Silas shared the good news about Jesus with the jailer and his entire family, and they all became believers. The jailer washed Paul and Silas's wounds and gave them food to eat. Then he and his family were baptized. The jailer was overjoyed, for he and his family had come to believe in Jesus!

The next day an order came from the authorities telling the jailer to release the men, but Paul and Silas refused to go.

"No," they replied. "We were beaten in public without being given a trial, and then we were thrown into prison, even though we're Roman citizens. Do the authorities really expect us to leave quietly as if nothing happened? No! Let them come and personally escort us out of prison!" they demanded.

When the authorities learned that Paul and Silas were Roman citizens, they became worried and immediately came to the prison to apologize. After being escorted out of the prison, Paul and Silas returned to Lydia's home to encourage the believers before leaving Philippi.

Footwork

Read Acts 16:36–37 in your Bible. Why do you think Paul and Silas refused to leave the prison quietly? Do you think they were getting even with the officials? Because they were able to praise God in their circumstances, we know that wasn't the case. Rather, Paul and Silas knew that receiving an official apology would help protect the other believers in Philippi from being treated in the same way.

Fruit

When you're unfairly blamed, do you concentrate on your own problems, or are you concerned about others? Take a moment to consider the example of Paul and Silas. They could have become bitter, but they didn't. When given an opportunity to escape, they wouldn't. Instead, they saved the life of one of their enemies and chose to look out for the needs of fellow believers. Think about how you can follow that example in a situation you may be facing right now. Then do it—with God's help.

comes into power. ● AD 46–48 — Paul an

Great Results!
Taken from Acts 19—20

Foundation

Spend some time in prayer, asking God to examine your heart and life. Also ask Him to help you understand the importance of your actions and the effect they have on others. Then ask Him to change the things in your life that need to be changed.

Focus

Have you ever noticed how one person's actions often influence the actions and attitudes of others?

Apollos was in Corinth when Paul returned to Ephesus on his third (and final) missionary journey. For three months Paul spoke boldly about Jesus in the synagogue, but the nonbelieving Jews began causing trouble. Because of their actions, Paul stopped coming to the synagogue and met instead with the believers in another place, where he continued preaching for two years.

During this time God did wonderful miracles through Paul. He cast out demons and proclaimed God's Word with boldness. Even handkerchiefs that touched him brought healing to those in need. Because of Paul's actions, interest in Jesus spread. Even those who didn't know Jesus tried using His name, hoping for extra power over evil spirits.

One day the seven sons of a Jewish priest named Sceva (who weren't

Barnabas embark on Paul's first mis-

followers of Jesus) tried casting out a demon using Jesus' name.

"I know Paul and Jesus," the demon said, "but I don't have any idea who you are!"

Then, as quickly as the demon had spoken, the demon-possessed man attacked the men with a burst of supernatural power. Screaming, naked, and bleeding, the sons of Sceva ran out of the house in fear for their lives. When word about this spread around Ephesus, people treated the Lord's name with greater honor, and many people believed in Jesus, openly confessing their evil actions. Those who practiced magic and sorcery brought their scrolls to be burned, and many people became more devoted to knowing and honoring Jesus. This new attitude, however, didn't please everyone.

Demetrius, a silversmith who crafted false gods, was particularly upset. "If this Christianity keeps up, it will ruin our business!" he said, challenging the other idol makers. "This man Paul says that our gods aren't really gods at all, and people have stopped buying our idols! Now even our great goddess Artemis is being robbed of her place of honor in our city!"

> **Check out Acts chapters 21–28 for details on what Paul faced after leaving Miletus. He was determined to live his life to honor God— regardless of the consequences.**

Greedy and angry Demetrius ignited a disturbance against Christianity and Paul, and soon the whole city was in an uproar. Like a huge tidal wave, the town rushed into the theater chanting, "The goddess Artemis of the Ephesians is great!" They shouted for two solid hours as the crowd formed into a riotous mob. Not until a city official came and spoke to the people did they eventually calm down and go home.

Despite this disturbance, Paul continued preaching the Word of God wherever he went, and he made a point to encourage fellow believers. Upon reaching Miletus, Paul asked the leaders of the churches in Ephesus to join him there. The Holy Spirit had warned him that he would face hardship and prison in the days ahead, so Paul knew that this would be his last chance to say good-bye.

"You know that I was never afraid to speak the truth, and my only desire now is to finish the task the Lord has given me—the task of proclaiming His gospel.

After I leave, others will rise up within the church and twist the truth. So stand firm and be on your guard! I turn you over to God and the power of His Word, which builds you up …"

After Paul prayed for them, he set sail for Jerusalem. Once there, he was arrested and left to rot in prison for many years. When he was finally granted a hearing, Paul was sent to Rome to stand trial before Caesar. While en route to Rome, Paul not only survived a shipwreck, but he also spent several more years imprisoned in Rome awaiting his trial. During this imprisonment, the Lord used him to write the New Testament books of Ephesians, Philippians, Colossians, and Philemon.

Footwork

Whether we realize it or not, our actions affect those around us either for good or for bad. Look up Acts 19:18–20 in your Bible. What happened as a result of former sorcerers burning their scrolls when they became believers? (See verse 20.)

Fruit

Take a quick inventory of your life. How do you think God is using you? (Is He able to use you?) Do your actions and attitudes point others to Jesus, or do they point people away from Him? Tell God about it. Ask His forgiveness for the things you've done recently that weren't honoring to Him.

Romans

Paul wrote this letter (which we call the book of Romans) while staying in Corinth for three months during his third missionary journey. He addressed his letter to all believers—Jews and Gentiles—living in Rome.

Since Paul hadn't been to Rome to share the gospel, where did these believers come from? Perhaps some had traveled from Rome to Jerusalem and became believers during Pentecost (Acts 2). Others may have been believers who moved to Rome during the twenty-seven years after Pentecost but before Paul's writing of this letter.

Paul's purpose in writing this letter was to provide a detailed explanation of the gospel message he proclaimed. Because he hoped to go to Rome after delivering gifts to the church in Jerusalem (Acts 21), he was preparing the believers in Rome for a visit. Paul eventually visited Rome, but not in the manner he had intended.

Romans is an exciting book to journey through. It's much like climbing to the top of a mountain and being able to see everything around you for miles. It helps us understand the big picture. As you read through Romans, learn from the foundation it provides. Take a look around you. Romans describes what you (and all people) are like and what God has done and desires to do for you.

is work would later influence

Did You Hear?
Taken from Romans 1—5

Foundation

Before you read today's lesson, make sure your heart is in the right place. Ask God to forgive any bad attitudes you may have so that your heart and mind will be pure and teachable.

FOCUS

Do you ever wonder, If God is loving, how could He send people to hell? *or* What about the people in Africa who have never heard about Jesus?

Paul had so much to share with the believers in Rome. The message of the gospel burned in his heart as he gripped his pen and began writing. "I am not ashamed of the gospel, because it is the power of God for the salvation of everyone who believes," Paul passionately wrote to the Romans. "In this gospel, God has made known to us a righteousness that doesn't come from us, because all of us have sinned against Him and have fallen short of His glory. Not one person is righteous in his sight … not one person truly seeks him. We have all gone our own ways…. No one becomes righteous by keeping the law because the law merely points out our sin and can't save us from it."

Paul paused for a moment to collect his thoughts before continuing. "But God makes us righteous through faith in Jesus Christ. It's freely given to everyone who believes."

Paul also explained to the Roman believers the importance of the gospel message and how everyone must hear about it, even those who live in the far-away places of the world. He told them that no one can claim that they don't know anything about God, because God has shown the whole world His divine nature and power through the things He created. No one can look at nature without recognizing the existence of a God who designed it all.

"But instead of acknowledging God as God," Paul wrote, "people began worshipping what God created, and they even bowed down to images made by their own hands. They thought they were wise, but they were really fools, so God let them have their evil desires. And as a result of their sinful ways, their hearts were hardened by unbelief, and their lives were filled with jealousy, selfishness, anger, pride, lying, and greed. But just when humans were at their worst and completely powerless to help themselves, God showed His love for us by sending Jesus to bear the punishment we deserved and pay the penalty for our sins—death.

"It's because of Christ's blood," Paul reminded the believers, "that we can be declared 'not guilty' and escape God's judgment. This is the gospel message I'm not ashamed to preach. This is the message everyone must hear."

Why is Christ's blood mentioned so often? Blood carries life throughout our bodies. When our skin is cut, our bodies bleed, cleaning out our wounds so that infection won't set in. Blood washes away dirt and floods the wound with healing agents. Christ's blood does the same for us, but on a spiritual level. It "washes away" our sin and "heals" our relationship with God so that we can stand before Him blameless and holy.

How can you be a "sent" one?

S—Seek opportunities to share about Jesus.

E—Evaluate the needs of your listener.

N—Never rely on your own strength.

T—Trust God to give you the right words.

Footwork

God never sends anyone to hell. He desires for all to come to know Him. Because of this, He has shown Himself in simple ways so that all people will know that He exists. He also provided a way for our sins to be forgiven so that we wouldn't have to experience eternal punishment in hell.

Look up Romans 3:22–24 and read it. What do you think this says about people who have never heard the gospel message? Verse 23 says that all people stand guilty before God, even those who have never heard about Jesus.

Thought: If God is big enough to provide for people's sins, isn't He also big enough to provide an opportunity for people wanting to know Him to hear the gospel?

Fruit

Everyone is under God's judgment, regardless of whether he or she has or hasn't heard the gospel message. Paul raised an urgent matter in Romans 10:14–15. Turn there in your Bible and read these verses. Are you willing to be used by God to share the gospel with others? If you are, tell Him right now that you are one person who is willing to be "sent" to tell others about Jesus—whether people in your own neighborhood or people in another part of the world. Mark this passage in your Bible and put today's date next to it. Refer to it often as a reminder of the commitment you made.

I Give Up!
Taken from Romans 6—8

Foundation

Stop and spend some time talking with God before you begin today's lesson. Don't be afraid to admit your shortcomings to Him. He already knows about them anyway. Thank Him for His love, power, and strength that are available to you.

Focus

Has living the Christian life ever seemed impossible to you?

"What I want to do, I don't do, and the evil I don't want to do, I end up doing!" Paul wrote to the Roman believers. Paul wasn't writing to complain but rather to comfort. Even though God had done great things in and through him, Paul still struggled with sin. "The fact is, even though I want to do what's right and good, it seems like sin is always right there beside me, tempting me to do what's wrong. My heart desires to do God's will, but my mind and my body are waging war against me, creating great difficulties and making me a prisoner to my sinful desires."

Beads of sweat dripped down Paul's face and onto the parchment. Paul wrote from his heart as God directed his words. "What a miserable person I am! Who will save me from my own body intent on death? Thank God through our Lord Jesus Christ!"

The words flowed from the tip of Paul's pen as he explained how Christ

> *Faith is an everyday thing, not just a salvation thing. It's believing in God's character rather than in my own. Here's an easy way to remember what faith is: F-A-I-T-H = Forsaking All I Trust Him.*

> *Righteousness (and the power to live the right way) is a gift of God's grace; it isn't something we achieve by our own efforts.*

sets people free from being helpless slaves to sin. "For sin is no longer our master. We have been set free from it and are no longer under its all-controlling power."

Paul paused for a moment and thought about his own life—his victories and his struggles. Then he continued writing. "Yet, we must still wrestle with our sinful nature (our natural desires toward self-centeredness), but we don't have to be defeated! The Holy Spirit gives us the help and strength we need to overcome sinful desires in our lives. Even when our struggles are so great that we don't know how to pray for ourselves, the Holy Spirit prays for us in ways that can't be expressed in mere words. Things that are impossible for us become possible with God. As we depend upon the Holy Spirit, He will help us live in a way that shows our love to God and honors Him. There will be difficult times in our lives, but we must never forget that God makes everything work together for our good. He is in control. If God is on our side fighting for us, then who can defeat us? Nothing in this world, or even in the entire universe, can tear us away from God's love, and because of what Christ Jesus did for us, we have His power to defeat whatever comes against us. And we have the power to live the way God wants us to live."

"I'm absolutely certain," Paul wrote with joy, "that nothing can keep us from God's love in Jesus, whether life or death or angels or demons or the realities of today or what's to come in the future."

Footwork

Read Romans 8:8 in your Bible. Now skip down to verse 14 and compare the two verses. By whom should we be led?

letter of James is written by James (Jesus

Fruit

As you walk with God, there will be times when you forget to depend on His strength and try to live the Christian life on your own (by your own efforts and resources). When you do, it only results in defeat and self-centered living. Instead, ask God for His strength so you can live a God-centered life—a life that is honoring and pleasing to Him.

It's Not My Problem!
Taken from Romans 14—15

Foundation

Stop and pray before you read today's lesson. Ask God to show you any areas in your life that might be affecting others in a negative way, turning them from Him rather than to Him.

Focus

Does it ever make you angry when you see someone trying to act big and bragging about what he or she has done or is allowed to do?

Paul picked up his pen and continued writing his letter to the believers in Rome. He had so much to tell them! They had been enjoying great freedom in Christ, yet with that freedom came responsibility. Some believers, who were weak in their faith, were still holding tightly to the Law. And as they did, they were tempted to think of themselves as more religious than other believers.

> **Paul called some believers "weaker brothers" because they still wanted to earn God's favor by keeping Jewish laws and traditions.**

Those who were stronger in their faith enjoyed their freedom in Christ without thinking about how it might affect those whose faith was weaker. The stronger Christians knew that meat itself wasn't evil. It was merely food—even meat that had once been offered to idols. Nothing in Scripture forbade them to eat it. But the believers whose faith was weak wrestled with this idea. They not only refused to eat any kind of meat, but they also struggled in their hearts with those who did. Without knowing it, the stronger Christians were causing problems for the weaker Christians.

"Even if what you're doing isn't wrong," Paul wrote, "it causes others to have difficulties, so it then becomes wrong. Don't judge or blame one another, but determine in your heart to build each other up. You who are stronger believers should be willing to stop doing something that causes weaker believers to stumble in their faith—even if what you're doing isn't wrong."

Paul paused a moment, then continued. The words flowed onto the parchment as the Holy Spirit guided Paul in his writing. "Don't destroy what God is doing in another person's life just because He's given you the freedom to do something. It would be far better not to do that thing than to do it and damage someone else's faith."

Why did Paul have to address this issue? The Christian church began in Rome and was made up of both Jewish and Gentile believers. When Emperor Claudius expelled the Jews from Rome (Acts 18:2), only the Gentile believers remained in the church there. After Claudius died, the Jewish Christians returned to Rome (Romans 16:3) only to discover that their cultural way of expressing faith in Jesus was different from the way the Gentile believers did.

Footwork

Check out Romans 14:12–13. To whom will we have to answer for our actions? What two things are we not to do to our fellow brothers and sisters in Christ? Now skip down to verse 19 and read that. (It's a great verse.) *Edification* means "to build up or strengthen another."

eets to decide whether or not to

Fruit

When you have an opportunity to do something God has given you the freedom to enjoy, but you know it might cause a fellow believer to struggle in his or her faith, what will you do? On a piece of paper list some of the things you have the freedom to do as a Christian. Then examine that list and think about those around you—your family, friends, neighbors, acquaintances. Ask God to clearly show you what might be a stumbling block for them and to help you do the right thing out of love for them.

nd to follow all Jewish laws.

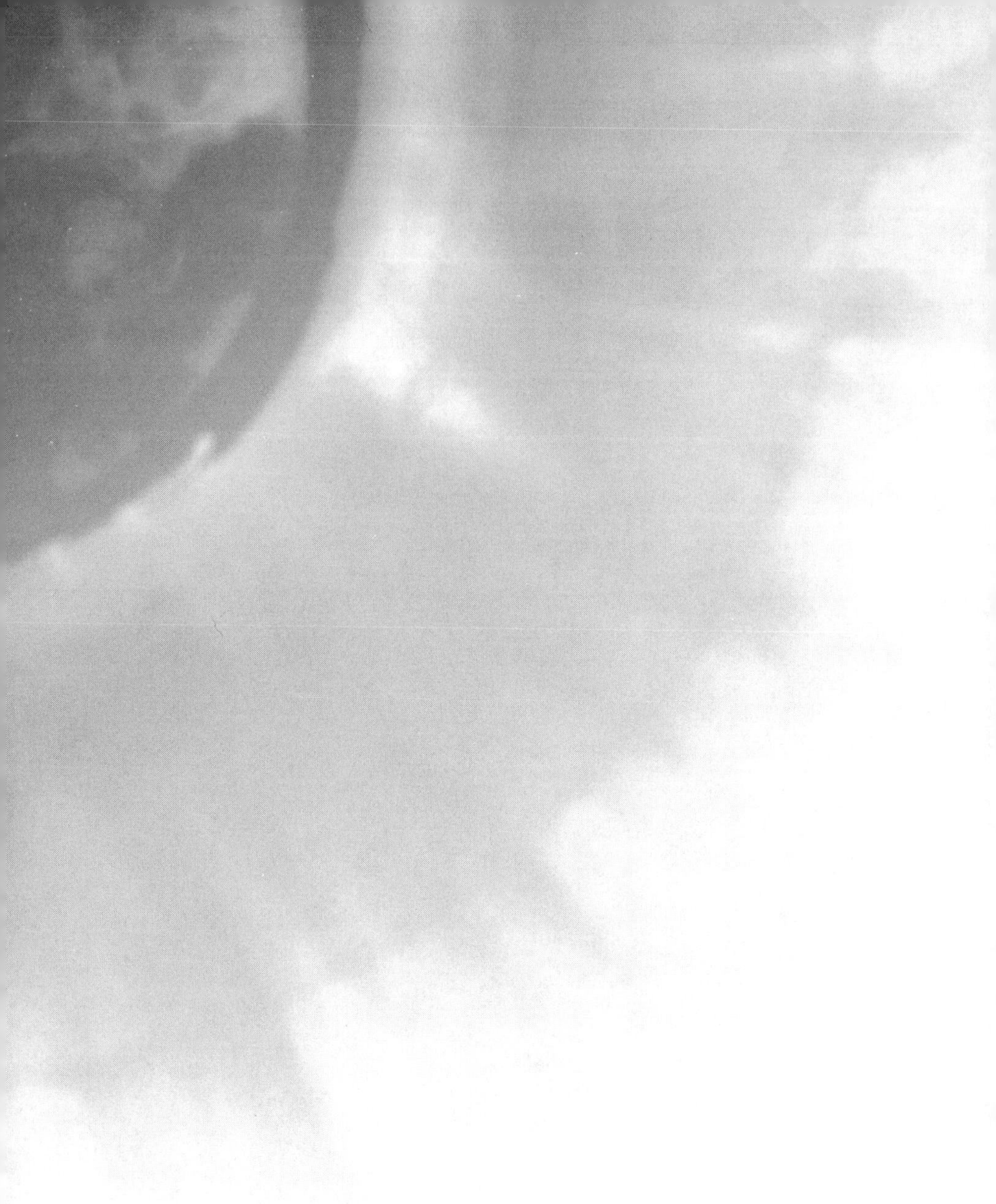

AD 50 - Nazca civilization (Peru) makes

Corinthians

First Corinthians is a letter Paul wrote to the struggling church in Corinth. He wrote it during a two-and-a-half-year stay in Ephesus while on his third missionary journey (Acts 19).

At that time Corinth was one of the greatest trading and commercial centers in the world. It was located on an isthmus (a narrow strip of land joining two larger bodies of land) that was four miles across. In order for people to travel from the northern part of Greece to the southern part, they had to pass through Corinth. Because it was dangerous to sail around the southern tip of Greece, sailors often dragged their ships out of the water at Corinth, put them on rollers and hauled them across the isthmus. If the ship was too big to be rolled across, the cargo was unloaded and carried across the isthmus (through Corinth) and placed in a ship waiting on the other side.

Because of all this activity, Corinth became famous for its trading and its markets. Luxuries came into the city from every land imaginable. People living in Corinth became known for their love of drinking and their idol worship. Temples for idol worship abounded throughout the city.

In the midst of all this evil, the church in Corinth was struggling with its own set of problems. Paul received word about those problems and wrote 1 Corinthians in response to them.

As you read through 1 Corinthians, take note of the issues these believers were having. Do you see some of the same problems believers and churches face today?

iant patterns of animal, insect, and

"Oh Yeah? Well, I . . ."
Taken from 1 Corinthians 1—3

Foundation

As you prepare to read today's lesson, ask God to examine your thoughts, actions, and attitudes. Then ask Him to change what needs to be changed so you can live a life honoring to Him. Thank Him for the help He gives through His Holy Spirit.

Focus

Do you ever hear people brag about how great they are because of the church they go to?

"Oh yeah? Well, I follow Paul's teaching!"

"That's nothing. I follow Apollos; he's really good."

"No way! Peter is the best."

"Oh yeah? Well, I follow Christ! So there!"

Arguments like these arose in the church at Corinth. Those who claimed to follow Paul were probably Gentile believers who had heard the gospel through him. Apollos was a very intelligent believer from Alexandria. Those who claimed loyalty to him were the intellectuals who thought they had more information than others. Jewish believers stood behind Peter (also called Cephas), since he had brought the gospel to the Jews. And those who wanted to outdo the others proudly stated that they followed Christ. No one could argue with that! There was only one fault with this last group: They were really saying that Jesus belonged to them—and them alone—not that they belonged to Jesus.

All of this arguing back and forth was ripping the church apart, and it needed to be stopped immediately.

"Don't you realize," Paul wrote, "that Apollos, Peter, and I are nothing? I may have planted the seed of the gospel, and Apollos may have watered it through the information he gave you, but God is the One who has made your faith blossom and grow. God and God alone is the One who should receive glory."

Paul continued. "Remember what you were like before you came to know Christ. None of you were overly wise, of royal birth, or the most important people in society. Why do you think of yourselves that way now? Don't you realize that God chooses the things the world considers weak to make the strong feel shame? He does this so that none of us can stand before Him and boast about ourselves. If we're going to boast at all, we should boast in the Lord."

Paul tapped the table a few times with his pen as he searched for the right words. "The first time I came to visit you, I didn't speak eloquently or persuasively. I came preaching the simple message of the cross of Christ. I didn't even try to impress you with human wisdom because I didn't want to in any way diminish the powerful message of the cross itself. Instead, I came relying on the Spirit's power so that you would believe because of God's work in your hearts and not because of my wisdom and persuasive powers."

"But you've taken your focus off Christ and have put the focus on

In 1 Corinthians 1:31, when Paul challenged the Corinthian believers to boast only in the Lord, he was actually quoting from Jeremiah 9:23–24 in the Old Testament. In that passage God states, "'Let not the wise man boast of his wisdom or the strong man boast of his strength or the rich man boast of his riches, but let him who boasts boast about this: that he understands and knows me, that I am the Lord, who exercises kindness, justice and righteousness on earth, for in these I delight,' declares the Lord."

yourselves. Because of this you quarrel with one another. You're being controlled by your sinful nature rather than by God's Holy Spirit, and God isn't honored. When I came to you, I laid down a solid foundation built upon Christ. Each of you has this foundation to build your faith upon, but be careful how you build! Stop boasting about men and start boasting about God, for the thoughts of even the wisest person are foolishness to Him."

Footwork

Read 1 Corinthians 3:11. A foundation is the most important part of a building and gives the building its value. Without a solid foundation, a building will crumble.

Jesus is the true foundation for our faith. Go back a few verses and read 1 Corinthians 2:5. What is the result of such a foundation? This verse really puts things into perspective!

Fruit

When you're tempted to brag, will you brag about yourself or your church, or will you brag about your God? What foundation are you building upon? Think about it.

It's My Business
Taken from 1 Corinthians 5—6

- *Foundation* ───────────────────

Don't rush through this section. Use the time to prepare your heart for today's lesson. Get quiet before God and invite Him to speak to you.

Focus

> *Have you ever had a friend tell you, "Leave me alone! What I do is my own business, not yours!"?*

Paul sat back in his chair. He had just written to the Corinthian believers about one problem in their church, but he knew that other problems needed to be addressed before he sent his letter. With a sigh, he leaned forward over the parchment and continued to write.

"I've heard reports that someone in your church is actually practicing an immoral act. Yet you proudly stand by and allow him to do such a thing, boasting about the love you're showing him. Instead of boasting, you should be filled with grief and expel him from your fellowship so that he might think about his sin and come to realize the damage it has caused. All this boasting of yours is doing damage too. Just as it takes only a little bit of yeast to spread through a whole batch of dough, it takes only one believer living in sin to do great

> **Yeast is a substance that's mixed into dough so that the dough grows, spreads, and multiplies. You can see yeast working when bread rises or is being baked. It changes the entire shape of things—literally!**

> *Slander, idol worship, theft, drunkenness, greed, and immorality are all actions based on choices that reflect how a person thinks—or doesn't think! All of these choices stem from a lack of love for God.*

damage in the church. Don't have anything to do with those who call themselves believers yet continue to live in sin. The loving thing to do is to cut them off from fellowship so that they will realize their sin and turn from it. Don't be afraid to act as judges in these matters. God is the judge of unbelievers outside the church, but He wants you to deal with problems inside the church."

Paul set his pen down and rubbed his eyes. How could he communicate the importance of living a God-honoring life that stands as an example for others to follow? He knew the Corinthian believers were taking one another to court and airing their complaints and arguments in front of unbelievers. Rather than working things out among themselves, they were demanding their rights in secular courts. Paul wrote, "I'm saying this to your shame. One of you takes another believer to court—and this is being done in front of nonChristians!"

Paul reminded these believers of the evil Jesus Christ had rescued them from. "Before you came to Christ, you were slanderers, idol worshippers, thieves, drunkards, immoral, and greedy people! But now your sins have been washed away. Through Jesus you have been made holy before God and stand blameless before Him. This gift of God wasn't free or cheap—it cost Jesus His life! So be careful how you live and what you do with your body, because God's Spirit lives in you. Each of you must choose to honor God with your body and your actions, for what you do has an effect on others."

Footwork

Turn to 1 Corinthians 6:19–20 in your Bible. When we become Christians, God gives us His Holy Spirit to live in us. According to verse 19, how does God view our bodies? What should we do as a result (verse 20)? A good way to make God-honoring choices is to ask yourself this question before acting: "If Jesus were standing here, would He approve of what I'm saying? Would He join in on what I'm doing?"

Fruit

Because God's Holy Spirit lives in you, His presence is always with you. Wherever you go, He goes. Whatever you do, He's there. Whatever you say, He hears. Whatever you think, He knows. He's intimately acquainted with everything about you, including all your fears and failures. And He chooses to stick with you (and me) anyway. So before you say or do something, do you ask yourself, "What would Jesus do?" Or does Jesus have to ask you, "What are you doing?"

No Problem!
Taken from 1 Corinthians 10

— ᖴoᴜɴᴅᴀᴛɪoɴ —

Spend some time in prayer, asking God to teach you from His Word. Thank Him that His strength and help are always available to you.

Focus

When you're tempted to do bad things, do you ever give in and do those things, thinking you can just ask God to forgive you later?

"As I mentioned before," Paul wrote to the Corinthian believers, "don't think that just because you have forgiveness in Christ, you have the freedom to sin. The freedom you have is freedom from the mastery of sin!"

Paul knew that the believers in Corinth were tempted to sin and to live solely for pleasure. They reasoned that if their sins were forgiven, no harm could come from adding a few more to the list. Because they mistakenly thought this way, they became overconfident and self-centered. They took their eyes off the Lord and focused their attention on themselves and their desires. "Live and be happy" became their motto as they gave in to temptations. They seemed to have forgotten about God's presence in their lives.

Paul's pen moved slowly across the parchment as his thoughts traveled back in time to God's chosen people. He thought about all they had done against God in spite of His presence with them. "I don't want you to be uninformed," Paul wrote. "The Israelites, under Moses' leadership, knew they were God's people (just as you are), yet God was displeased with them. They continuously

Silas as his new partner. He meets Timothy

sinned by loving other things more than they loved Him. They served idols and put God's love for them to the test. Wanting to satisfy their own pleasures, they gave in to temptations and complained about the leadership God placed over them. Because of their sinful behavior, God punished them to bring their hearts back to Him. Some He even put to death because their sins against Him were so serious. What happened to the people of Israel stands as an example and a warning to us."

Paul continued. "Know that the temptations you face are common to all people. You don't have to be mastered by them, for in the face of temptation, God remains faithful to you. He won't allow you to be tempted beyond what you can withstand, but He offers you His strength and help. Call to Him whenever you face temptation, and He'll provide a way for you to escape it. So whatever you say or do, commit everything to God and do it all for His glory."

> *The New Testament is so rooted in the Old Testament that it's impossible to fully understand the New Testament without spending some time in the Old Testament. In 1 Corinthians 10:1–13, Paul wrote about the warnings we need to take from Israel's history. Check out the Old Testament and Israel's history in* **Faith Factor OT**—*or simply read the Old Testament stories for yourself in Exodus 17:1–7 and ch. 32; Numbers 16; 21:4–9; and 25:1–9.*

Footwork

Turn to 1 Corinthians 10:13. What does this verse say? Read it again, emphasizing the words *no, but,* and *God.* What two things does God promise to do for you when you face temptation and ask for His help?

Fruit

Write 1 Corinthians 10:13 on an index card and memorize it. Keep the card handy to review the verse as needed. It's a promise you'll need to remember and rely on for the rest of your life.

I Love You Anyway
Taken from 1 Corinthians 12—13

— *Foundation* ————————————————

Spend a few moments alone with God. Thank Him for loving you with a love beyond imagining and for giving you a special place in the family of believers.

Focus

When people treat you like a nobody and act as if they're more important than you, have you ever been tempted to believe them?

"Nobody is a nobody in God's kingdom," Paul wrote to the Corinthian believers. He was aware of the temptation by some in the church to look down on others. They compared their God-given spiritual gifts with the gifts of others and rated them in order of importance.

"Don't you understand?" Paul wrote. "The same Holy Spirit lives in each of you. He doesn't give gifts so you can build yourselves up, but rather so you can build others up and have the ability to do God's work in God's way," he explained. He then listed some of the gifts with which the Holy Spirit empowers believers.

"Each person has a special place in the family of believers, and each person is given special abilities. We're like a body working together. Every part of the body needs all the other parts. So if the eye were to say to the hand, 'You aren't needed,' that wouldn't make the hand any less a part of the body. And if the foot were to say, 'I don't belong to the body because I'm not

First Corinthians 13:13 states, "And now these three remain: faith, hope and love. But the greatest of these is love." Why is love the greatest? When we see Jesus face-to-face, there will be no need for faith and hope. Love, however, will remain. It's the greatest.

a hand!' that wouldn't make it so. No! If all the parts were an eye, then how could the body hear? If all were an ear, then how could the body smell? All parts of the body are equally important, no matter how visible or hidden their role. We're all part of the body of Christ, and each of us has been given different abilities," Paul stated.

"Therefore, don't seek certain gifts thinking they'll make you more important. That kind of thinking is sinful and selfish. Instead, desire to live a life showing God's love. For if I had the gift of speaking in tongues but didn't have love, I would only be like a noisy clanging instrument. And even if I could do the greatest and most wonderful things for the glory of God, but didn't have His kind of love in my heart, it would be as if my life counted for nothing. God's kind of love changes lives. People who have God's kind of love in their hearts are patient and kind. They don't envy others and don't boast or act in a proud way. They aren't rude and don't selfishly want the best for themselves. They aren't hotheaded or quick to become angry, and they don't keep a list of the wrongs that have been done against them. God's kind of love enables people to rejoice in the truth rather than delight in evil. It always defends and protects; it always has faith; it always holds on to hope; and it always hangs in there no matter what. God's love never fails."

Paul paused for a moment, then continued writing, "God has given many kinds of gifts, but they will all pass away—they are only temporary. Only His love will remain forever. Those who have learned to love with God's kind of love are those who desire the greatest thing of all. Faith, hope, and love are what matter, but the greatest of all of them is love."

Footwork

Turn to 1 Corinthians 13:4–5. In these two verses alone, Paul lists nine descriptions of real love. Based on what you've already learned about the Corinthian believers, which of these nine rules on how to love were they guilty of breaking?

Fruit

Referring to your Bible, write down these nine rules of love on an index card or a piece of paper. Then put a small *x* by any rules that are hardest for you to keep. (Remember, loving others with God's kind of love is something we can do only by relying on His strength and help.) Next, get down on your knees and tell God about your areas of struggle. Ask Him to forgive you and to provide the strength to love with His kind of love. For the rest of this week, find practical things to do that fit under the areas you marked. Then, with God's help, do them.

2 Corinthians

Second Corinthians can almost be viewed as part 2 of a letter written to the church in Corinth. Although the church had corrected one of the problems Paul wrote about in his first letter, other problems quickly developed. Some who tried to cause trouble in the church attacked Paul's character. In response Paul wrote this letter to defend himself—not for his own sake but for the sake of the Corinthian believers. He knew that if they questioned him, they would also question the gospel message he proclaimed.

While reading through 2 Corinthians, remember that Paul wrote it while on his third missionary journey. Because of a riot by the silversmiths in Ephesus (Acts 19), Paul found himself in the region of Macedonia where he met up with a fellow believer and church leader named Titus and received news of the church in Corinth. The general well-being of the church was good, although there was bad news about a group in the church who were rising up against Paul.

As you read through this book, notice Paul's love for the church even though it caused him great pain. Notice how he handled some of the problems and encouraged believers to remain true to the Lord by living in a God-honoring way. Think about your own life and how it measures up.

He was easily swayed by bribes and

Read My Life
Taken from 2 Corinthians 2—5

— *Foundation* —

Take a few minutes to tell God about the struggles you have with others.
Open your heart and speak honestly, for He has a listening ear. Then ask Him
to point out any areas in your life that make other people struggle. Don't be
afraid; God loves you with a perfect love, and He will never give up on you.

Focus

Do you sometimes have a hard time getting along with other Christians?

Paul's letter contained some harsh words to the Corinthian believers. It seemed
that the problems in the church were getting worse! Since his first letter more
trouble had arisen, and the church was now torn with other difficulties. Though
the believers had obeyed Paul's instruction about disciplining the man living in
sin, they were now unwilling to forgive him. Even though he had turned from
his sin and asked for forgiveness, some in the church insisted on even harsher
punishment. A great argument arose, causing disunity and bitterness.

"The punishment first given was enough," Paul wrote, "for it was successful in
turning this man away from his sin. Now, however, you should forgive him and
seek to comfort him. Welcome him back into your fellowship and don't hold a
grudge against him, because this only causes division among you that will
result in bitterness and an opportunity for Satan to gain a victory."

leaned toward cruelty. • AD 53-58 — Paul'

Paul went on to explain how the believers' lives were like a living letter people could read. They weren't meant to be individual letters, but one letter, working together in unity to communicate one message—and that to the glory of God. Their ability to love and forgive one another would carry a strong message to the world that couldn't be easily ignored.

Paul knew that it didn't take much for them to look at their failures and become discouraged. But even though the church had some serious problems, these believers still belonged to God, and He had greater things ahead for them.

"Our goodness and our abilities come not from ourselves but from God," Paul reminded them. "And He chooses to carry His message in us much as we use jars of clay to carry treasures. Through Jesus, God brought us to Himself, and He desires to use us to carry this same good news and hope to others. So fix your eyes on what you can't see—those things that are eternal—not on the problems you have with one another. Make it your goal to live a life pleasing to God, and forgive the one who has turned from his sin. Whatever you do, don't forget that all believers will stand before Jesus one day and be judged according to what they have done—both good and bad."

In John 13:35, Jesus said, "By this all men will know that you are my disciples, if you love one another." Christians didn't have high social status in the culture. Instead, they had a remarkable ability (if they relied on and obeyed God) to love others. That alone would turn the world upside down.

Titus, a Greek convert and trusted friend of Paul, carried Paul's first letter to the Corinthians and would also deliver this one. It was through Titus that Paul learned the good news (that the man living in sin had repented) and some troubling news (that the church was hesitant to welcome him back).

Footwork

Look up 2 Corinthians 3:18. What do we reflect? Whose likeness should we find ourselves being changed into? Do you think this is something we're responsible to do on our own? Is it something we can take any credit for? Explain.

Fruit

Our lives are like letters that others read, and yet in and of our own strength, we are like frail clay pots. There will be times in your life that you will have a difficult time forgiving or loving a brother or sister in Christ. Instead of focusing on your own feelings, think about what your actions and life might be saying to those who are watching. Turn the situation over to God and ask Him to change your heart so you can do what He would have you to do.

Oops!
Taken from 2 Corinthians 8—9

Foundation

Stop and pray before you begin today's lesson. Thank the Lord for His work in your life—even in the smallest of details. Ask Him to continue to help you live a life honoring to Him.

Focus

Have you ever promised to give money to your church or to a good cause and then failed to follow through?

Paul continued writing to the believers in Corinth while he stayed in a region called Macedonia. He had started three churches in Macedonia—one in Philippi, one in Thessalonica, and one in Berea. The believers in these churches knew that Paul was collecting an offering for the needy church in Jerusalem, and without being asked, they had promised to give generously.

There were many problems in the church at Corinth, but the believers there eagerly wanted to show their love and concern for the poor in Jerusalem. As a matter of fact, they were the first to respond with a promise to give. Now a year had gone by, and they hadn't followed through on their promise. Paul knew they needed to be encouraged.

"Brothers, I want to tell you about gracious gift the Macedonian churches gave out of their love for God," Paul wrote, holding them up

ecomes ruler at age sixteen.

189

A tithe is an Old Testament rule of thumb that involves regularly giving 10 percent of what you earn. An offering is anything given above and beyond the tithe as an act of worship, and the amount is determined by the giver's heart.

The first offering of a tithe is recorded in Genesis 28:20–21. Check out who promised to give a tithe and for what reason. The phrase "If God will be with me ..." is better translated "Since God will be with me...." Read Genesis 27 to understand the whole story.

as an example. "Even though they themselves were poor and suffering, they not only gave whatever they could, but they gave even more than they could afford to give! They came to us on their own and pleaded for us to let them share in this ministry of giving to the needy church in Jerusalem. They did so much more than we expected. Because of their example, we have urged Titus to visit you so that you might have the opportunity to give what you promised earlier.

"Please understand that I'm not ordering you to give, but rather I'm encouraging you to show that your love is sincere and real. I know since last year that you were ready to give. I even boasted about it to the Macedonians, telling them of your eagerness to help. Your example inspired many of them to give to the cause too," Paul told them.

Then he clarified, "I'm sending Titus and some of the brothers to you ahead of us so that our boasting about you won't prove empty, and that you'll be ready to give as I said you would be.

"When the brothers arrive, don't have a bad attitude and give because you feel you have to or because everyone else is giving. Give the amount that your hearts tell you to give," Paul wrote, encouraging his readers, "because God loves those who give willingly. When you give, you'll not only be helping meet the needs of God's people, but everyone will give thanks to God for your generosity. Not only that, but the hearts of those who receive your gift will be with you because of the work of God's grace in your lives."

Footwork

Read 2 Corinthians 9:7–8 in your Bible. Then read it a second time aloud. According to these verses, what does God promise to do for you when you give with a willing heart?

Fruit

Think about what you promised to give to your church or to other causes but never did. Perhaps it was a portion of your allowance for a Sunday school project or the support of a missionary or a needy child. If at all possible, try to make it right and pay what you promised. Know that God will be honored and you will be more blessed than those who receive your gift.

dvises him, Nero becomes a power—

And Here's the Proof
Taken from 2 Corinthians 10—13

— Foundation —

Before you read today's lesson, ask the Holy Spirit to teach you and help you understand God's Word. Thank the Lord for His faithfulness and power to help you change what needs to be changed in your life.

FOCUS

Do you know people who think better of themselves than they should?

Paul's hand was steady and sure as the words poured from his pen. These were the last thoughts in his letter to the Corinthians, and he had saved the most difficult issue for last.

Ever since Titus gave Paul the report of a group rising up against him in the church, the news burned in his heart. The men opposing him were false apostles who accused Paul without just cause. He knew that these false apostles were only trying to gain power and influence for themselves and that they really had no love for the church. Paul also knew that they were preaching a different gospel that wasn't at all about salvation through faith in Jesus. Because of this, Paul needed to speak up and put the matter to rest, not for his own sake, but for the sake of the Corinthian believers.

Though Paul disliked talking about himself, he knew he needed to go to some extreme measures to make his point. So he put his pen to the parchment and continued to write. The false apostles had accused him of being bold in his letters

hungry tyrant, later ordering his mother

but cowardly in person. They also criticized him for not living off what the Corinthian believers could provide for his needs. On top of that, they even accused him of possibly dipping into the money collections for the church in Jerusalem!

"You need to know that we will back up our letters with action when we are with you in person. We are fully equipped to destroy any argument or idea that opposes God's truth," Paul wrote. He thought about how the false apostles were taking advantage of those in the church. "As for not accepting your support of my ministry, you know that I never wanted to become a burden to you. Why should I rob from the poor? Let it be known that I came only to give, not to take for myself—which is something those who speak against me do," Paul continued. He knew that the false apostles boasted about themselves and their pretend accomplishments. They even carried special papers telling others how great they were. (See also 2 Corinthians 3:1.) "They come to you boasting about themselves, but I come to you boasting about Christ. Let him who boasts boast in the Lord." Then Paul went on to describe how the false apostles took credit for work done by God, and how they made themselves look official and important.

"They boast in a worldly way," Paul began, "so just for this moment I, too, will boast this way so that you may fully see and understand what I'm talking about.

"They're Hebrews? Well, so am I. They're Abraham's offspring? I am too. And they claim to serve Christ? I've served Him much more. I've worked much harder, been imprisoned more often,

> *It has been thought that Paul's thorn in the flesh was fading eyesight or even severe headaches.*
>
> *In Paul's day the wealthy often hired their own teachers. Paul chose not to be associated with teachers who were only interested in making money off those who hired them. Instead, he supported himself as a tent maker, an "artisan." Artisans were often viewed as lower-class people.*

been beaten with rods and the thirty-nine lashes, faced death many times, and was even stoned once and left for dead. Not only that, but I've been in shipwrecks three times, was adrift in the ocean a day and night, and have been forced to move around constantly. I've faced many dangers, including dangers from rivers and oceans, from outlaws and robbers, and from Gentiles and Jews and so-called Christian brothers who turned out not to be. I've faced danger in both the country and the city. I've lived through many times where I've had no food to eat or water to drink; I've shivered from cold and nakedness, and I've gone without sleep. And on top of all that, my heart is often filled with worry and concern for the churches I oversee."

Paul paused a moment before continuing. "Even if I could have boasted about these things to you, I did not do so in the past, for I didn't want anyone to think more of me than they should. Also, to keep me from becoming proud of all the amazing things God has revealed to me, He gave me a weakness, "a thorn in my flesh," that forces me to depend on Him and His strength. Because of this I gladly boast about my weaknesses, because it's only through them that Christ's power is perfected in me. I've learned that when I'm weak in myself, then I'm strong through Christ's strength."

Then, as Paul began to wrap up his letter, he told the Corinthians, "The reason I write all this is not to defend myself but to strengthen you. And these things about me you already know. Don't be taken in by false apostles or listen to a gospel other than what I preached to you. Look closely at your hearts and lives to see if you've really put your faith in Jesus."

Footwork

Look up 2 Corinthians 13:5 in your Bible. What does it say? (Don't guess at this or skim over it. Read it for yourself.) A good way to test yourself is to check your motives for what you do and say. Why do you do what you do?

Fruit

If you were put on trial and had to give an account of yourself to the judge, would you need to say anything, or would the sincerity of your life and actions speak for themselves? On what side of the fence does the proof of your life fall? Take time to examine your life.

Galatians

The book of Galatians is a letter Paul wrote to the believers in the Gentile region of Galatia. These churches began as a result of Paul's first missionary journey (Acts 13—14) when he visited the cities of Pisidia—Antioch, Iconium, Lystra, and Derbe. As you may remember from your study of Acts, these cities held great adventure and trials for Paul as he faithfully preached the gospel before being run out of town or stoned.

Paul wrote this letter to the Galatians from his home church in Antioch right before the meeting of the council of Jerusalem. He had just received word that some Jewish believers were trying to force their Jewish rules on the new believers. Paul wrote to remind the believers of how they had come to Christ.*

Galatians is a foundational book for the Christian faith, much like the book of Romans. It has sometimes been called a "short Romans" because it's packed with important facts about our faith (called *doctrine*). One such doctrine states that none of us can earn our way into heaven by trying to keep God's rules. Salvation from the penalty and power of sin comes only through God's grace, not our own efforts.

As you read through Galatians, keep your eyes open and see how many other faith facts you can discover.

*Note: This letter was written before the letters to the Roman and Corinthian churches, even though in our Bibles it comes after them. Don't let this confuse you. The New Testament isn't put together in the order it was written. That's why it's important for you to get your bearings before you read through a book of the Bible. Knowing the background first will help you better understand what you're reading. ——————

Nice Work
Taken from Galatians 1—3

Foundation

Take some time to pray, asking the Lord to give you a teachable heart so you can learn from His Word and grow even closer to Him. Thank Him for what He has done for you through Jesus Christ. If you aren't sure what all that is or what it means, take a moment and turn to the back of this book. There's a special message there just for you.

Focus

Do you know anyone who follows the rules to try to impress others, including God?

Paul's anger burned. A group of Jews were going around the churches in Galatia trying to convert the believers to Judaism. "You must first become Jews in order to have salvation," the group called Judaizers stated. "Then you must dedicate your life to carry out all the rules of the Law, since that's how you can win God's favor," they proclaimed. (See Acts 15:5.) The Judaizers believed that they alone had been given the special privilege of salvation, and they proclaimed a false gospel, telling other believers to depend on the Law of Moses for salvation. They even went a step further and accused Paul of making religion easy in order to win the favor of men. These were the issues that caused Paul to write with a sense of urgency to the churches in Galatia—churches that were being taken in by this false teaching.

"I'm shocked that you're turning away from the one true God, the One who called you to Himself through the grace of Jesus Christ and are turning instead to another gospel, which isn't the true gospel! If anyone comes to you preaching something other than what you heard from me and accepted, may God condemn him for all eternity! Even if I myself or an angel comes to you with a different message, don't listen. For the gospel I gave you isn't man-made; it's from God," Paul wrote.

"What people say about me makes no difference, for my Master is God," Paul defended himself. "If I were trying to win the approval of men, as the Judaizers accuse me of doing, I wouldn't be serving Christ. Let it be known that I bear the marks of being His servant on my body. I'm now living my life by faith in Jesus, who laid down His own life for me because He loved me."

Paul sat back and thought about the possible results of the Judaizers' false message. He knew it was turning people's hearts from faith in Christ to a false religious faith that deceived them into thinking they could become good enough to impress God and earn their way into heaven.

"That's wrong!" Paul screamed in his heart as he picked up his pen and started writing. "It's only through faith in Jesus and His works of righteousness that we can be holy enough to stand before God! God gave His laws to show us His standards of righteousness. These laws can't deliver us from our sin, for they were intended only to point out our sins. If we could become righteous by keeping God's law, then Jesus' death was meaningless."

Paul wrote, "Oh, friends—are you so foolish? Did God give you the gift

> **Legalism** *is the act of trying to add our own works to faith in an attempt to earn God's approval. It's like saying that Jesus' death on the cross wasn't good enough. In Ephesians 2:8–9, you'll find God's reason for faith. Check it out!*

> *Since righteousness comes through Christ alone, the same requirements for salvation apply to both the "chosen" Jews and the "outsider" Gentiles— much different from the Jews' original idea that they had a privileged position before God through Abraham.*

of the Holy Spirit and do miraculous things in your lives because you were perfect or because you put your faith in Him? You started out depending on the Spirit to help you live a righteous live. Why are you now insulting God by going back to thinking that you can impress Him with your own works of righteousness?"

Footwork

Look up Galatians 3:1. What do the first few words say? (*Hint:* It's an exclamation.) Now skip down to verse 3. What did Paul say they were doing?

Fruit

Some people say you can't please God unless you keep a certain number of religious rules—or at least the rules they live by! Don't believe them. Live for Christ, and your life will automatically honor and please God.

Fruit Anyone?
Taken from Galatians 5

Foundation

As you prepare your heart for today's lesson, ask God to quiet your thoughts and keep you from being distracted. Ask Him to honor your time with Him and to teach you through His Holy Spirit.

Focus

Have you ever been in a situation where there were no rules or people to tell you what was right?

Paul had already told the Galatians that it wasn't necessary to live by the Law in order to impress God. Their righteousness came through faith in Christ alone. Since the Law was no longer their master and they were no longer slaves to it, did it mean they now had the freedom to do anything they wanted to?

"Jesus Christ set us free so that we can live in freedom," Paul wrote. "This freedom is a freedom from sin, not a freedom to sin! So don't use your freedom to do whatever you want, but use it instead to do what is right by serving others in love."

Paul continued. "If you live under the control of the Spirit you won't end up doing what your sinful nature desires, such as behaving in ways

> *Our "sinful nature" is the self-centered way we are naturally, without God. Sometimes Paul referred to it as "the flesh," the desire we have toward sin and toward running our lives without God.*

that make you unfit to come before God; desiring pleasures so much that you don't care what others say or think; loving something or someone else more than you love God; engaging in witchcraft; hating other people; arguing; selfishly trying to get ahead at the expense of others; wanting what someone else has; having outbursts of bad temper; looking out only for yourself; not getting along with others; and living for your own enjoyment. Those who live by the desires of the sinful nature will never enter the kingdom of God."

> *The word picture of "bearing fruit" is rooted (no pun intended) in the Old Testament. Check out Hosea 14:8 as just one example of many.*

Paul thought for a moment and then wrote, "Those who belong to Jesus don't live by the sinful nature and its desires; they live by the Spirit. The fruit of the Spirit is much different than the acts of the flesh. The fruit of the Spirit seeks nothing but the best for others (even if others seek only the worst for you); it has confidence and peace in difficult times; it accepts others (faults and all); it shows kindness and allows God's goodness to shine; it trusts God; it's teachable (not proud); it respects others; and it doesn't give in to temptations and sinful desires. Since we have new life by the Spirit, let's walk by the Spirit's power and not by the sway of our sinful nature."

Footwork

Read Galatians 5:16 in your Bible. How can we keep from doing the wrong thing, even when there seem to be no rules? Now skip down to verses 22–23. What are the results of living by the Spirit?

Fruit

Look back at verse 22. Notice that it says the fruit of the Spirit, not the fruits! This isn't a shopping list from which to pick and choose. A good test to see if you're walking in the Holy Spirit's power is to write the list of fruit on an index card, review it often, and measure your life by these qualities.

If you fail in one area, you can be sure you aren't living a Spirit-filled life. When you see this happening, talk to God. Tell Him what you've done wrong and ask for His forgiveness. Ask to be controlled by His Spirit rather than by your own sinful nature. God is faithful and will answer your prayers, even when you fail over and over and have to keep coming to Him. For the next five days, start each day by asking the Holy Spirit to be in control of your thoughts and actions, making sure you do your part by seeking to please God in whatever you say and do. See the difference this makes in your life.

Count Me Out
Taken from Galatians 6

Foundation

Before you finish Galatians today, take a moment to thank God for the Holy Spirit who lives in you (if you have trusted Jesus as your Savior) and for the way He helps you live a life pleasing to God.

Focus

Does it ever seem unfair when others get away with things they shouldn't?

"Friends," Paul wrote to the believers in Galatia, "if a believer accidentally slips and falls into sin (we all make mistakes), those of you who know how to rely on the Holy Spirit should help that believer get back on the right track again. This help needs to be given in a gentle and loving way, not with a prideful or harsh spirit that's only interested in punishment. As you help your brother or sister, think about yourself so you don't become vulnerable to temptation as well. Those who think they can't be tempted are only fooling themselves."

Paul thought for a moment, then continued his warning. "All of you should compare your own actions to God's standards. Those who compare themselves to others become taken in by a prideful attitude and begin thinking better of themselves than they really ought to.

"Don't deceive yourselves: You can't fool God! Those who seem to get away with things they shouldn't don't get away with them forever. They will always reap the results of what they sow," Paul wrote, thinking about the nearby farmers.

When a farmer plants a seed, it doesn't look like anything is happening for a few weeks because the seed is growing underground. Roots are being sent down and outward to seek out nourishment for the plant, and soon a tender shoot pops up through the soil and sprouts leaves. Anyone looking at a developing plant can tell what kind of seed the farmer planted in the ground.

"So it is with your life," Paul observed. "Whoever sows to satisfy the desires of the sinful nature will reap what the sinful nature produces—destruction. But whoever sows to the Spirit will reap everlasting life. So don't compare yourselves to others, or you may become proud. And don't become discouraged and stop doing good," Paul wrote, encouraging the believers. "For just like the farmer who planted seed and eventually reaped a crop, you'll also reap a crop of eternal blessings if you're patient and don't give up."

> *To reap is to experience the results or rewards of an action. (Sow a tomato plant; reap tomatoes.) It's a common law of physical nature around us (ask any gardener) as well as a common law of human nature (ask God).*
>
> ---
>
> *According to Proverbs 11:18, "the wicked man earns deceptive wages" (something that promises gain but leads to poverty), but the one "who sows righteousness reaps a sure reward" (a definite and guaranteed gain!).*

Footwork

Look up Galatians 6:9. This applies to each of us personally, especially when we compare ourselves with others or begin to get discouraged. What does this verse tell us to do? What is the reward, if any?

Fruit

In your lifetime you'll see people doing wrong and seeming to get away with it. Don't become discouraged, defeated, or deceived by what you see. Sooner or later they'll experience the consequences of their actions. Instead, keep your focus on Christ; that's what matters most. He sees and He knows.

shipwrecked on island of Malta while

being taken to Rome. ◆ AD 60–62 – Pau

Ephesians

Paul wrote Ephesians while he was a prisoner in Rome after his third missionary journey. This letter differs greatly from his others; many say it's Paul's greatest writing. Perhaps one reason for this is that Paul wasn't writing to correct any church problems. As a prisoner, he had plenty of time to write about the things on his heart and to share his thoughts not only with the church at Ephesus but also with other churches in the neighboring areas.

Reading through Ephesians is much like exploring a gold mine. Each verse is loaded with great nuggets of truth waiting to be discovered. Ephesians reminds us of the spiritual blessings we have in Christ and the privilege we have of standing before God in righteousness because of what Jesus has done for us. It also gives us instructions for living the Christian life and fighting spiritual battles.

As you read though this book, take your time. If you see a gold nugget that catches your eye, stop, dig it up, and examine it. One way to do this is to ask questions. Then, using a Bible-study tool, such as a concordance (usually found in the back of a Bible), look up a word and read the other verses in Scripture where that word is used. If you didn't find an answer to your question, ask your parents, your Sunday school teacher, or your pastor to help you. Who knows, God could use your question to teach them something too!

remains in Rome under house arrest.

What a Picker-Upper!
Taken from Ephesians 1

Foundation

Before you begin today's lesson, ask the Lord to forgive you for not always appreciating what He has done for you. Thank Him for how deeply and completely He loves you.

Focus

Do you sometimes wish you could be someone else rather than who you really are?

Paul wrote to the believers in Ephesus, "May you experience the grace and peace God offers you." He sat back and thought about the wonders of God's love, then he picked up his pen and began flooding the parchment with words.

"Praise God! In Christ He has blessed us spiritually so that we lack nothing. Before He created the world, He knew us and set us apart for Him, and in His eyes, we stand before Him spotless and without fault because of Jesus. Because of His love for us, He planned our adoption into His heavenly family. And He has freely showered His grace on us through Jesus who forgives our sin."

Then Paul thought about God's incredible grace. "God keeps pouring out the riches of His grace upon us in His wisdom and understanding—even today! He allows us to know His will, and He brings everything together under the leadership of His Son, Jesus Christ. God, who works out everything according to His will, chose us in Jesus, and we exist to bring glory and praise to Him. When we believed in Jesus, God gave us His Spirit to live in us forever. He is God's guarantee to us that we have an inheritance in heaven with Him."

Paul paused for a moment and then continued to write. "In all my prayers for you, I continually ask God to reveal Himself to you and give you wisdom and understanding so that you will grow in your relationship with Him. I also ask Him to fill your hearts with the hope He has given you in Jesus, with the many riches of being an heir of eternal life, and with the awesome power He has given those who trust in Him!"

Paul's heart yearned for the believers to know and experience all the blessings God had for them. He knew if they could only understand who they were in Christ, it would keep them from great difficulties, disappointments, and temptations. No longer would they feel unimportant or want to be like others. No longer would they have the need to compare themselves with others or strive to win God's favor or approval. In Christ they had all they needed to live a victorious life, but they needed to live each day in dependence on Him. If they could only understand who they were in Christ, they would realize that they stood complete, totally loved, and fully accepted in God's sight through Jesus. And they could begin to experience a joy that words could never describe! *If only they understood,* Paul thought.

> *In Christ you have been chosen, planned for, adopted, forgiven, guaranteed an inheritance, empowered, loved, and accepted. Never forget that!*
>
> ---
>
> *The worth of something is based on the value so-called experts give it. God is the greatest Expert. Believe what He says about your worth.*

Footwork

Don't skip over this section! Check out Ephesians 1:18–19. These are great verses. What three facts can we stand on?

Fruit

Your feelings about yourself will come and go, and they will change many times as you mature. Don't trust them! Feelings are just that: feelings. They aren't fact, and they don't usually tell the true story. Don't rely on them. Instead, remember that you belong to God. If He thinks this highly of you, should you think any less of yourself?

Rescued!
Taken from Ephesians 2—3

Foundation

Stop and pray before you begin today's lesson. Ask God to use His Word to remind you of the most life-changing thing that can ever happen to a person: receiving salvation. Ask Him to keep your heart teachable and excited about Him, no matter how old you get.

Focus

Have you ever been heroically rescued from something?

"Lying, cheating, stealing, disobeying, fighting, being selfish, being proud, being unkind to others, being impatient, loving something more than you love God—these are the desires of human nature," Paul wrote.

He leaned over the parchment as he continued writing to the believers in Ephesus. Paul knew that he didn't need to explain what sin was; they already knew. "When you used to follow the desires of your sinful human nature, you became like a dead person because of your sins," he wrote. Then he went on to explain how people are unable to change themselves. "All of us were guilty of sin, and none of us on our own could make ourselves holy enough for God. We were like dead men, hopelessly trapped in our own evil desires and behavior, waiting for the death sentence.

"But then," Paul wrote in larger letters, "God did something to save us from the penalty of our sins! Because He loved us so much, He acted in mercy and rescued us. And not only did He rescue us, but He also gave us new life in Christ! Remember it's only by God's grace that we have been saved through faith in Jesus, and this faith isn't even something that comes from us or that we work at. It, too, is a gift from God, not something we can boast about as if it originated with us!"

> **What's the difference between God's grace and His mercy? It has been said that grace is getting what we don't deserve (God's love), while mercy is not getting what we do deserve (punishment).**

Paul then went on to remind them how they once walked in the darkness of sin, but now they were walking by the light of God's will. "For God crafted us and created us in Christ Jesus to live in ways that please Him and help others, ways He prepared for us ahead of time," he told them.

Before God saved them, they had been hopelessly trapped in their sins, unable to help themselves, just like everyone else in the world. But through the blood of Christ, God forgave their sins and brought them near to Him. What God did, He did for everyone in the world, so that through faith in Him, people could experience His grace and the incredible things He wanted to do in and through them.

Then Paul wrote, "I pray that you might understand the love of Jesus and how wide and long and high and deep it is, and that you might know and experience this love that goes beyond the greatest things you can imagine! May God be glorified forever! His incredible power is working in our lives, and He can accomplish so much more than we would ever dream possible or think to ask!"

Paul placed his pen next to the parchment and stood up to stretch. He couldn't help but think of his own life and how he had been rescued from the darkness of sin. "Praise God," he breathed with a sigh of relief.

Footwork

Turn to Ephesians 2:4–5. What does verse 4 tell us about God? According to verse 5, what did this prompt Him to do for us?

Fruit

Don't put your Bible aside yet! Turn to Ephesians 3:20–21. These verses speak about God and His abilities. What is God able to do? More than what? Stop now and thank Him for His character and for what He has done for you.

Grow Up
Taken from Ephesians 4—5

— *Foundation* ———————————————

Ask God to examine your heart as you prepare to read today's lesson. Invite Him to point out and help you change areas in your life where you need to grow.

Has anyone ever said to you, "Why don't you just grow up?"

Paul had already explained the great spiritual blessings God gives to those who know Jesus. He had reminded the believers in Ephesus of their sinful heritage and of all that God had done for them so they could come to know Him. Now he needed to remind them of one more thing.

"But God has given His grace to each of us," Paul wrote. "We have all been given gifts and abilities to use in building one another up so that we might become more mature in Christ. We shouldn't be like babies, not knowing what we believe or why, but instead, we need to grow up in Christ and tell people the truth with love."

Paul continued, explaining how believers are called the "body of Christ," how Jesus is the head, or leader, of the body, and how all believers come under His leadership. Just as a body is connected by ligaments and muscles that work together, so believers are to work together. And as each believer does his or her part, the body grows in unity and is built up in love.

"So every one of you must start telling your brothers and sisters the truth. Stop lying and deceiving one another, because we all belong to Christ and are part of His body! If you become angry with someone or about a situation, don't go to bed angry. Instead, seek to make it right immediately. If you don't, a root of bitterness will spring up in your heart and it will give Satan a perfect and destructive foothold in your life," Paul warned.

> *A foothold is an area in our lives where Satan can firmly stand and move around with confidence. Paul warned believers not to give Satan any footholds in their lives.*

Paul's pen flowed across the parchment, leaving a trail of challenging words behind. "Do not say anything that could do harm. Instead speak to build up others and benefit those who are listening to you. And don't grieve God's Holy Spirit by tuning Him out or disobeying God. Also, get rid of all bitterness, anger, fighting, back-talking, and other actions that aren't honoring to God," Paul instructed.

"Instead, imitate God as His dearly loved children. Seek to live a life that models Christ's kind of love; he not only loved us, but He also gave up His life for us, dying in our place. This kind of love is a love of actions. Don't be content to remain as a baby Christian or to live in darkness anymore. Get rid of your old attitudes and behaviors and let God give you a totally new attitude and help you become more like Jesus so that you can live a righteous and holy life."

Footwork

Look up Ephesians 5:1–2 in your Bible. According to this passage, what two commands sum up what you just read in the Focus section? (*Hint:* Each verse begins with a command.)

Fruit

Take a moment to ask yourself, "Am I still a baby Christian, or am I becoming more and more like Jesus?" Becoming an imitator of Christ doesn't just "happen" by living life. You have to put effort into it. Do you have goals for your spiritual walk? Take a moment now and write down four things you can actively do (or not do) that will help you "grow up" to be more like Jesus. Be specific, and begin putting these things into practice today.

This Means War!
Taken from Ephesians 6

Foundation

Take a moment to look at the things around you. There's more to life than what you see—literally! Because we're human, we can't see the spiritual world with our eyes. Ask God to help you live in such a way that you never forget about the things you can't see.

Focus

If you were a soldier, would you find it hard to believe that you were under attack if you couldn't see, feel, or hear the enemy?

"Last of all, stand strong in the Lord and in His awesome power!" Paul wrote as he closed his letter to the Ephesian believers. While in prison he quietly observed all the pieces of armor that Roman soldiers wore. Paul knew that each piece had a special purpose, enabling the soldier to stand against an attack from his enemy.

Before a Roman soldier put on his armor, he put a belt around his waist to hold his clothes in place. This belt gave a soldier the ability to move about freely and was also a place where he could hang his sword. Next came the breastplate, which protected the soldier's heart and vital organs from an attack. Sandals were also important, giving him the ability to go anywhere sure-footedly. To protect himself against arrows and other flying objects, the soldier carried an oblong shield made of two pieces of wood

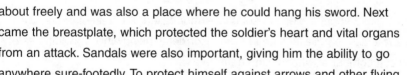

glued together and covered with linen and leather. It was about two and a half feet wide and four feet long! Because of the shield's construction, fiery arrows would simply sink into the thick wood and be extinguished. The soldier's helmet was hot and uncomfortable, and he used it only when facing danger. The only weapon a soldier carried for attacking his enemies was a sword—actually, a short dagger, which he used in close-up battles.

Observing all this armor, Paul couldn't help but think of the protection God has given to each believer. "Put on God's full armor so you can stand against Satan and his schemes," Paul wrote, as he thought about the armor of God and what it protects believers from. We do not struggle with an enemy we can see, but with an enemy we cannot see. Our war is not against flesh and blood, but against the powers and forces of Satan, the evil one who is at work in your world. Put on the armor of God so that when you are attacked, you may be able to stand your ground."

Paul knew believers must understand what God had equipped them with, so he compared spiritual armor to the Roman soldier's armor. He began with the belt, calling it "the belt of truth." Paul knew that as believers walked in God's truth and in integrity, they would experience a great sense of freedom. They would experience God's power in their lives and would be able to use the sword of God's Word, kept at their side on the belt.

Next came "the breastplate of righteousness." Believers who stand in the righteousness of Christ and allow Him to change their lives will have pure hearts and be protected from evil.

The believer's feet should also be protected with the gospel—sure footing for all situations.

Next, Paul described the shield, calling it "the shield of faith." Only faith has the ability to protect a believer from the temptations (fiery arrows) and evil schemes of Satan.

Paul also spoke about a piece of spiritual armor called "the helmet of salvation." Salvation protects the believer's head from incorrect thinking while providing safety during difficult combat or when facing death.

The final piece of armor is "the sword of the Spirit," the Word of God. This is a deadly weapon when used against Satan, the only weapon that can put him in his place.

river up to Sudan. James, the Lord's

220

"Put on God's complete armor," Paul told the believers, knowing that many would forget these things and attempt to stand against the Enemy in their own strength. Then he instructed, "Pray in all situations with the Holy Spirit's help, and don't be afraid or ashamed to tell God about anything. Remember to pray for other Christians. Be on your guard and understand the battle you're up against. Know and stand in the strength that God lovingly provides."

Footwork

According to Ephesians 6:10–11, what should you be strong in? How are you supposed to do that, specifically?

Fruit

Satan is a defeated enemy but only because of Christ's power. Don't try to fight the war in your own strength, or you will be defeated. Put on the armor God provides (know it, believe it, and act upon it), and you'll be able to stand—and withstand—anything! God already has the victory. Walk in it!

is released from his imprisonment in Rome.

Philippians

Like Ephesians, Paul also wrote the book of Philippians while imprisoned in Rome. He wrote to the believers in Philippi—a church started as a result of Paul's second missionary journey (Acts 16). As you may remember, Paul sang hymns of praise to God while in jail at Philippi and was miraculously delivered! When the jailer saw this, he and his household became believers in Christ. Paul also shared the gospel with Lydia, a woman who sold fine purple fabric, and she believed along with her entire household. The church in Philippi was born from these new believers.

Ten years later, after hearing the news of Paul's imprisonment in Rome, the church in Philippi sent Epaphroditus (their pastor) to comfort Paul and deliver a gift of money to make his stay in jail more comfortable. While visiting Paul, Epaphroditus became ill—almost to the point of death. When he recovered, he took Paul's letter back with him to Philippi.

As you read through Philippians, you'll see that Paul's main reason for writing was to thank the Philippians for their concern. He also used this opportunity to write about a concern he had for them. It seems that some in the church thought too highly of themselves. Others did right things for the wrong reasons and wrong things with the right motives. Paul included these concerns and corrections in his letter to the Philippian believers. ————

Let Me Pray for You
Taken from Philippians 1

Foundation

Before you begin today's lesson, ask the Lord to show you areas in your prayer life that need growth. Thank Him that He is a God who answers prayers.

Focus

Are you ever at a loss for words, not sure what or how to pray when someone asks, "Can you please pray for me?"

Ten years had passed since Paul visited Philippi on his second missionary journey. Ten years, and yet his love for the believers there was just as strong as if he'd seen them only yesterday. Epaphroditus had recently come with gifts from the Philippian believers and also reported on their well-being. Now, with pen in hand, Paul responded to their kindness and the report Epaphroditus had given him.

The order of words in Paul's greeting "Grace and peace to you ..." is an important reminder. We must first respond to God's grace to be in relationship with Him before we can enjoy the peace He gives.

"To all the believers in Philippi: May God the Father and Jesus Christ grant you grace and peace," Paul wrote as he began his letter. Rather than introducing himself as an apostle in his customary way, he introduced himself as a servant of Christ. The loving tone in his letter seemed to flow from his heart, through his pen, and onto the parchment.

"Every time I think of you, I thank God. I have

prayed many prayers for you, and I always pray with great joy because of your part in receiving and sharing the gospel. What's more, I have no doubt that God will continue to do a good work in your lives until Jesus Christ returns, just as He has been doing from the beginning.

"My thoughts toward you are full of love. Only the Lord Himself knows how deep my feelings are for you; for the love I have for you is a love that comes from God," Paul wrote as he sat back in his chair. He was so far away from them, yet he held them close to his heart.

"I pray that God will make your love grow to overflowing so that you may experience more of His love and show it to others. I also pray that you will grow in knowledge and be able to understand God's ways better. I pray this so that you will be able to test everything that comes into your lives and choose what's best over that which is simply good. I also pray that you will be sincere and without fault—pure before God. As far as your fellow brothers and sisters in Christ are concerned, I pray that you will be able to get along with one another. May your lives be filled with the fruit of the Spirit, and may God be glorified because of the way you live for Him," Paul wrote, silently praying the words he penned.

> *"The day of Christ" is a phrase Paul often used to describe the time when Jesus will come back to earth to take all the remaining believers with Him to heaven.*
>
> ---
>
> *The apostle Paul had two names: Saul, his Hebrew name, and Paul, his Gentile name. Since his mission was to carry the gospel message to the Gentiles, we know him as Paul— what he was most commonly called.*

Paul had seen God do many miraculous things in and through his own life because of prayer. He knew by experience that many of the battles Christians face in life are won while on their knees in prayer. Paul wanted the Philippian believers to know how he prayed for them. Perhaps they would follow his example and pray for one another.

Footwork

Look up Philippians 1:6 in your Bible. Who is doing the work in you? You can stand confident because you do not stand alone. God began a good work in you, and He'll finish the job.

Fruit

Make this a project: For the next several days, secretly pray Paul's prayer for a member in your family. (You can find this prayer in Philippians 1:9–11.) Sometimes God works in small, quiet ways, so don't expect to get out a ruler and measure progress. Remember, too, that God is working in your life at the same time.

What's the Catch?
Taken from Philippians 1—2

Foundation

Before you begin today's lesson, stop and pray. Ask God to show you any wrong motives or attitudes that may hide in your heart and to help you change them.

Do you ever do something good but for the wrong reason?

Paul wrote to the believers in Philippi to thank them for their gift and to remind them of his prayers for them. In his letter he expressed his joy that Jesus was being preached among them, even though some preached Christ for the wrong reasons.

"I want you to know that because of my imprisonment in Rome, the gospel has been spreading. I have no doubt this is why God has allowed me to be here in prison, and as such, I don't mind these living conditions. Because I haven't hesitated to tell everyone I can about Jesus Christ—including the entire palace guard—many have put their faith in Him! May you be encouraged as you hear what God is doing," Paul wrote.

"Some of you who were once timid about preaching the gospel are now speaking out boldly. I praise God for this, as you are speaking the Word of God more courageously and fearlessly than ever before. Others are preaching the gospel out of envy, secretly hoping to cause me greater difficulties."

Paul was referring to a few in the church who were envious of him. Since Paul was in trouble for preaching the gospel, they thought they could increase his suffering by helping the gospel to spread. They were doing something good (preaching the gospel) for a wrong reason.

> **Sin *is an archery term. In ancient times when an archer shot an arrow at a target, someone would tell him whether it hit the target or "sinned," meaning a miss. Missing God's target of holiness is something we're all guilty of; we have all "sinned."***
>
> ---
>
> *Not sure whether you're sinning? Here's a simple test using the letters S-I-N. Look at the letter in the center of the word. What is it? Sin is when* **I** *get centered on myself.*

Although Paul could have responded in bitterness or demanded that they stop, he didn't. Instead, he gave thanks to God! "What does it matter if they try to cause me harm?" he asked. "The most important thing is that the gospel of Christ is being preached, and because of that fact I can rejoice."

As Paul reflected about the privilege of serving God, he couldn't help but think about the Master-Servant, Jesus. With his pen, Paul leveled a challenge to the Philippian believers to follow Christ's example and serve one another in love.

"Don't just look out for your own interests, but look out for the interests of others as well. That's what Jesus did, and you should strive to be like Him not only in your actions but in your attitudes," Paul stated. "For even though Jesus is God, He humbled Himself and came to earth, willing to take the form of a human. In doing this, He set aside all His privileges and honor as God and didn't demand His rights as God's Son. Even though Jesus knew that His actions would mean suffering, being mocked, being misunderstood, and eventually being killed, He did it anyway. He didn't do it for personal gain. Instead, He did it for us. He did it out of love.

"Therefore," Paul concluded, "since Jesus, being God, could humble Himself to become a servant, do we dare to think that we're somehow above such things? May it never be! Let us not do things from selfish ambition, wrong motives, or for our own personal comfort or gain. Instead, let us have the same attitude as Christ Jesus our Lord—the attitude of humility."

Footwork

Turn to Philippians 2:4–5 in your Bible. What does this passage instruct you to do? This is a good practice that will keep your motives pure—guaranteed!

Fruit

Wrong motives are dangerous killers because they're silent and hard to detect. They can easily ruin something that started out good, so don't allow them in your life. Ask God to show you any wrong motives you may be harboring so that you can confess them to Him and take steps to deal with them.

Fire burns two-thirds of Rome. Nero

Look At Me
Taken from Philippians 3

Foundation

Spend some time in prayer before today's lesson. Thank the Lord for His loving patience toward you. Ask Him to help you delight in Him more.

Do you ever want to be cool or well thought of by others?

"Finally, friends," Paul wrote, "be full of joy in the Lord! I don't mind repeating this, and I will do it as often as necessary. Our confidence isn't in who we are or what we can do," he urged, fully aware of the Judaizers who looked down on others and gloried in their own self-importance. "But rather, our glory is rooted in Christ Jesus and what He has done for us!

"I don't place any confidence in my own achievements or standing in the church, although I might be able to do so if I wanted to," Paul admitted, comparing himself to the Judaizers as an example of choosing not to boast.

"For I'm a pure-blooded Jew, circumcised eight days after birth, according to Jewish law. I can trace my family history back to Abraham, and I myself am from the tribe of Benjamin," Paul informed them. (The Jews held anyone from the tribe of Benjamin in great honor and importance because Israel's first king, Saul, came from this tribe.)

Paul went on to carefully detail his past and the things he used to be proud of. "As for being a Hebrew, I was born a Hebrew son of Hebrew parents. I was also a Pharisee, a member of the strictest group of Jews, who strongly upheld the Law of

Moses. I was zealous for the old laws and gladly killed those who spoke against them or who followed Christ. In my own eyes I was faultless in keeping the Jewish religious rules."

He paused to clear the past from his thoughts before continuing. "I want you to know that even though I have reason to think more highly of myself than the Judaizers, I count all my credentials and accomplishments as trash compared to the incredible value of knowing Christ. Instead of making a place for myself in society, I'm confident of the place Jesus has made for me in heaven. That's what really matters. Righteousness doesn't come from keeping the law or because of our own importance; it comes through faith in Christ," Paul clarified.

He then continued, telling the Philippians how he would rather know Christ than be known by others. "I don't look at myself as having already arrived, but one thing I do: I keep moving forward, striving to reach the goal of knowing Christ and winning a heavenly prize, because my real home is in heaven. I encourage you all the more, dear brothers and sisters, to stand firm in the Lord and not to set your minds on earthly things that amount to nothing."

Judaizers were Jewish teachers who sought to make the Gentile believers obey all the Jewish rules and regulations. Paul dealt with them in Galatia.

In Greek races, runners didn't compete to cross a finish line. Instead, each runner tried to be the first one to reach a wooden goal. Paul's goal wasn't wooden; it was Jesus, and his running was to draw closer to Jesus in order to know Him better.

Footwork

Read Philippians 3:7 in your Bible. What was Paul's response to the things that made him seem cool or more important than others? Now skip down and read verses 8–11. What did Paul value most?

AD 64 — Paul writes his first letter

Fruit

In the race of life, what goal or prize are you competing for?

Where do you stand with Jesus today?

Think about It
Taken from Philippians 4

Foundation

Before you finish Philippians, take a moment to think about whether your thoughts are pleasing to God. Ask the Lord to help you in this area.

Focus

Do you ever struggle with thoughts you can't seem to get out of your mind no matter how hard you try?

Paul's final words to the Philippian believers were words of personal experience. They were words Paul had tried, tested, and found to be true—words of comfort and help to those who read them.

"No matter what comes your way, rejoice in the Lord. Praise Him in every situation, for even though you may not know what is going on, the Lord is always with you. When difficult times arise and you think that everything is going against you, don't be anxious or fearful. Instead, trust God. Pray and talk to Him about everything. Tell Him all your needs; be thankful that He's a God who cares and that you can come into His presence. Don't be afraid to request specific things, for it's only when you come to God that He can truly help you. When you do these things, God's peace will comfort your hearts. It's a wonderful peace that words can't describe!" Paul wrote.

In his own life Paul had many opportunities to become worried, angry, and feel hurt. He had been lied about, made fun of, and tortured. It would

etter to Titus while in Nicopolis.

233

Philippians has been called "the book of joy" because the words joy, rejoice, and glad occur numerous times throughout its four short chapters. This is especially interesting since Paul's circumstances didn't naturally lead to happiness.

Joy and happiness aren't the same. Happiness is rooted in circumstances (everything going in a favorable way for you). Joy is a deep, settled contentedness, even when circumstances are bad. It's also a fruit of the Holy Spirit (Galatians 5:22).

have been easy for him to think about these things and become bitter or to anxiously worry about how everything was going to work out. But rather than being controlled by his thoughts and feelings, Paul chose to be in control of them.

"Whatever things are true (reliable and trustworthy), noble (worthy of respect), right (fitting to God's standards), pure (wholesome and not immoral), lovely (encouraging peace rather than conflict), admirable (building up rather than tearing down something or someone)—these are the type of thoughts you should dwell on. These thoughts are the kind that are excellent and worthy of praise," Paul wrote, challenging his readers.

Paul didn't know how much longer he would be alive, and he desperately wanted the Philippian believers to understand the joy that is found in living for Christ. Even though at times Paul was hungry or poor, he also experienced times when he was well fed and rich. He didn't let his circumstances control his love for the Lord or his thought life. "I've learned to be content in any and every circumstance God allows me to be in," Paul wrote. Instead, he kept turning everything over to God. "God gives me strength to handle whatever situations I face, and through Him I can do anything."

Footwork

Read Philippians 4:6–7. Notice the words, "but in everything." What are you supposed to do with everything? If you do this, what will God's peace do for you?

Fruit

Will you let your thoughts be filled with peace, which will guard your heart and mind in Christ Jesus, or will you let thoughts fill your head that turn your heart from Him? Your life is a reflection of what occupies your mind.

Colossians

The book of Colossians is another one of Paul's letters, written while he was a prisoner in Rome. Colossians is unique in that Paul wrote it to a group of believers in Colosse whom he had never met. How did these believers hear the gospel message, and how did they know Paul?

Apparently, Paul had sent a man named Epaphras on his behalf to share the gospel with those in Colosse and start a church there. When Epaphras returned to Rome, he told Paul about the Colossians' great love for the Lord.

Unfortunately, a false teaching had entered the church in Colosse and was turning the believers away from the truth. This teaching emphasized following Old Testament laws and ceremonies and involved the worship of angels. It also excluded many people. But worst of all, it denied that Jesus was God. This last teaching prompted Paul to write this letter, which contains some of the greatest verses about Christ's deity found anywhere in Scripture. Paul also wrote to challenge the believers to grow in their spiritual walk.

As you read through Colossians, keep your eyes open to the practical things Paul told the believers to help them grow in their walk with the Lord. Also notice how he took them back to their foundation and their roots. ———

Awesome!
Taken from Colossians 1—2

Foundation

As you begin your walk through Colossians, ask the Lord to open your heart so that you will gain a better understanding of Jesus and your relationship with Him.

Focus

If someone challenged you to name at least eighteen things that describe who Jesus is and what He does, could you?

Paul's heart greatly rejoiced when Epaphras returned with news. The good news was that the believers in Colosse had a strong love for the Lord. The bad news was that a false teaching was spreading, and Paul feared it would get into the church. This false teaching was of the worst kind, actually denying the deity of Christ by saying that Jesus wasn't really God! Paul felt an urgent need to warn the Colossian believers about such false teaching, or heresy.

> *Being rooted means to know your foundation, to dig in and stand on it, and then to grow. Just as a plant without roots can't grow, we can't grow in our walk with God unless we're rooted in Jesus.*

Paul began his letter by telling the Colossians how often he prayed for them since hearing of their love for the Lord. "Every time I pray, I pray that God will give you His wisdom so that you can know and understand His will for you. I pray that your life will be pleasing to Him: that everything you do will bear the fruit of the Holy Spirit, that you will come to know

God better, that He will empower and strengthen you so you won't give up in difficult times or seek revenge in times of anger, and that you will always be filled with joy as you thank God for all He has done."

Paul then reminded them of their spiritual roots and of all Jesus is and had done for them. "Nothing compares with Christ and knowing Him! In Jesus, we have redemption and forgiveness for our sins. He is the mirrorlike image of God's qualities. He existed before creation, and He created everything in heaven and on earth for His glory. Jesus is over all things, holds everything together, and is the head of the church. He set the pattern for resurrection and is to have first place in everything. In Jesus the fullness of God dwells. And through His blood, His death on the cross, we have been made holy and are able to have a relationship with God. Jesus gives us peace and presents us to God as holy people so that we can stand before Him without shame."

Colosse was approximately one hundred miles east of Ephesus and was known for its unusual stony deposits. Colosse possibly came from the word Colossus, which was a large statue.

Epaphras was a shortened version of the name Epaphroditus from Philippians 2:25 and 4:18.

But Paul knew that it wasn't enough to just know this truth. The believers in Colosse needed to stand on it to grow. So he told them, "Just as you came to know Jesus, you need to live each day in His power. Sink your roots deep into Him and build yourselves up in Him the way you've been taught. And let God strengthen your faith in Him. Keep your life overflowing with thankfulness for what Jesus has done for you. Don't let anyone trick you with empty religion or with man's wisdom. Remember that you were like a dead person when you were away from God and lost in your sins. But God raised you to life, just as He did with Christ, and forgave all your sins. In fact, He even took away the Law that condemned us as sinners and nailed it to the cross. Only Jesus could do this for you, because He has all God's characteristics and power."

Footwork

Turn to Colossians 2:6–7. Verse 7 talks about being "rooted and built up" in Jesus and growing in your faith. Verse 6 tells us what the starting point is. How and when do you become rooted in your faith?

Fruit

How and when were you rooted in Jesus Christ? Do you recall a specific date when you asked Him to be your Lord and Savior? Since you gave your life to Jesus, are you being built up in your faith? How is your relationship with Jesus coming along? Take a few minutes to examine your heart. Then ask Jesus to help you in your walk with Him. There's so much He longs to do in and for you.

New and Improved
Taken from Colossians 3

— Foundation —

Spend some time in prayer, asking God to help you deal with any old thoughts and bad habits that keep dragging you down. Thank Him that He's able to give you the power and strength to change.

Focus

Do you ever get distracted or taken in by what the world has to say or offer?

Paul knew that he could write more about who Jesus is and what He has done, but he didn't. Instead, he wrote about the next step the Colossian believers needed to take in their faith.

"Since God has raised you from the dead with Christ, don't set your hearts on earthly things any longer. Instead, focus your hearts and minds on heavenly things. For you have a new life in Christ. So consider yourselves dead to your old nature and its sinful practices; your old nature is no longer your master. Things such as anger (which is a smoldering hatred), sudden outbursts of rage, the desire to see others suffer, speaking evil of them, saying filthy things, and lying—these are all part of the old nature, which you need to get rid of."

Paul tapped his pen lightly on the parchment, looking for the right words. "Just like taking off a dirty shirt, you have taken off that old sinful self of yours and have clothed yourself with the new self, the new person

In the Bible behavior is often compared to wearing clothes. Your behavior is what you choose to show yourself wearing. Just as you sometimes judge others by their clothes, people judge you by your behavior. There are two standards for behavior: the world's and God's.

Paul's letter to the believers in Colosse was also to be read to the believers in Laodicea, who claimed to know God but were conceited, self-sufficient, and halfhearted about following Jesus. Revelation 3:14–22 records God's strong words against them.

you are in Christ. This new self needs to be refreshed and renewed daily—and this only comes through getting to know Jesus better. The goal of the new self is to become more like Christ," Paul explained.

Paul knew that the believers were tempted to behave just like those around them. They needed to know that such behavior wasn't fitting for those who belong to Christ. Paul wrote, "Just as God loves you dearly and has made you His chosen people, set apart to be used by Him, you are to be different from the world and should not live by its standards. Instead, put on garments of compassion (seeing the needs of others) and kindness (doing something about those needs). You should be humble and gentle toward others; be patient when angered, and put up with others who don't show these qualities. Forgive any complaints you may have against others, just as Christ has forgiven you. And above all, love one another.

"Allow God's peace to have full control of your hearts and have an attitude of thankfulness. Be filled with God's Word so that you'll be able to teach and encourage other believers with His wisdom."

Paul had written many specific things the Colossian believers should be doing. Since they had a new life in Christ, they needed to live that new life every day, and they needed to grow in their faith. Only by taking practical steps to get rid of their old self and put on the new self could they have victory in their lives. This type of living would rise far above the world's standards.

Summarizing his thoughts, Paul wrote, "Make it your goal to do and say everything in Jesus' name so that you will bring glory to Him."

He knew that the greatest way for believers to glorify God is through changed

against Roman persecution. Artists begin

lives, and the greatest test of spiritual maturity is allowing ourselves to be changed.

Footwork

Look up Colossians 3:2 in your Bible. What does this verse challenge you to do?

Fruit

Are you living a new and improved life, or are you still living by the old self? Take a moment and think about your life. On a piece of paper, write down one or two areas of struggle for you. Then ask a trusted friend, your parents, and/or your pastor to ask you on occasion how you're growing in those areas. This is called *accountability*. It will help you as you strive to put Colossians 3:2 into practice.

painting on canvas. Paul writes his

Hey, Didn't Anyone Notice?
Taken from Colossians 3—4

Foundation

Spend a few minutes alone with God in prayer. Tell Him you're trying to live a life pleasing to Him, and ask Him to help you rely on His strength. Thank Him that He takes notice of you—even if no one else does.

FOCUS

Do you ever feel frustrated or resentful when others are recognized for the good things they do, but you aren't?

The words kept flowing from Paul's pen. He thought about the territory he had already covered in his letter to the Colossian believers. Perhaps the greatest thing he did in his letter was to remind them of all that Jesus is and had done for them. Once he had reminded them of that, Paul then challenged them to continue growing in their faith and living a life worthy of their calling. Now Paul had come to the last details of his letter, the important tidbits he didn't want them to forget.

"Make wise choices about the way you live. Be especially aware of your actions and the effect they might have on any nonbelievers. Live for Jesus all the time, even when no one is around or seems to notice. You should live in such a way that you're always ready and able to talk about the Lord. Make sure that what you say is always pleasing to God and that your words are pure and meaningful. If they are, they will be like salt and will make others thirsty and interested in

Paul called Epaphras his "fellow prisoner in Christ" (Philemon v. 23). He visited Paul while Paul was imprisoned in Rome.

knowing why you're different," Paul instructed.

He paused briefly before continuing, "Epaphras sends you his greetings. He's always praying that you will take a firm stand in doing God's will and that you'll grow and mature in your faith."

The description of Epaphras's humble service was an example for the growing believers of how to act. Epaphras didn't pray for others because it brought him recognition, appreciation, or praise. Until Paul mentioned it, no one had even known what Epaphras was doing on their behalf. He was acting out of love for God rather than for the praise of people. Using Epaphras as an example, Paul challenged the Colossian believers: "No matter what kind of work you do, do it all wholeheartedly as if you're doing it for the Lord rather than people. In fact, you really are serving Jesus, and He will reward your efforts with an eternal inheritance."

Feeling that enough had been said, Paul added some final greetings to his letter, signed his name, and prayed that his words would find their mark.

> *Epaphras founded the Colossian church and worked under Paul's direction. Although Paul wanted to visit Colosse, he never made it, but he did keep informed about the church's condition. (See Colossians 1:3–4, 9; 2:1.)*

Footwork

Turn to Colossians 3:23–24. How are you to work? Read these verses again. God sees your actions, and His rewards are great.

Fruit

You'll have many opportunities throughout your life to live for the praise and recognition of other people, but it only results in frustration, impure motives, and a temptation to give up. Don't let your heart fall into that trap! Instead, do your work for God and for Him alone. Nothing ever escapes His notice—or His rewarding love. Nothing.

AD 68 — Nero dies and Galba rules

Rome for one year. • AD 67-68 — Paul i

Thessalonians

If we were to list Paul's writings in the order they were written, Galatians would be first, followed by 1 Thessalonians.

Paul wrote this letter to the church in Thessalonica, which started as a result of his second missionary journey (Acts 17). As you may remember, Paul had a vision of someone in the region of Macedonia calling out for help. Because of that vision, Paul changed his travel plans and ventured into Macedonia, stopping at Philippi, the first major city in that region (Acts 16:9–12). Leaving Philippi, Paul then followed the major Roman road, which led straight into the city of Thessalonica.

After arriving in the city, Paul started preaching in the Jewish synagogues, as was his custom. His gave a simple message, proclaiming what the Old Testament taught about the Messiah who would suffer, die, and be resurrected. He also explained that Jesus fulfilled what the Old Testament prophecies had said. Because of Paul's message, many Jews, Gentiles, and wealthy Thessalonian women became followers of Christ. This angered the nonbelieving Jews, who then started a riot against Paul. One thing led to another, and Paul was ordered to leave Thessalonica before he had a chance to finish his work (Acts 17:1–5).

Leaving Thessalonica, Paul traveled to Berea, burdened with a great concern for the new believers he had left behind. In fact, Paul was so worried about them that he sent Timothy back to check on their well-being. Timothy rejoined Paul in Corinth and gave his report. In response to this report, Paul sat down to write the letter we now know as 1 Thessalonians.

As you read through this book, see if you can discover what Paul encouraged the believers to do. Also, see if you can put your finger on any problems he may have been addressing in his letter.

It's Pleasing to Me
Taken from 1 Thessalonians 2

— *Foundation* ———————————————

As you begin today's lesson, ask the Lord to speak to your heart and help you understand what He wants you to learn.

Do flashy TV preachers turn you off?

Paul couldn't believe it! The nonbelieving Jews who had caused the riot that forced Paul to leave Thessalonica were now spreading misinformation and lies about him. They said that Paul was preaching the gospel only so he could live an easy life and fatten his wallet. Since he had left in a hurry, they accused him of being a coward and a hypocrite! The report sickened Paul. That was the exact opposite of how he lived! Although these lies were personal attacks, Paul knew that if he didn't correct them, they would bring shame on the name of Christ. So, with pen in hand, he set out to write.

"You yourselves know our visit to you wasn't a failure. Even though we had been insulted in Philippi and suffered, we still dared to tell you the gospel in Thessalonica. We didn't preach from impure motives or use flattery to cover up greed. For we weren't trying to please men but God! As apostles of Christ, we could have lived off your hard-earned money, but we didn't. Instead, we lived in a gentle way among you, looking out for your needs. We not only preached the gospel among you, but we also worked day and night, earning our own living so we would not burden anyone," Paul reminded them.

He knew that he had gone above and beyond what was necessary—even denying himself privileges and rights he had as a missionary—in order to live as an example among them. Even in those days, false preachers went around living off whomever they could. But Paul had determined to live in such a way that he could never be confused with one of them.

Paul's life was one of giving, not taking. He wasn't flashy, preaching the gospel with false motives; his motives were pure. Instead of making money from preaching, he actually suffered for the sake of the gospel.

Paul continued writing, challenging the believers to remember the example of how he had lived his life among them. He not only lived it, but he also urged them to live in a manner worthy of God. He reminded them that when they first heard the gospel,

> *Paul's life demonstrated true ministry as "doing God's work in God's way." Ministry isn't about big organizations or traveling off to exotic places. It's simply "being God's person, at God's time, in the life of another person."*

they accepted it as God's message to them, not as the words of men. The Thessalonians knew that Paul had left them not by choice but because he had been persecuted and ordered to leave. Paul brought them back to that fact and encouraged them to live blamelessly for Christ, just as he had sought to do while with them.

Footwork

Look up 1 Thessalonians 2:4 in your Bible. How are you able to live a blameless life? Who should you strive to please? Why?

Fruit

Some preach the gospel and go into ministry for impure motives or personal gain. They set bad examples and often hurt the cause of Christ. Carefully examine their lives. Don't be fooled; their ministry may not be of God.

suspended by iron chains. Emperor

Now That's Really Livin'!
Taken from 1 Thessalonians 3

— *Foundation* —

Stop and pray before digging into today's lesson. Preparing your heart isn't just a mindless routine thing like tying your shoes. It's your time to talk to God, and His time to get your attention so He can talk to you.

FOCUS

Is there something in your life that brings you great joy and satisfaction, something that makes you feel like you're "really living"?

Paul looked at the parchment spread in front of him. Having dealt with the false things, now it was time to deal with the truth. Since being forced to leave Thessalonica in a hurry, he had only been able to give the new believers a small amount of teaching. His concerns for them were growing because he knew that they would no doubt face the same persecution he had faced. Would they be able to stand their ground? Did they have enough teaching so they could at least begin to grow in their faith? What would happen to the new church?

But Paul's concerns about these things vanished when Timothy arrived with his report. It was with great joy that Paul wrote the next section of his letter, admitting the worry and concern he had for them.

"I had longed to come to you again and again, but I was prevented from doing so! When I couldn't stand being separated from you any longer, I sent Timothy to you, for Silas and I didn't want you to be discouraged by the trials you were experiencing. Even when we were with you in person, we often told you that persecution would come, and so it did, as you well know. Out of concern for your well-being, I sent Timothy to see how you were doing in your faith and to offer you strength and encouragement. I feared that perhaps Satan might have tempted you in some way and that our work among you might have been destroyed. But, I'm glad to see that isn't the case!" Paul wrote. "Even though we were followed by troublemakers and angry crowds were stirred up against us, we have great encouragement because Timothy has told us about your faith. Word has gone out about how you not only turned from idols to serve a living and true God but also continued on, even in the face of persecution, to stand firm in your faith. This is a great encouragement to us! We can think of no greater blessing or joy. Now that we know you're standing firm in your faith, we're really living! We're overflowing with thanks to God for the great joy we have because of you," Paul expressed.

He continued, telling the Thessalonian believers that they were in his prayers both day and night and blessing them with these words: "I pray that just as our love for you overflows, the Lord will also cause your love for one another to grow until it overflows." He then prayed for their hearts to be strengthened so that they would live blameless lives, dealing with their sin as God required and never being open to a charge of doing wrong. He also prayed that they would be holy—separated for God's use. Paul's joy wasn't in what he had done among them; it was in the fact that he could see God working in their lives.

The word **unsettled** *in the phrase "unsettled by these trials" (NIV) is the same word used to describe a dog's tail wagging back and forth. Paul feared that the new believers would go back and forth in their faith because of the trials they faced.*

Silas, a Roman citizen and a leader of the church in Jerusalem, held the office of an inspired teacher (Acts 15:32). He accompanied Paul on his second missionary journey. (Check it out in Acts 15:40—17:10.)

Footwork

Look up 1 Thessalonians 3:8–9 in your Bible. Apart from seeing God work in the Thessalonians' lives, what specifically brought Paul satisfaction?

Fruit

Think of the people who have made a spiritual impact on you (parents, teachers, youth-group leaders, friends, and so forth). Does your life bring them joy? Write one of these people a note of encouragement, telling that person how he or she touched your life and expressing your thanks. Deliver it today.

100 Percent Pure—
Guaranteed!
Taken from 1 Thessalonians 4

Foundation

As you begin the lesson today, ask God to speak to you. Invite Him to point out areas in your life that aren't honoring to Him, and ask Him to help you live by His rules.

Focus

> *Do you sometimes feel that God's rules and guidelines are only meant to ruin your fun?*

Paul knew of the many ungodly influences in the city of Thessalonica. Although the Jewish synagogue there was strong, the main people group in the city was Greek. The Greeks lived very openly and loosely. Part of their religion actually included acts of immorality! They thought it nothing at all to be sexually intimate with anyone and everyone, and some used their bodies in ways God never intended.

Paul knew of this destructive influence and wanted to encourage the new believers in Thessalonica to be on their guard. They needed to love God with their whole heart and strive to live in a way that pleased Him. "We gave you instructions for living a God-honoring life, just as you are now doing, and need to do all the more. For our instructions came not

scrolls> in caves at Qumran before

Sexual impurity (or immorality) is doing sexual things as an unmarried person which God says should be saved for marriage. It's also doing such things with others instead of with your marriage partner.

Temptation often strikes at the most opportune moments—when you're feeling tired, frustrated, discouraged, or alone. Guard your heart!

Almost all ancient literature presents its heroes as flawless. But the Bible shows its heroes as they really were, failures and all. Feeling discouraged? Check out the Old Testament and discover for yourself how God is a God of grace, mercy, and second chances!

from us but from the authority of the Lord," Paul wrote. He knew God's rules were given to protect them so that they could experience life in the most meaningful way rather than accepting the world's cheap substitute.

"Each of you needs to learn self-control, setting your body apart for God's use and managing it in an honorable way. Those who don't know God allow themselves to be ruled by sexual desires. They do immoral acts because they want something their way instead of God's. They think they are gaining everything when really they're missing out. They dishonor not only themselves but also the others they involve in their sin. They hurt themselves, wrong the other person, and sin against God. But as you know from our warnings, He will punish them for such things. You, however, are to live a life of purity. God called you to live a holy, purposeful, and satisfied life. His rules are for your benefit and personal growth," Paul instructed.

Tapping his pen on the parchment, Paul stopped and thought for a moment. The pen was soon in motion again as he challenged them to lead a peaceful life, not one ruled by desires, passions, or circumstances. The believers needed to examine their own lives, making sure they were following the will of God rather than comparing themselves with others or examining other people's lives. They also needed to set a good example of working rather than depending on others to provide for them. This type of living would show the purity of their hearts and their love and commitment to following God's rules. His rules and guidelines weren't given to destroy their fun; they were meant to protect them from destroying themselves.

Footwork

In your Bible, turn to 1 Thessalonians 4:7–8. According to verse 7, what did God *not* call us to? If we ignore Him and do it anyway, who are we really rejecting?

Fruit

Temptation takes many forms. It can come through doing something you shouldn't, viewing things you'd be ashamed of if others found out (such as surfing particular Internet sites), or not doing something you know you should do. What will you do when the temptation to be impure comes knocking at your door? Pull out the index card of 1 Corinthians 10:13 that you made while reading through that book. If you lost it, write the verse on another one. Review the verse and then say it aloud from memory. (If you didn't commit it to memory earlier, do it now.) Notice the words "God is faithful…. When you are tempted, he will also provide a way out."

The next time you find yourself in a tempting situation, look for God's exit sign (He always provides one) and leave!

Who? What? When?
Taken from 1 Thessalonians 4—5

Foundation

Things don't always happen when we want or expect them to. Spend a few minutes thinking about God's timing. Then thank the Lord that He's in control and that His timing is perfect.

Focus

Do you ever wonder how and when Jesus will come back to earth?

In Paul's day people believed that evil spirits lived in the air between heaven and earth. The air was Satan's territory. Because of this, Satan has been called "the ruler of the kingdom of the air" (Ephesians 2:2). When Jesus comes back again, believers will rise to meet the Lord in the air—Satan's turf! This great reunion with Jesus will take place in Satan's territory, marking a stinging defeat for Satan while proclaiming Jesus' triumphant victory. When will all this happen?

Paul warned the believers to be ready. "For the Lord Himself will come from heaven with a shout, with the voice of the archangel, and with God's own trumpet. Believers who have died will rise first. Then, those of us who are still alive will be caught up together with them. We will meet the Lord in the air and then be with the Him forever!"

Paul knew that the Thessalonians had questions about this. They had been taught that Jesus promised to return to earth for His people, and they wanted to know when this would take place. Paul knew there was danger in trying to figure out the exact time. People who think they have all the time in the world become caught up in pleasing themselves and don't care about the future. They become foolish. Those who don't know the time of the Lord's return are more watchful, living to make their days count, not knowing whether today will be their last on earth. That's how believers are to live—daily looking forward to the Lord's return. The day of the Lord is something no person has the privilege of knowing. God, who knows the character and weaknesses of humans, planned it that way. No one could possibly calculate days or claim to be wise enough to figure it out.

> *Trumpets (shofars, rams' horns) were used in the Old Testament to either gather an assembly of people or to give orders for battle. In this passage they're used for both.*

> *In Matthew 24, Jesus gave one of the longest statements about the future and the events that will happen before His second coming. Check it out! (Note: Jesus also reminds us in verse 36 that no one will know the day or hour of His return.)*

Paul continued to write, "We can't tell you the exact time or date when this will happen, for Jesus Himself said that no one would know. Rather, the day of the Lord will be like a thief breaking into your home in the middle of the night. It will come when people least expect it—suddenly, unplanned for, and by surprise. So be on the alert and live self-controlled lives. Encourage others to do the same, and build one another up."

Jesus will return according to God's timetable and pleasure. He planned it that way to protect us from ourselves. Jesus (who) will return (what) at a time only God knows (when).

Footwork

Read 1 Thessalonians 5:2 in your Bible. What does it say? Now turn back to Mark 13:32–33 and read Jesus' own words about His return to earth.

under his wise and practical ten-

Fruit

Although we can clearly see that the time of Jesus' coming is drawing near, this is all that's clear. None of us could (or should) be so bold as to say that we have God's timetable figured out. To do so would be to call God a liar, for He specifically says that no one knows. (Reread Jesus' words in Mark 13:32–33.)

You will undoubtedly hear people make predictions about when Jesus will come back. They might even use charts and a handful of Bible verses or fulfilled prophecies to support their views. Don't get caught up in their foolish predictions. It will only lead to disappointment and distract you from living for Him each day that He gives you here on earth.

You Look a Little Green
Taken from 1 Thessalonians 5

Foundation

As you finish your study of 1 Thessalonians, take a few minutes to think about the new Thessalonian believers and their need for spiritual growth. Ask God to show you areas where you need to grow spiritually.

Focus

Do you ever wonder what it really takes to grow spiritually and live according to God's will?

Paul knew that his last words to the Thessalonian believers would be important; last words are what most people remember. Paul paused for a moment, as if to sum up everything.

"Respect the spiritual leaders who are responsible for you. They work hard on your behalf and should be loved and greatly honored. Listen to what they say, for they are responsible to God for your care," Paul instructed.

"Continue to live peacefully with one another, not stirring up fights or problems. I urge you to warn those who neglect their daily responsibilities, encourage those who are easily discouraged, strengthen those who haven't yet learned to lean on the Lord as they should, and treat everyone with patience. Don't repay the wrongs done to you, but purpose in your hearts to show kindness to everyone. This can be done only through God's love working in and through you," he wrote.

ust prior to 70 AD, possibly by

The Thessalonians were new believers. Though on the right track and doing a good job, they needed to push onward and grow in their walk with the Lord. Knowing this, Paul then became more specific about God's will for them.

"Always be filled with joy," Paul instructed. "Rejoice in the blessings of Jesus rather than depending on circumstances to bring you a temporary happiness.

"Live your lives in an attitude of prayer," he reminded, encouraging them to talk with God throughout the day and about everything, just as they would a close friend. "And thank God in every situation, for giving thanks shows that you trust Him. It also shows that you accept both the good and the bad things that come into your lives, trusting that Jesus is in control and knows what He's doing," Paul stated, speaking from personal experience.

> *Since many people couldn't read in Paul's day, letters were often read aloud. In verse 27 of this chapter, Paul specifically instructed the church to have his letter read to all the believers in Thessalonica.*

Paul then gave them a warning. "Don't ignore the Holy Spirit's teaching in your life. When He puts it in your heart to do something, do it."

Paul's mind flooded with thoughts of those whose hearts had been hardened and whose faith had been shipwrecked because of disobedience. He pressed on. "Test whatever comes your way to make sure it's in line with what the Scriptures say." Even in his time false ideas floated around, confusing the uninformed and ungrounded and competing for a place in people's hearts. "Always hold tightly to what's good, and stay away from whatever is evil."

Having written these words of encouragement and caution, Paul finished his letter with a passionate prayer: "May God continue to change you into what He wants you to be. May you continue to grow in your walk with Him so that your lives will be blameless and full of honor when our Lord Jesus Christ comes again. For God has called you and will faithfully bring this about in your life."

Having said all that was needed, Paul laid down his pen. It was now up to the believers to put his words into practice.

Footwork

Take a look at 1 Thessalonians 5:23–24. As you do your part, God works in your life to bring about spiritual growth. According to verse 23, we're kept blameless for what event? And when is the work in our lives completed? (Don't guess at this one but see what God actually says about it.)

Fruit

A simple law of nature exists in a vegetable garden: Green things grow; ripe things rot. Your life is the same. "If you think you're green, you'll grow; if you think you're ripe, you'll rot!" In your walk with the Lord, which do you think best describes your life lately?

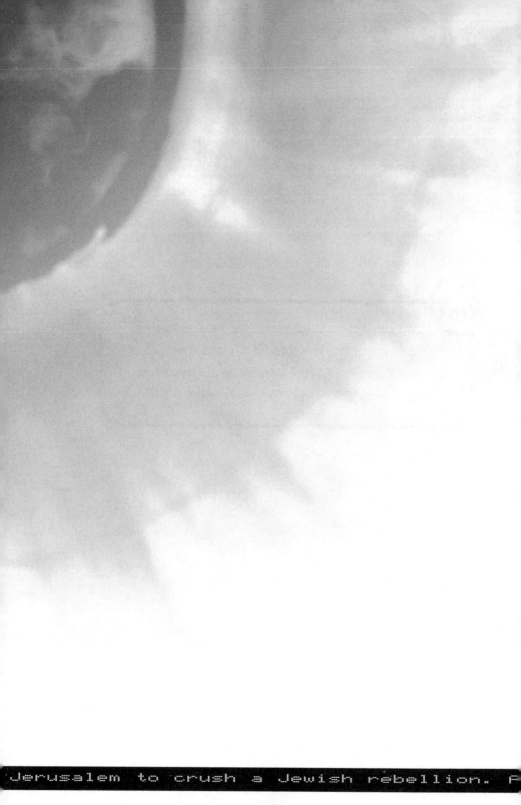

Jerusalem to crush a Jewish rebellion. P

2 Thessalonians

Paul wrote 2 Thessalonians within a year of writing 1 Thessalonians. He wrote his second letter to the believers to praise them for their continued spiritual growth and to correct a false teaching concerning the day of the Lord. Paul not only corrected this bad teaching but also warned the believers of the consequences of it.

You Mean, Work?
Taken from 2 Thessalonians 3

— *Foundation* —————————————————

Before you read through today's lesson, think about your attitude toward chores, homework, or just plain work. Ask God to help you have a better attitude in this area.

Focus

Have you ever heard the phrase, "If you don't work, you won't eat!" and wondered where it came from?

Due to incorrect teaching, some of the Thessalonian believers had begun thinking the wrong way. *Why should I bother doing that? If Jesus is coming back at any time, then it really doesn't matter if I do this or not!* they reasoned.

"Quit your jobs! The Lord is returning tomorrow!" was the false message they heard. Since many didn't think their work made much difference if the end of the world was near, they quit their jobs altogether, leaving the workload for others to shoulder. "We'll just wait for Christ's return," they told themselves.

Others believed that Jesus had already returned. And in the midst of all this, some lazy believers merely watched others work and then came around later asking for favors and food. In his first letter Paul challenged them to work, but apparently the idle people hadn't obeyed. With this false teaching conditions had gotten worse, and Paul decided that he needed to address the issue.

"You remember how we lived among you when we were there. We always paid for the food we ate, and we never took anything from others. Instead, we worked hard to earn our keep. Even though we had the right and privilege as missionaries to be supported by you, we didn't become a burden. Instead, we lived as an example for you to follow," Paul began. Then his words turned more serious as he thought of those who were living off the hard work of others.

> **Idle** *means "unmoving, lazy, not going anywhere or doing anything." Sometimes this word is used to describe a car with a running engine that's out of gear and going nowhere.*

"We have heard there are some in your fellowship who aren't doing anything productive. They're idle. Instead of being busy with their own lives and responsibilities, they're busy interfering in the lives and business of others. I instruct you to stay away from them. They must learn to work for the food they eat. Don't socialize or spend time with them so they will feel shame and turn from their sinful ways. But don't think of them as enemies; instead, warn them as you would warn a brother or sister," Paul instructed.

"As for you, follow the example we set and don't become weary or discouraged about doing the right thing. Keep working diligently," he wrote, encouraging his readers.

Paul knew that it was difficult to keep working hard when those who were lazy seemed to do as well, if not better, than those who were working diligently. "Remember our example to you and live by the standard that God has set for us: "If a person refuses to work, then he or she won't eat."

Footwork

Look up 2 Thessalonians 3:11. What does it say? Who does it describe?

Fruit

Evaluate your actions over the past week. Would those who know you best say that you are busy or a busybody? Make a list of those things you've been putting off doing, and do one of them today.

Rome begins using locks with keys of

1 Timothy

First Timothy is one of Paul's pastoral letters or epistles. In it, Paul gave counsel, advice, and encouragement to his coworkers who were serving as leaders (pastors) in the regions of Crete and Ephesus. Timothy, one of these coworkers, became Paul's closest friend to the very end.

One of Paul's stops on his first missionary journey was Derbe, Timothy's hometown (Acts 14). Timothy, who was eighteen or nineteen years old at the time, heard Paul's message and became a believer. When Paul returned to Derbe on his second missionary journey, he saw great promise in the young man and took him on as an assistant. Having begun with small tasks as Paul's travel companion, Timothy soon became a valuable coworker in sharing the gospel message, staying behind to work with new believers while Paul traveled on to other areas. Timothy was a loyal, trusted friend.

As you may remember from the close of Acts, Paul was imprisoned in Rome. He had spent many years traveling on his missionary journeys only to return to Jerusalem and be thrown in prison for preaching the gospel. It took him five years to work his way through the Roman court system, which eventually brought him to Rome (where Acts leaves off).

By piecing together information from Paul's other letters, we discover that Paul spent two years imprisoned in Rome. Taking Timothy, he revisited the churches he had started on his earlier missionary journeys. After visiting Ephesus, Timothy stayed behind to provide much-needed leadership while Paul visited the other churches. In this book, Paul wrote to Timothy, checking on how things were going. It's a personal letter full of love, instruction, and encouragement.

As you read through 1 Timothy, see if you can discover what Paul had to say about sound teaching, prayer, leadership, personal godliness, and contentment.

In My Opinion
Taken from 1 Timothy 1

— *Foundation* —

Spend a few minutes in prayer, thanking God that His Word is truth and His ways are right. Thank Him that He has called you into His kingdom.

Focus

Do you know anyone who likes to talk about religion but doesn't have a serious interest in God?

"Is not!"

"Is too!"

"Is not!"

"Is too!"

"Well, in my opinion …"

Some in the Ephesian church involved themselves in discussions and arguments that led nowhere. They delighted in debating over fables, family histories, and even religious teachings different from those Paul taught. Everyone had an opinion, and each thought his or her opinion was right. Believers argued only to prove who was right and who was wrong, and their debates were over things that didn't even matter! Instead of building one another up, people were left confused. The pointless, unproductive arguing had nothing to do with sound doctrine (God's truth).

"Timothy," Paul wrote, "continue to stay in Ephesus and command those teaching different doctrines to stop. They are causing arguments and confusion

of the Colosseum in Rome begins. ⊛ AD

rather than promoting the work of God that is accomplished by faith."

Paul continued. "I'm aware that some there have strayed from God's truth. They no longer seek to live with a clear conscience, a clean heart, or an honest and sincere faith. Instead, their talk is empty and meaningless, and they have no idea what they're saying or what they're agreeing with. They aren't true teachers of the Law; they only teach and argue to convince themselves that they're more important and more knowledgeable than others.

Sound doctrine isn't referring to noise. Sound means "that which is right." It's solid, firm, sure, true, and trustworthy. The word doctrine *simply refers to the foundation and building blocks of what we believe. It represents the facts our faith is built upon.*

"Timothy," Paul wrote, "keep fighting with all your heart for the faith. Cling to the solid teaching of God's truth, for this is what real faith is built upon. As you anchor yourself on God's sound doctrine, you'll be able to maintain a clear conscience."

Paul paused a moment before penning words of warning. "As you know, some have turned away from God's truth, and as a result, their faith has been dashed against the rocks and shipwrecked," he wrote. "Therefore, Timothy, stand firm and do not allow empty arguments and foolish teachings to be found among the believers."

Footwork

Turn to 1 Timothy 1:5. What three things are important to faith? Now skip down and read verse 17. Who receives the honor for our faith?

Fruit

Many talk of God when they really know very little about Him. Some talk about Him as if He were a hobby. They look for someone they can confuse, disturb, or tear down with questions that seem unanswerable. Don't get trapped in their foolish arguments, but stand firm on God's truth. If you talk with someone like this, present the gospel and leave it there. Don't try to win the person over by arguing or debating. Our strength isn't in our own clever arguments but in the Lord and the power of His Word! As God brings this person to mind, faithfully pray for him or her, and then leave the rest in God's hands.

is attacked by Romans. Its 960 Jewish Zealo

270

God Bless
Taken from 1 Timothy 2

— Foundation —

Before reading today's lesson, think about prayer for a moment. Ask God to show you His plan in praying for others and the benefits of taking time to pray.

Focus

Do you ever stop to pray for our president and the leaders of our nation, even though you may not like them or agree with them?

Nero, the emperor of Rome, turned cruel toward the end of his reign. He did many bad things and blamed them on Christians. He even tortured people—and Christians were his favorite victims. Though many people said he was a madman, Paul said that he was worthy of prayer but not because of who he was or what he accomplished. Nero was worthy of prayer simply because God placed him in a position of leadership over the people.

Continuing his letter of encouragement and instruction to Timothy, Paul wrote, "I strongly encourage you to pray for all people, including those in positions of authority."

Paul knew that this would be difficult for many believers to do, so he went on to explain. "God

> *Second Corinthians 11:23-33 reminds us that Paul knew how difficult it can be to live under harsh rulers. He endured imprisonments, beatings, lashing, and even a stoning.*

defenders commit suicide before fac—

placed men in authority over us and He is in control. Just like all men, these leaders need God, and we must see their need for Him and pray in their behalf. We're to pray for them and thank God for them," Paul wrote.

"When we pray for our leaders, we benefit. God will answer our prayers for them and will bless us with peace as we seek to live holy and godly lives," Paul instructed. "I want people in every part of the world to raise their hands in prayer with holy hearts, not with anger or arguing."

Footwork

Check out 1 Timothy 2:1–4. What does it say about prayer? What does it say about God?

Fruit

Praying for our nation's leaders is important. You may never know how your prayers are answered, but rest assured, God answers prayers! He wants everyone to be saved and to know the truth. When you pray for national and local government leaders, you're praying in line with God's desires. Spend the next few minutes specifically praying for our president. Pray also for the governor of your state.

ing capture.   ◆   AD 74 — China opens up

To Be or Not to Be
Taken from 1 Timothy 3

— Foundation —

Stop for a moment and pray. Ask God to help you understand His point of view on leadership, and thank Him for His standards.

Focus

Have you ever thought that a particularly skilled or likeable person would make a good leader?

Paul knew that Timothy was facing many things in the large church at Ephesus. Questions about selecting leaders would soon surface. How would leaders in the church be picked? Who would make a good leader?

"I am writing these things to you," Paul explained in his letter, "so you will know how people who are part of God's household should behave." Paul used the word *household* to describe the church, for all believers are part of God's family. The church is made up of those who believe in Jesus; it isn't the building in which believers worship. For now, however, Paul compared the church to a building.

"God is the pillar of truth that holds up His church," Paul wrote, knowing that the Ephesians had a great understanding of pillars.

It was in their city that one of the Seven Wonders of the World, the Temple of Artemis, was located. Built to honor the false god Artemis, this temple was known for its many pillars. These pillars—127 in all— were made of marble, studded with jewels, and overlaid with gold. They

`a silk trade with Egypt, Mesopotamia,`

The Greeks believed that Artemis was the goddess of hunting, nature, and the moon (giving the land fertility and sustaining life). The temple that housed Artemis took 220 years to build!

When Paul compared the church of God to a pillar of truth, the believers would have compared themselves to the massive Temple of Artemis with its 127 sixty-foot-tall pillars supporting an enormous marble roof four times the size of the Parthenon! They would have had a hard time forgetting the word picture and reminder that they were to be pillars of truth in a world of lost and searching people.

caught the attention of everyone for miles around.

Paul said that the church is the pillar and supporter of the truth. Just as the pillars of the Temple of Artemis could be clearly seen, the church is to present the truth in all its glory to be clearly seen by everyone. Paul knew this could only be accomplished as godly leaders in the church influenced and encouraged other believers. For this reason, Paul included the topic of leadership in his letter to Timothy.

"Leaders in the church shouldn't be chosen based on their popularity or talent," Paul instructed. "Instead, they should be chosen according to God's standards. Leaders should be self-controlled and not given to quarrels or violence. They are to be respected by the people and sincere in their words and actions. They must be able to get along with their families; otherwise, how can they be expected to get along with those in the family of God? A leader must be able to teach others but also be willing to learn. He must not be greedy or love money, but rather he should use whatever resources he has to serve others. These are the qualifications of a good leader," Paul wrote.

Paul's words of instruction clearly showed that leaders were to be picked not because of their abilities but because of their character. They were to be picked not by man's measure but by God's standards. Such leaders would help and encourage believers to be pillars and supporters of the truth throughout the world.

Persia, India, and Rome (known as famous

Footwork

Turn to 1 Timothy 3:5. What does it say? Why do you think that being able to manage one's own family is so important? Managing one's family describes the ability of the head of the household to get along with the family. It involves giving respect and being respected. It's been said that the rules you live by privately (in your home) determine how you live publicly (in front of others). Or, more simply put, what you're like at home is what you're really like. Leaders need to be of proven character.

Fruit

If you were measured by God's standards of leadership, would you be picked to be a leader? What, if anything, is holding you back from being all you can be for God? Tell Him about it.

And Now for Exhibit A
Taken from 1 Timothy 4

Foundation

Take a moment to think about your life and the example you set. Is it a good example, or does it need a little work? Tell God your answer to this question, and ask Him to help you in areas where you are weak.

Focus

Have you ever been mocked or made fun of because you're trying to live a life that honors God?

Paul knew he had given Timothy a big job. Leading the church in Ephesus was no small task. Also, Timothy was considered young for the responsibilities he had taken and prone to timidity and fear. Paul wrote his next words to encourage Timothy.

"Timothy," Paul wrote, "stand strong in the teachings and truth of the faith in which you were trained. Continue to teach these truths as you have been doing, and have nothing to do with the godless myths and old wives' tales that some are teaching. Instead, become godly through spiritual discipline and training, train yourself to be godly, and continue to live a life that is honoring to Him."

Paul specifically used the word *train* so that Timothy would be reminded of athletes who spent time disciplining their bodies for a specific physical goal. Timothy's goal was spiritual: to become godly. Paul knew that physical training was good, but it was also limited. Physical training could develop only part of the person, and its effects lasted for just a short while. Training in godliness, however, develops the whole person—body, soul, and mind. It's good not only for this life but

son of Vespasian, becomes Emperor of

also for the life to come. Paul made sure that Timothy took careful note of this.

Paul continued, "You have put your hope in the living God who is the Savior of all men. Continue to spread this message, and don't let anyone look down on you because you are young," Paul wrote. "Instead, be an example for the believers in your words, in your actions, in love, in faith, and in purity."

> *In Paul's day, the word youth was used to describe anyone of military age—forty years of age or younger.*

Paul knew that the church sought to have leaders who were over fifty years old. Most believed that until people reached this age, they weren't mature enough to lead and set an example for others to follow. Paul told Timothy not to feel timid because he was only a youth. Instead, he was to show his maturity and set an example for others by living a godly life. No matter what people said or thought, Timothy was to stand firm and to live for his Lord.

Footwork

Look up 1 Timothy 4:12. According to this verse, how should you handle those who look down on you? In what five areas can you be an example for others?

Fruit

On an index card or piece of paper, list the five areas you read about in verse 12. Think of a practical way you can be an example in each of these areas, and write it down next to the word. (*Example:* Speech—I won't talk back to my parents when I disagree with them.) Practice the things you listed for a week, keeping your list handy as a reminder.

Rome. Mount Vesuvius erupts, burying

I'm Content
Taken from 1 Timothy 6

Foundation

Ask God to speak to your heart and help you become more godly in your hopes and desires.

Focus

Do you ever wish you could become rich?

As Paul finished his letter to Timothy, he expressed the same concerns he mentioned at the beginning. "If people teach anything that isn't in line with the truth of our Lord Jesus Christ, they are teaching false doctrine. Not only that," Paul stated, "they are filled with self-importance and only love arguing about spiritual matters so they can pretend to know about God. Their real love is engaging in controversies and quarrels. They stir up arguments and doubts that cause friction. These false teachers are filled with pride and are completely empty of God's truth. They think they can gain something or become rich by acting godly! How little they know!"

Paul knew that the truly godly don't demand riches for themselves. They don't look for what they can gain, but rather for what they can give. They understand that their possessions aren't their life. They're completely satisfied and content with God alone, even if it means not having anything else. Godliness doesn't lead to great gain; godliness itself is gain.

> **Godliness *means* acting the way Jesus would act and doing the things He would do. It's the act of becoming more like Him.**

Paul continued, warning Timothy about the dangers of loving money. "Loving money is the starting point for all kinds of sin and evil desires," he stated. "Some people, who were greedy for money or the promise of having the best of everything, have strayed from the faith. Their lives have been torn apart by the very things they seek.

"Timothy," Paul wrote, "as a man of God, you must run from all this and strive instead to be righteous and godly, full of faith, love, endurance, and gentleness. Command those who are wealthy and have nice possessions not to be proud or boastful. They shouldn't put their hope in what they own, for it is uncertain and won't last. Instead, their hope should rest in God, who provided those things for them. They should use their possessions as God-given things to enjoy and use to benefit and build others up. They should be rich, not with things they have or own, but in good deeds. Their lives should be characterized by contentment, generosity, and a willingness to share with others, knowing that God is the One who meets their needs."

> *In Proverbs 30:7–9, the writer pleas with God to give him neither poverty nor wealth. The writer feared that if he were poor, he would be tempted to steal in order to survive and thus dishonor God; he also feared that if he were rich, he would be tempted to find "happiness" in his possessions and thus forsake God.*

Footwork

Turn to 1 Timothy 6:17. What two dangers do the rich face? What should they fix their hopes on? Why? Have you set your hopes on things you want, or is your hope in God?

Fruit

Take the contentment challenge. First, grab a piece of paper and pen, and write down seven things that describe who you are and what you like. Then examine your list. Does it revolve around your character or around your possessions?

taly and killing 30,000 people.

AD 79 - The colosseum in Rome opens and i

2 Timothy

Paul wrote 2 Timothy under different circumstances than his first letter to Timothy. By the time Paul wrote 2 Timothy, he was back in Rome as a prisoner for preaching the gospel—only this imprisonment wasn't like the first one. During Paul's first imprisonment, he stayed in a rented house under guard (sort of like being grounded by your parents). This was called house arrest.

Now, however, Paul found himself in a dark, damp dungeon. After he appeared before the wicked emperor Nero, the outlook for Paul wasn't good. Knowing that death was certain, Paul wrote what would be his last epistle (letter) and addressed it to Timothy. This letter contains Paul's last words of instruction, warning, and encouragement to the young pastor.

As you read through this book, notice Paul's love and concern for others despite his own circumstances. See how he encouraged Timothy and the believers to remain faithful to God, even in the face of hardship. ————

Here I Stand

Taken from 2 Timothy 1

Foundation

As you begin 2 Timothy, think about your walk with God. Are you experiencing His joy and peace? If not, ask God to show you why, and invite Him to change and rearrange things in your life.

Focus

Do you find it easier to run from difficulties than to stand and face them?

The darkness and dampness of the prison cell surrounded Paul like a death grip, threatening to choke out any remaining hope. In a Roman dungeon he was awaiting execution. Despite his circumstances, Paul kept his thoughts on things greater than his own difficulties. With pen in hand he set out to write his final words to Timothy.

"Paul, an apostle of Jesus Christ by the will of God," he boldly wrote, never regretting or wishing it were otherwise. "May God's grace, mercy, and peace be with you. I thank God as I constantly remember you in my prayers. How I long to see you."

Paul felt anxious to see Timothy before winter. It seemed that almost everyone had abandoned him, and he was very lonely. Only Luke and Onesiphorus weren't ashamed of Paul or his prison chains. Despite the danger of associating with a criminal, they had taken the risk and searched for Paul in Rome.

atres. ◆ AD 80 — Fire breaks out in Rom

Paul continued his letter, encouraging Timothy to remember his training in godliness and to depend upon the gifts and abilities God had given him to accomplish His work. "For God doesn't want us to be cowards, but to be confident, resting in the power, love, and self-control He gives us."

Paul knew that Timothy might feel ashamed of having to defend a prisoner. He might also become fearful of proclaiming the message of the gospel. Paul didn't want this to happen. "Don't be ashamed of the message about the Lord Jesus or of me as a prisoner for His cause. In times like these we can know and experience the power of God as we suffer on behalf of the gospel. God called us to be holy—not by our own works and efforts but according to His will and grace. This was God's plan from the beginning of eternity and has been made known to us through Jesus, who destroyed the power of death so that we can live forever with God."

Paul continued. "I'm suffering because of the gospel, but I'm not ashamed, because I know the One I believe in, and I'm absolutely certain that He will take care of all that concerns my life."

Why was Paul jailed again? In AD 64 on July 19, Rome went up in flames. Many suspected that Nero (who had become a madman) did it, but he simply blamed the Christians. As a result, anyone who was a believer and proclaimed Christ in Rome was viewed as a criminal and tried.

In Acts 16:1, we learn that Timothy was trained by his mother and grandmother who were Jewish believers. (His father was a Gentile).

Paul knew that no matter what happened, he could stand firm on the fact of the gospel and on God's character, trusting Him in spite of hardship, difficult times, or even death. His main concern was that Timothy would stand firm too with his courage rooted in God, and that he would follow Paul's example of holding fast to the Lord, unashamed to testify about Him.

Footwork

Look up 2 Timothy 1:12. What did Paul know? What did he say he was convinced of? This is something Paul personally experienced in his life and found to be true. Notice how he wrote, "I know *whom* I have believed," not what. Paul could stand firm because of his personal relationship with God.

Fruit

Tough times will come your way in life. At some point it may become life threatening to be known as a Christian! The only way through difficult times is relying on your personal relationship with God. Get to know Him and experience His faithfulness now so that you'll be able to stand confident in times of trouble.

I Can Handle It
Taken from 2 Timothy 2

Foundation

Take a few moments to really talk with God. Share with Him what's on your heart and mind at this moment. Ask Him to take away your concerns or bad attitudes so you can have a clear mind and a pure heart that He can teach.

Focus

Do you ever long to be a better example of a believer in Christ but don't know where to begin?

Be strong ... be strong ... be strong! These words kept flooding Paul's mind, finding their way onto the parchment. "Strengthen yourself in the grace that Jesus gives us," he stated. "Not only be strong in His grace but teach faithful men about Him so that they can teach others. Don't be afraid to suffer difficult times with me as a good soldier of the Lord."

Since Paul had spent so much time in the company of Roman soldiers, he knew a great deal about them. And he used that knowledge to describe what a believer in Christ should be like. "No soldier gets tangled up in things that distract him," he stated, knowing that soldiers were first and foremost soldiers—in heart, soul, and mind. They ate, lived, and breathed being soldiers. Believers should do the same as soldiers of Christ.

> *The soldier, the athlete, and the farmer all work for a future reward: the soldier, for victory over an enemy; the athlete, for the hope of winning the prize; the farmer, for the coming harvest. The believer also works toward a future reward: to hear God say, "Well done, good and faithful servant!" (Matthew 25:21).*

Paul also knew that soldiers were trained to obey their commanders. They did what they were supposed to do without necessarily knowing all the reasons. They trusted in their commanders, who saw the big picture and knew the reasons.

Soldiers were also willing to suffer and sacrifice for their ruler's cause. Even in the face of death they remained faithful. This is a picture of how the believer should be, serving the God who made the universe.

Paul continued with another image of a believer as an athlete who trains hard for a race. It isn't an example of a person who does just enough to get by; it's an example of someone who strives to compete for a prize according to the rules and standards of excellence.

Athletes aren't lazy; they constantly set standards for themselves and train their bodies accordingly. Believers are to do the same. They shouldn't lower their standards, but rather they should live their lives within them, ever striving for excellence.

Paul's last example was that of a farmer who knows there are no quick results from his labors. His work is never done. And after planting and working the soil, he must wait for the rewards. That's how believers are to be—always at their job of being a Christian.

"You are to follow the example of the soldier, the athlete, and the farmer," Paul instructed. "Don't get distracted by useless arguments, empty talk, or trying to win the approval of others. Instead, be concerned about God's approval. Believers should stay away from evil and live life in such a way that they are always available to be used by God. Much like a vessel that is kept clean so it can be ready and useful, you are to be full of honor—set apart and available to be used by the Lord—not a cause for shame."

Footwork

Look up 2 Timothy 2:15. According to this verse, what two qualities describe a person God approves of? (Don't merely guess at the answer from what you've read above. Examine God's Word for yourself.)

Fruit

Handling the Word of God correctly means spending time in it and knowing your way around its contents. As a result, you will have a changed life and will set a good example of how to live as a believer. Have you been faithful to look up all the verses in the Footwork sections, or did you just look up those you were most interested in? Did you skip any questions because you didn't want to look up the verse and couldn't guess the answer? Stop now and go back through any Footwork questions you may have skipped or neglected. Look up the verses in your Bible and do your best to answer the questions. Then commit in your heart to know and spend time in God's Word. In the book of Jeremiah (in the Old Testament), we learn that God's Word is like a fire that can ignite a life and bring about change and like a hammer that shatters rock (a description of a hard heart). (See Jeremiah 23:29.) Allow His Word to work in your life.

This Is Getting Ugly
Taken from 2 Timothy 3

Foundation

Spend a few minutes thinking about God's comfort and help. Thank Him that He is always near and ready to help you weather any storm, no matter how ugly it gets.

FOCUS

Do you ever feel that you're purposefully picked on, hurt, or denied your right to free speech because you try to follow Christ?

Paul knew firsthand what persecution was like. In his lifetime he had been in the center of riots, falsely accused, beaten, driven out of cities, imprisoned, threatened, stoned, and even left for dead! He had been treated as a hero and then sentenced as a criminal. He faced great suffering, but it didn't stop him from loving his Lord or serving Him. As Paul faced death, his heart went out to Timothy. He wanted Timothy to continue to stand strong in his faith and not back down, even in the difficult times to come.

"Realize that in the last days there will be difficult times. People will follow their own desires rather than seeking after God. They will be selfish, doing things only to bring themselves pleasure. They will love money and wrap their lives around all that it allows them to buy and enjoy. People will talk better of themselves than they really are, and they will make promises they can't or won't keep. In their pride, they will stir up arguments and fights with others. They will be out of control, ungrateful for what they have, unloving toward others, disobedient toward their parents, and disrespectful toward God. They will be unforgiving, holding grudges against people, and they will freely gossip and slander others."

Paul also knew that these people would target Christians. "Don't be taken by surprise," he warned Timothy "These people will be cruel toward you. Don't trust them! They will lie by saying one thing and then doing another. Their hearts are full of conceit. They laugh at others and live only for their own pleasures. Some may even try to look godly, but they don't have God's power. They may know about God, but they don't really know Him. But it won't be long before their wrong ways become known to all," Paul reassured.

Paul described to Timothy some of his own sufferings at the hands of such people. "As you know, I suffered great persecution in Antioch, Iconium, and Lystra. And you also know that the Lord delivered me from each and every difficulty." God didn't keep Paul from experiencing persecutions, but he helped him in the midst of them and delivered him.

> Humanism *teaches that each person decides what truth is for himself or herself. Since what is true for one person may not be true for another, our society forces us to be "tolerant" of the beliefs and standards of everyone. The trend toward tolerance in our society is based on a denial that there is a God who has absolute standards, and anyone who even suggests that fact is silenced. (How intolerant!) Don't be confused. And don't be bullied into silence!*

Then Paul gave Timothy another warning. "Know in advance that all who are determined to live a godly life as believers in Christ will be misunderstood and persecuted, and those who do evil will only get worse. But don't be discouraged, Timothy. Instead, continue in your walk with the Lord and keep living a godly life, no matter what. Hold on to the Scriptures, because they are able to give you the teaching, correction, wisdom, and strength you need to live in this ungodly world and to face the challenges that come your way."

Footwork

Look up 2 Timothy 3:12. Why do you think believers who want to live godly lives will be mistreated and persecuted? Now turn back a few books to 2 Corinthians 12:9–10 and read what it says. What comforting verses! Remember them and take courage.

Fruit

In our society it's becoming more and more difficult to live for Christ or speak about Him. One thing Satan strives for is to silence believers. Why? Because he wants to keep the good news of the gospel quiet. One way this happens is through "tolerance" and "diversity training" (accepting others who may believe differently than you). Remember, you can accept others without embracing their beliefs or letting their beliefs silence yours! When you speak out for Christ, you will be persecuted. Expect it—and be prepared for the possibility that things could get ugly. People like to make up their own rules (we call that *humanism*) and don't like to be told there is only one way—God's way. They will seek to belittle and silence you. So the next time you face persecution for being a Christian, will you be shocked, or will you be ready to stand? Remember, when you're at your weakest, God is there to make you strong. Stand for Him, and He will stand with you!

Check It Out
Taken from 2 Timothy 3—4

Foundation

Before you finish your study of 2 Timothy, think about the part you allow Scripture to play in your life. Be honest. Ask God to forgive you for the times you leave His Word behind—unread, unheard, and unheeded.

Focus

> Have you ever heard someone say (or have you yourself thought), "The Bible is just an old outdated book that has nothing to say about life here and now"?

"Timothy," Paul charged, "hold on to the Scriptures, because they are able to give you the teaching, correction, wisdom, and strength you need to live in this ungodly world."

Paul didn't make up these words to convince Timothy to think highly of the Scriptures. Paul had personally experienced, tested, tried, and found those words to be true. The Scriptures are God's words of comfort, encouragement, instruction, and correction to us. They aren't the words of men; they are God's love letter of communication to all people. The Scriptures are special, holy, dependable, and true because they come from God.

"God has breathed all Scripture," Paul wrote, explaining how God put into the minds of godly men what to write. God carefully guided every thought so that the Scriptures became God's words to people—accurate

alled the aeolipile. His device is

> *"God-breathed" is another way of saying "inspired by God." It means that the words we read in the Bible are His communication to us— true and without error.*
>
> *Hebrews 4:12 says that the Word of God "is living and active. Sharper than any double-edged sword [like a surgeon's knife] ... it judges the thoughts and attitudes of the heart."*

and without any mistakes. "And it is useful," Paul explained. The Scriptures are words specially designed for us—practical, purposeful words. Since God made us, He knows us best. His words are like an instruction book or owner's manual about our lives and how we operate best.

Paul's next words describe the many things Scripture accomplishes in our lives. "[It] is useful for teaching, rebuking, correcting, and for preparation and teaching in righteousness." God's Word instructs us how to live God's way (teaching). If we get off track, it shows us where we went wrong (rebuking) and points out how we can get back on track again (correcting). God's Word applies to how we live here and now. It's able to train us in righteousness so that we can "be ready and able to do every good work."

Through God's Word we see who we are (and aren't!) and get a glimpse of all that God is. We see our weaknesses and His strength, our problems and His solutions, our selfishness and His love, our faltering and His faithfulness. God's Word isn't just any old book written long ago; it's God's message to each of us—personally.

Footwork

In your Bible, turn to 2 Timothy 3:16–17. In what ways, if any, have you seen God's Word doing each of these things in your life?

Fruit

The next time you hear a friend say that the Bible is just an outdated book of little or no value, what will you say in response? Take a few moments to think about what you know and have learned about God's Word or have personally experienced.

Then on a piece of paper or an index card, finish the following statement: "The Bible is not just an ancient book of little or no benefit. I know because_____." Make it a point to share what you wrote on your card with a family member, a friend, a teacher, or a coworker today.

becomes Emperor of Rome and rules fiftee

Titus

Titus was a Gentile believer who served and traveled with the apostle Paul. He was dependable, willing, and able to do any task set before him. So when Paul needed a trusted messenger to deliver a harsh letter to the troubled church in Corinth, he sent Titus.

After Paul's release from his first imprisonment in Rome, he took Timothy and Titus with him on his journey to revisit the churches. After leaving Timothy at Ephesus, Titus and Paul traveled to Crete where Titus stayed behind to help bring needed changes to the church there. The book of Titus is Paul's letter of instruction to Titus, reminding him of what he is to teach the Cretan believers.

As you read this book, notice the important thing Paul reminds Titus to teach. It's something the believers' entire walk with God was built upon. ——

years. He is last of the twelve

Don't Forget
Taken from Titus 2—3

Foundation

As you read through today's lesson, think about your life. Think about the things you did and thought before you became a Christian. (If you're not sure you are a Christian, turn to the back of this book and read the special message just for you.) Ask God to remind you of what He has done in and through your life.

Focus

When you see pictures of yourself as a young child, what memories come to mind?

Paul thought for a moment while his pen rested on the parchment. The churches in Crete were struggling to know what and in whom to believe. Titus had stayed behind, tending to this matter, yet Paul still felt heavyhearted. He knew he needed to write a letter of encouragement and instruction to Titus, telling him what to remind the believers of and what to teach them.

"Tell the believers to pay no attention to the nonbelieving Jews who have rejected the truth. They claim to know God, but by their own actions, they deny Him. Challenge the believers not to listen to such men but to stand firm in the truth," Paul wrote.

"Teach older men to live lives that are worthy of respect, to be self-controlled, to endure hardship, and to show great love and faith. In the same way, older women should live in a way that honors God, not slandering others with their words but teaching what is good," Paul instructed.

He went on to describe how young men, young women, and even slaves were to act as believers, and then he summarized how all believers should live. "For God's grace, which offers salvation to everyone, instructs us to turn away from ungodliness and sinful desires so that we can live righteous, godly, and self-controlled lives here on earth. We're to live such lives while we wait for Jesus Christ to come back again in all His glory!"

Paul paused, thinking back on what he and these fellow believers had been like before committing their lives to follow Jesus. "We were once foolish people, laughing at the thought of someone dying on a cross for our sins. We thought we were smart, but in reality we were deceived, not knowing the truth. We thought we were free, but actually we were slaves to uncontrollable desires. We constantly lived in envy of others, not wanting them to have good things or to succeed. We not only hated other people, but they also hated us in return.

Crete is a mountainous island located southeast of Greece. Paul never visited Crete while on his missionary journeys.

Where did the believers in Crete come from? It is believed that they traveled to Jerusalem during the time of Pentecost and returned home to Crete as Christians.

"But in the midst of this, God came and did something about it. In His great kindness and love, He saved us from our sins, not because we ourselves were righteous or had done anything good, but because He is full of mercy. Not only did He save us, but he also gave us His Holy Spirit so that we would have the power and ability to live godly lives here on earth and be filled with the sure hope that we will spend eternity with Him.

"Titus, teach the believers to be devoted to doing whatever is right and good. Teach them to live lives worthy of God by calling to mind all that He has done for them. Remind them of their past so they will continue to live for God in the future."

Footwork

Look up Titus 2:14 in your Bible. According to this verse, what were the two results of Jesus giving Himself for our sins? How should we live because of this?

Fruit

Sometimes it's good to look back and remember what you were like before Jesus saved you. Remembering helps you become more thankful for all He has done and is doing for you.

Take a piece of paper and draw a line down the middle. On the left side, draw a big circle. In that circle write words that describe what you were like before you came to know Jesus. (Or draw pictures if you prefer.) Now, on the right side, draw another big circle. In this circle write or draw descriptions of what God is helping you become.

Next, read Titus 3:3–5. Under the circle on the left, write the words "Titus 3:3." Under the circle on the right, write the words "Titus 3:4–5." Now, draw a big *X* through the circle on the left. It's because of God's work in your life that you no longer have to live like that. Take a few moments to thank God and tell Jesus that you love and appreciate Him.

AD 89 — Romans establish the former

Philemon

Paul wrote the book of Philemon during his first imprisonment in Rome, around the same time he wrote Colossians. This prison letter is a personal letter addressed to a man named Philemon, who lived in the city of Colosse.

Philemon was a wealthy Christian in whose home the church met. He had become a believer through Paul's ministry. Apparently, Philemon owned slaves (as did all wealthy people at the time), and one slave, named Onesimus, stole from Philemon and ran off to Rome to become lost in the crowds.

While in Rome, Onesimus met Paul and became a believer in Christ. Even though he had become very helpful to Paul, Paul knew that Onesimus must make right the wrongs he had done. So Paul sent Onesimus back to his master in Colosse with a letter in hand, asking Philemon to forgive Onesimus and welcome him home, not as a slave but as a brother in Christ. As you read through the short book of Philemon, notice the theme of forgiveness. Notice, too, how Paul (who had done no wrong) offered to pay any debts Onesimus might have owed his master. Paul's offer is a great example what Jesus did for us on a much grander scale when He gave His live for us on the cross. —————

Will You?
Taken from Philemon v. 1–25

--- Foundation ---

Spend time in prayer, asking God to speak to your heart through today's lesson. Ask Him to show you anyone you might need to forgive.

Focus

Is asking for forgiveness and forgiving others sometimes difficult for you to do?

As Onesimus walked along the road, he clutched Paul's letter tightly. His heart was pounding as he wondered how Philemon would respond. Yes, he had done something terribly wrong against his master, Philemon—he had stolen from him and then run away. Although slaves were often treated as mere property, Philemon had never mistreated Onesimus. Yet Onesimus hadn't thought twice about what he was doing at the time; he just wanted his freedom. That was then; this was now.

Now, Onesimus had freedom but of a much different kind. Never had he known such peace. Although physically he was a slave, he was no longer a slave spiritually. He now served a new Master—the Lord Jesus Christ.

Onesimus continued to walk, not knowing what lay before him. The letter he carried from Paul asked Philemon to forgive and accept him back, not just as a slave but as a brother in Christ. "For the sake of love," Paul wrote, "I ask you to do what is right. I'm writing concerning your slave Onesimus. He was once of no use to you, but I'm sending him back to you now as a brother who is useful

base for their border-protection system.

in a new way," Paul explained. The name Onesimus was a common name for slaves and it meant "useful."

Having become a believer, Onesimus helped Paul while he was imprisoned. He was such a great help that Paul had wanted to keep Onesimus rather than send him back to Philemon. But Paul knew that he needed to do the right thing. "He is very dear to me," Paul wrote, "so welcome him back as a brother in the Lord; welcome him as you would welcome me."

Paul knew that this might be a difficult thing for Philemon to do. Rebellious slaves were usually killed. Runaway slaves were branded on the forehead with a hot iron so that everyone would know of their disgrace. Not only did Paul ask Philemon to accept Onesimus back, he asked Philemon to forgive the slave and honor him as a brother in the Lord! Philemon would have no time to think it over. Onesimus would be right there, delivering the letter in person. "If Onesimus has done you any wrong or owes you any money, I will personally pay it back," Paul offered. He knew he could trust Onesimus, and he knew he could expect Philemon to do what was right in God's sight.

Onesimus clutched the parchment in his hands as he neared Philemon's house, wondering what Philemon's response would be.

Sixty million slaves lived in the Roman Empire during the time Paul wrote this letter. Soldiers kept a tight rein on slaves, fearing that such a large number might cause trouble. Rebellious slaves weren't tolerated. When Paul sent Onesimus back to Philemon, he was taking a great step of faith.

The name **Philemon** *means "loving"; apparently, it was a very fitting name for this man!*

Footwork

Turn to Philemon v. 7. (Since Philemon is only one chapter long, this is verse 7.) Look at the description of Philemon toward the end of the verse. What does this tell you about Philemon? Do you think he was one to forgive or one to hold a grudge?

Tradition has it that Philemon not only forgave Onesimus but also granted his freedom so he might return to Paul and help out in the ministry. It has been recorded that fifty years after this incident, there was a church leader in Ephesus named Onesimus. Could this have been the same man? It very well could have been!

Fruit

When a person who has wronged you in a hurtful way comes back to ask for forgiveness, how will you respond?

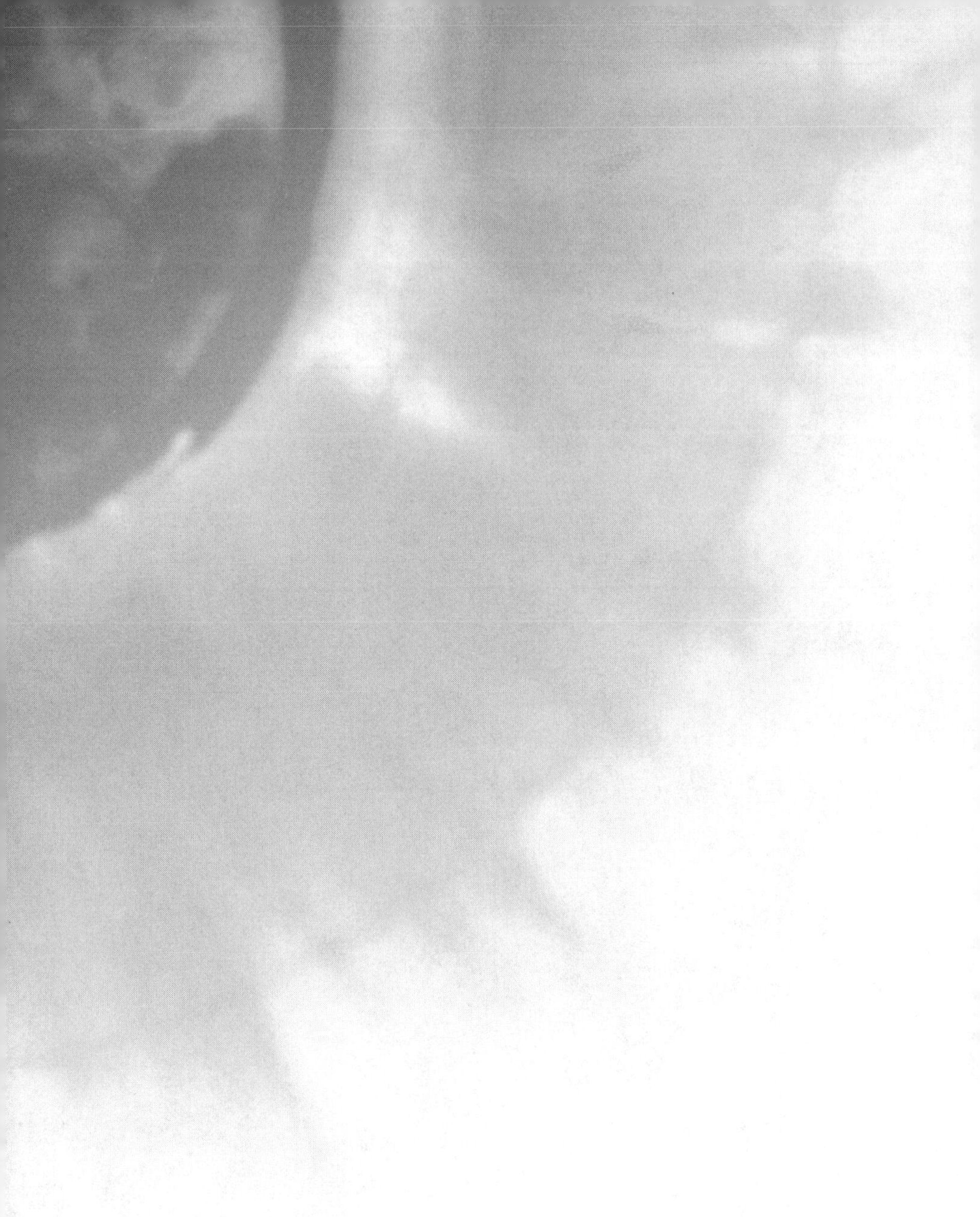

94 - Philosophers are banned from Rome b

Hebrews

Hebrews is a fantastic book because it allows us to see what Jesus is doing for us today. Unlike the other New Testament books, we're not sure who wrote the book of Hebrews. Some suggest that Paul wrote it, while others suggest a coworker, such as Barnabas or Apollos did. Although we know that the letter was written to Jewish believers sometime before AD 70, we can't be sure of the exact date or to whom it was actually sent. The important thing about the book of Hebrews isn't who wrote it, who received it, or even the exact date it was written. The important thing is that God wanted it to be part of the Scriptures. This book contains a special message from Him.

As you read through Hebrews, note that it addresses believing Jews who were in danger of going back to their old Jewish religion and turning their backs on Christ. A phrase that appears in this book is "consider Jesus, our great High Priest." Apparently, distractions were causing the believers to drift away from their relationship with Jesus. They needed to be reminded of who Jesus is and all He had done for them. ————

He Knows
Taken from Hebrews 4

— *Foundation* —

Stop and pray before you begin today's lesson. Ask God to show you areas in your heart where you may not be living truthfully—areas you may hope He doesn't notice.

Focus

> *Do you ever tell only part of the truth about something because you're afraid that if you tell the whole truth you'll get in trouble?*

No doubt about it—a number of Jewish believers were drifting from the Lord. Some were interested in angels, others in keeping the old laws and going back to meaningless ceremonies. "You must be very careful to pay attention to the gospel you heard so that you don't drift away from God's truth!" the writer to the Hebrews warned. "In the past God spoke through the prophets and the Old Testament Scriptures, but now He has spoken to us through His Son."

The writer explained how everything in the Old Testament points to Jesus. He also explained how Jesus is greater than anything or anyone, including Moses who gave the Israelites God's laws. Then he quoted Psalm 95—something with which the Jewish people were very familiar. It spoke of Israel's turning from God and the results of doing so. Warning the believers not to make the same mistake their forefathers did, the author wrote, "Make sure your hearts aren't filled with unbelief or sin so that you turn away from the living God. "No one can hide or try to keep anything from God, for nothing is hidden from His sight," the writer continued. "Everything is exposed and naked before Him." The believers would have understood the words "nothing is hidden from His sight" because they were wrestling words. They described what happened when one opponent grabbed another by the throat so that he couldn't move or escape. Instead, he had to gaze into the face of the one holding him.

The phrase was also used for skinning animals. When the outside skin of an animal was stripped away, everything that lay beneath the skin was exposed.

Finally, that same phrase described a criminal who stood trial with a dagger placed under his chin to keep him from bowing his head and hiding his face from his accusers.

So it is with believers. Nothing is hidden from God's sight. He looks past the outside things we see and looks straight into our hearts. He can't be fooled. God's people sinned in the past not only by turning their hearts from God but also by thinking that God didn't know any better!

The writer of Hebrews went on to explain how God's Word helps uncover things believers try to cover up or deny. "For God's Word is sharper than a two-edged sword. It is alive and actively working to cut through falsehoods and get to the heart of things. It's also able to judge our thoughts and heart attitudes."

Two-edged swords were razor sharp and very exact. They could cut through even the hardest and most dense objects with great ease.

Psalm 139:1–12 states that the Lord knows everything about you, including your innermost thoughts and words— even before they roll off your tongue! When David penned this psalm he expressed both praise and a humble plea for God to search his heart. Check it out! (To learn more about David's life, read 1 and 2 Samuel in the Old Testament.)

Footwork

Look up Hebrews 4:13. What does this verse tell you about God? Whom do we have to answer

to? Is God fooled? Now read verse 16. Knowing that God knows everything, how should we

respond to Him?

Fruit

When you mess up, you'll be tempted to try to hide from God. Don't. He already knows what you've done and all the thoughts that have gone through your mind. (Check out *Faith Factor OT* for living examples of this.) You can never tell Him half the truth; He already knows the whole story. So instead of running from God, *run to Him*. He wants you to draw near to Him so that He can help you. His mercy and grace are yours for the asking. Nothing can make Him love you any more than He already does, and nothing can make Him love you any less. Never forget that.

But Why?
Taken from Hebrews 4—10

— Foundation —

Stop and pray, asking God to help you understand and appreciate all it cost Him to offer you forgiveness.

Jesus died for our sins, but have you ever wondered why?

The writer of Hebrews answered this question for us by comparing Jesus to a high priest. The main theme of Hebrews is this: Consider Jesus, our great High Priest. But just what was a high priest, and what did he do?

In the Old and New Testaments, the high priest acted as a bridge between man and God. On the Day of Atonement, which took place once a year, the high priest, with great fear and reverence, went into the Holy of Holies in the temple to make a sin sacrifice for all the people. This was done only after he had completed several ceremonies to cleanse his own sin. Once inside the Holy of Holies, he made his sacrificial offering for the people and then left the presence of God as quickly as possible. But why did the high priest have to make a sacrifice for sin?

Long ago when God created Adam and Eve, He gave certain rules for their relationship with Him. When they broke those rules, sin entered the picture, and Adam and Eve could no longer keep their same relationship with God. As a result, they hid from God and tried to cover their sin. Big mistake! God forgave them, but the consequences of their sin remained.

> *The Holy of Holies in the temple was only a type, or model, of what the real throne of God is like in heaven. After Jesus offered Himself as a sacrifice, He went back to the (real) Holy of Holies in heaven, paving the way for us to follow one day.*

> *In both Old and New Testament times, blood was thought of as life itself. Today we know that blood cleanses our wounds and carries the necessary ingredients to help our bodies heal. The Bible tells us that the blood of Christ cleanses us, and we're healed by His wounds. (See 1 John 1:7 and Isaiah 53:5.)*

Knowing that Adam and Eve's feeble attempts at covering themselves with fig leaves would never do, God fashioned coverings for them—of animal skins. An innocent animal had to die on their behalf. This was the first animal sacrifice and the first time blood was shed. (See Genesis 3:21.) After that, God instituted the regular practice of having the high priest offer animal sacrifices as a covering for sin and a reminder to the people. But the high priest's sacrifices were only temporary. They had to be offered again and again, year after year, because the people kept sinning and breaking God's laws. Because the Law and animal sacrifices couldn't deal with the cause of sin, they were neither a permanent nor a perfect solution. At best, they just showed people's sins and failures all the more clearly and proved that they needed a Savior.

God intended the sacrificial system to be a picture of a Great High Priest who would someday come and offer a perfect once-for-all sacrifice.

Unlike the high priest who had to offer sacrifices for his own sins first—and who would eventually die like everyone else—Jesus, the Great High Priest, was sinless and had no need to offer sacrifices for Himself. Because He is God, He lives forever.

The high priest also had to continually offer sacrifices for the people's sins. His job was never done. Only once a year could he pass through the curtain into the Holy of Holies to make a special sacrifice on behalf of the people. But Jesus, the Great High Priest, offered Himself as a one-time sacrifice for everyone's sins, and then he sat down in glory in heaven to show that His work was finished. He passed through the heavens from the very throne of God to give Himself as that sacrifice,

tion under his reign. The Arch of Titus

312

then he returned to the heavenly Holy of Holies where He sits in glory.

More than just a bridge between God and man, Jesus is the key that opens the door so that you and I can actually go into the very presence of God on our own! Jesus was both the perfect High Priest and the perfect Sacrifice! Unlike animals sacrificed against their will, Jesus voluntarily gave His life for us. The animals were sacrificed because of God's law, but Jesus sacrificed Himself out of love. The animals didn't know what was happening; Jesus knew what He was doing. He wasn't a victim but did what He did fully knowing all it would cost Him.

Because of Jesus' sacrifice, our hearts can be washed clean and our lives freed from sin. Because Jesus acted as our High Priest, we can draw near to God and have the privilege of knowing Him as our heavenly Father.

Footwork

Read Hebrews 10:10. Through Jesus we have been made holy in God's sight once for all. Now skip down to verse 19 and then verses 22–24. What does verse 19 say? Since we have this ability to stand before God, what should be our response? (See the first part of verse 22, the first part of verse 23, and verse 24.)

Fruit

God wants us to draw near to Him with full assurance. It cost Him greatly to open a way for us to be able to come before His holy presence. Do you appreciate the opportunity and privilege you have to do this? Think about the time you spend in prayer. Do you just hand God your wish list when you pray, or do you take time to really worship and talk to Him? Spend a few minutes right now thanking Him for what He has provided and worshipping Him for who He is.

Sign Me Up
Taken from Hebrews 11

— Foundation —

Ask God to speak to your heart today so that you can clearly understand His Word. Ask Him to challenge you and help you in areas where your faith is weak.

Focus

Do you ever secretly wonder whether your faith as a Christian is the right one?

Not all faith is the right kind of faith. The value of your faith is only as good as the thing in which you put your faith. A good definition of the right kind of faith is "believing and trusting in God's character." That means believing that God is who He says He is and that He will do what He says He will do.

"Faith means that we're sure of the thing we're hoping for and the One we've put our hope in (God). It also means that we're absolutely certain that what we can't see is real and that God's promises will be fulfilled. This kind of faith is what some of our forefathers were praised for," the writer of Hebrews stated.

Then he described the great heroes of faith. "By faith, Abel's offering was accepted by God. By faith, Noah listened to God's warnings and obediently built an ark, even though there was no sign of rain. By faith, Abraham became a father—even when he was too old to have children—because God made a promise and Abraham believed Him. By faith, God's people crossed through the Red Sea on dry land while the Egyptians were drowned. And by faith they marched around the city of Jericho for seven days and then saw the walls

ture and sack of Jerusalem. The last of

314

come crashing down. All these people experienced great things in their lives because they knew and believed in the living God. Their faith was in the right One."

The writer of Hebrews continued by providing more examples of those who had placed their trust in God and weren't disappointed. "I haven't even mentioned Gideon, Samson, David, Samuel, or any of the prophets! Through their faith they gained victory over other kingdoms; they received what God promised; they were delivered from the mouths of lions; they survived the fiery furnace; they found their weaknesses being turned into strength; and they overcame their enemies through God's power! Still other believers were tortured and killed for their faith. Some were flogged and jeered at, while others were thrown into prison in chains. Some of them died by stoning or being sawed in half; others were killed by the sword. Some had the opportunity to be released, but they refused to deny their Lord. They knew the One they believed in and were willing to die before they would ever turn from their God."

Hebrews 11 has often been referred to as "the believers' hall of fame." It shows ordinary people who became heroes through their obedience and faith in God and God alone.

The Old Testament is awesome and is loaded with examples of great (and not so great) people you can learn from. It answers many questions and provides greater depth and meaning to the New Testament. Read it for yourself, or check out Faith Factor OT *for help.*

The writer of Hebrews penned powerful words. His readers would immediately know the stories behind the names he mentioned. They would see the great examples of the right kind of faith and understand even better that God was and is the only true God. As a result, their own faith would be encouraged. Perhaps even one day their own names would be added to the list of those who have found God to be all He says He is.

Footwork

Who or what you put your faith in is very important. In your Bible, turn to Hebrews 11:6. What two things do people who come to God need to believe? What pleases God?

Fruit

Everyone has faith in something. Those who don't believe in God have faith in themselves or a god they've created in their own minds. Some people make excuses for not believing and say that Christianity is a "blind faith." Such people are deceived and are only kidding themselves.

The changed lives of people who have gone before you are just one kind of proof that God is real and His ways are right. Stand confident in this. Look to Him and know that He will reward your faith. Keep your eyes on Him and live for Him. Follow the examples of the great heroes of faith who have gone before you—and some who may be living among you now.

I Think I Can
Taken from Hebrews 12

Foundation

Take a few minutes to talk with God. Thank Him for those who have gone before you and have set an example of how to follow Him with your whole heart. Ask Him to make you like that as well.

Focus

Do you sometimes start something but either lose interest or run out of steam before finishing?

Boredom. Distractions. Wanting rewards and results now. Busyness with other things.

All of these can keep people from finishing what they start. Little by little these things destroy people's desire to stick with what they're doing. And little by little these things pull people away from their goal.

The writer of Hebrews knew that all believers would face this struggle. Having already challenged them to follow in the steps of strong Christians who had gone before them, he went on to explain why and how to follow their example. Such strong faith is possible, and its rewards are far greater than anything imaginable.

Next, he directed the believers to focus on their own personal walk with God. He told them not to become lazy, thinking that everything would work out in the end. Instead, they must fix their eyes on the goal and keep running toward it, much like an athlete runs in a race.

and appointed emperor by the Senate,

Hebrews 12:1–2 lists three specific things you can do to get back on track when you're distracted or defeated in your walk of faith:

1. Release your heavy and sinful baggage
2. Refocus your attention on Jesus
3. Remember Jesus' sacrifice on the cross for you

The writer of Hebrews encouraged the believers to run the race of faith with freedom. "Let's get rid of everything that keeps us from running the race well," he wrote. It was unheard of for an Olympic runner to race with a backpack strapped behind him and his arms full of nonessential things. Everyone knew that a runner couldn't run well carrying extra weight, so he "threw off" everything and ran with only the necessary things.

Then he wrote, "Get rid of the sin that entangles you so easily and causes you to stumble." *Entangle* means that something falls down around your feet and trips you up—which is exactly what sin does! In ancient times a runner usually prepared for a race by removing any unnecessary clothes. As believers, we need to take off the sin we often allow ourselves to wear, not thinking it will cause any harm.

The writer continued, "After we've done this, we need to run with determination the race that is set before us. We need to fix our eyes on becoming more like Jesus. He's both the Author of our faith and the One who helps us live a life of faith." The writer knew that as believers, we shouldn't be strolling along in our walk with God. We should always keep heading toward the goal of becoming more like Jesus. We should be like pilgrims, forever traveling onward.

"Consider Jesus and all that He has done. For He was willing to give up His privileges as God and be beaten, misunderstood, and die on the cross for you. He made it possible for you to have a relationship with God. So don't become weary or discouraged, but keep your focus on Him and run the race to the finish!"

Footwork

In your Bible, look up Hebrews 12:2. What three things does this verse tell us about Jesus? What should our eyes be fixed upon? Jesus will help us run the race of life well for Him. He has already seen the track and understands the difficulties and uphill climbs.

rules Rome. During his two-year reign, h

Fruit

What type of runner will you be: one who is focused on the goal and wins, or one who gets tangled up, runs out of steam, and is defeated? Memorize Hebrews 12:1–2. Whenever you're tempted to be distracted or defeated this week, recite it and put it into practice!

ncreases aid to the poor and is the

It's My Choice
Taken from Hebrews 13

Foundation

As you finish the book of Hebrews, think about your possessions and your activities. Are you content? Spend a few minutes talking to God about it.

Focus

Have you ever been unsatisfied in life and felt that nothing you had or did seemed to be enough?

Like using a remote control to rewind a movie on a DVD player, the writer of Hebrews hit the rewind button and reviewed what Jesus did for believers in the past (and still does for us today). In chapter 11, he gave real examples of common people in the past who stood strong in their faith. Then, with a quick touch of the fast-forward button, he challenged believers to keep their eyes on the future goal set before them. Finally, as he closed his letter, it's as if he hit the play button and brought believers back to the present time and their current walk with the Lord. He gave them practical instructions, challenges, warnings, and encouragement before finishing his letter.

"Keep loving one another, and remember those who are suffering in prison," he wrote, engouraging the believers. He knew the degree to which they did this would show the depth of their walk with the Lord. "Keep yourselves sexually pure and don't be greedy or become enslaved by the love of money. Instead, be satisfied and content with what you have."

The writer knew how important it was that believers keep first things first and not

first to choose and train his own

seek after things that wouldn't last and couldn't satisfy. "Even if you have very little," he wrote, "you still have the Lord and His help, for God Himself has said, 'I will never leave you. I will never turn my back on you.'"

These important words would help believers when they faced the temptation of being dissatisfied. At times they would be tempted to compare themselves with others and become discontent. Perhaps they would even turn to other people or things to meet their needs. The writer told believers that they needed nothing more, for they had the very presence and help of God in their lives. Nothing man has to offer could bring greater satisfaction! "Because of this," he wrote, "we can boldly say, 'I won't be afraid because God is the One who will help me.'" Believers need not worry, for no one can take away what they have in God.

Finally he encouraged them again. "Remember those who have gone before you as examples in the faith and how the Lord met their every need. Jesus was the same yesterday as He is today and will be tomorrow! So let us keep praising God through and because of Jesus."

> *"I will never leave you nor forsake you"* and *"the Lord ... is my helper"* were quotes from two Old Testament passages: Joshua 1:5 and Psalm 118:7. They show that believers need nothing more because they have the help and the presence of God in their lives. Nothing is greater than that!

To choose well involves ...

C—Concern

H—Humility

O—Observation

O—Obedience

S—Strength

E—Energy

Footwork

Look up Hebrews 13:8. What does this verse tell you about Jesus? Everything you've learned about Him so far was true in the past, is true today, and will continue to be true in the future. Jesus is trustworthy. He has proven Himself, and He can meet your needs.

Fruit

If you could choose anyone or anything to meet your needs and build your life upon, who or what would you choose? Who or what have you chosen?

oman to do so> and frees those

unjustly imprisoned by Domitian. During

James

James is a dynamite book packed with very practical words on how to live. Some have called it the "Proverbs of the New Testament" because it's so rich in advice. James, the half brother of Jesus, wrote the book that bears his name. It is thought to be the first of the New Testament books written.

The fact that James wrote this book is very special because James and his brothers (Joses, Simon, and Jude) didn't believe in Jesus as Savior and Lord while Jesus lived among them. It wasn't until after Jesus rose from the dead that James became a believer (Acts 1:14). It's also interesting to note that James grew into Peter's position as leader of the church in Jerusalem (Acts 12:17).

James wrote this book as a letter to the scattered Jewish believers.

As you journey through James, watch where you step and how you walk, for the book of James stands as a challenge to the way you live—in your actions (or lack of them), in your speech, and in your conduct toward others. —————————————————————

this nineteen-year rule, the empire

You Can Do It!
Taken from James 1

— Foundation —

Ask the Lord to speak to your heart today and help you be a doer of His Word.

Focus

Do you ever see friends trying to act like someone else?

To be like someone else, people often try to copy the behavior of that person. They study that person and imitate his or her actions. They try to talk like that person. They constantly check out the other person so they can remember how he or she acts. Even though they may be imitating the wrong thing or person, their actions are a good practice!

Believe it or not, James wrote to the Jewish Christians about doing this very thing. He instructed them to observe the Scriptures then act upon what they knew, allowing it to change their behavior.

James wrote, "Don't just hear God's Word, thinking that's all that is necessary. Such thinking is wrong, and those who think this way deceive themselves. Instead, pay close attention to God's Word, and then become a doer of it. Examine it. Study it. Put it into practice."

James knew that it wasn't good enough just to know about God's Word; knowing about something never changed a life. Instead, believers needed to act upon what they knew. "Whoever just hears God's Word but doesn't put it into practice is like a man who gazes at himself in a mirror. He sees things about himself that need to be fixed, but instead of doing something about it, he simply walks away. Then he forgets what he looks like and the things that need to be changed. Even though he looked in the mirror, it really made no difference in his life."

"But God will bless those who give their full attention to looking into His Word and acting on what they see," James wrote. "Be like those people. Do what God's Word says; don't just listen to it," he warned.

This warning is a strong message to us as well. While some people try to act like somebody they're not, some Christians forget to act like the somebody they are! They do this because they aren't checking out God's Word and putting it into action. As for practical advice when it comes to God's Word, you need to remember only four words: You can do it!

> *A doer isn't someone who tries to tackle being perfect. It's someone who takes little steps of obedience and lets God tackle the rest.*

> *The very best of mirrors in Bible times were made of Corinthian bronze and were a luxury not everybody owned.*

Footwork

Read James 1:25. What is the promise for those who strive to put God's Word into practice in their lives?

Fruit

Have you learned or read something in the Scriptures that really challenged you? Is there something you know you need to do (or stop doing)? What is it? Have you done anything about it?

Often we don't act on something because we don't have a game plan or we don't commit in our hearts to do it. What is God tugging at your heart about right now? Write it down on a piece of paper. Ask God to forgive you for not dealing with what you wrote down. Then commit it to Him. Tell Him that you want to do something about it and that you need His help. Then the next time this issue comes up, demonstrate your sincerity by acting on what you know to do. God will be right there to help you.

Did I Say That?
Taken from James 3

- Foundation

Take a few minutes and think about the things people have said about you to your face or behind your back. If this brings up bad feelings, take them to God. Ask Him to heal your hurt feelings and help you not to use your tongue as a weapon.

Focus

Are you sometimes tempted to criticize and talk badly about others?

James thought for a moment as his pen rested on the parchment. He knew how powerful words could be. The way people used their words often showed where their hearts were. Believers were to use their tongues and their words to build others up and glorify the Lord, not to tear others down. But this wasn't the case with the believers to whom James was writing.

"Everyone stumbles in different ways," James wrote, "and perhaps the greatest way we all stumble is in the use of our tongues. This is an area where we all need work. For even though it's small, the tongue is very powerful. Just as a small bit in the mouth of a large horse controls and guides the animal wherever you want it to go and a small rudder steers large ships through strong winds, so it is with your tongue. It's

> **Whenever Jewish people heard the name of God being mentioned, they were required to stop and say, "Blessed be He!" This is the phrase James was referring to when he wrote, "With the tongue we praise our Lord" (verse 9).**

small, but it can easily lead you places you don't want to go."

James continued. "Even though the tongue is one of the smallest parts of the body, it boasts in big ways and gets us into trouble. Think about how just a tiny spark can set a whole forest on fire! In the same way, your tongue is capable of setting your life on fire and burning it to the ground. It ends up destroying everything in its path, including the things that were good.

"We use our tongues to praise God, but with those same tongues we also talk down about others who have been made in God's image and are precious to Him. This should never happen!" James said with emotion. "Can fresh water and bitter water come from the same spring? No! Why then do sweet words and bitter words come out of the same mouth? Just as it doesn't make sense for a grapevine to produce figs, it isn't right that bitter, destructive words come out of your mouth," James instructed.

Then he went on to explain how a believer's words were to be chosen and used with wisdom that comes from God and is pure, peace-loving, thoughtful of others, honoring, forgiving, and sincere.

Such control over the tongue and such wisdom isn't something that comes naturally; it's something we can do only with God's help. "Even though humans have been able to tame the wildest of animals, we can never tame our own tongues by our own efforts," James warned. To do so, we need the strength and help only God can provide.

Footwork

Look up James 3:9–10 in your Bible. What does God's Word have to say about using our tongues for both good and bad? (*Hint:* Look at the end of verse 10.)

into certain sects of Christianity. ● AD

Fruit

Look up Proverbs 15:28 and underline it in your Bible. This would be a good verse to memorize so you can always have it as a reminder.

The next time you're tempted to open your mouth and say something negative, don't!

Me? Angry?

Taken from James 4

Foundation

Think about what makes you angry and how you respond. Ask God to help you with this area of your life.

 Focus

Do you have a hard time controlling your anger?

Have you ever felt so much frustration and anger that you just wanted to scream? Most of us have felt that way. Anger is a fact of life. But why do we get angry? What causes it?

James had already written about the difference between hearing God's Word and obeying it by putting it into practice. He had also written about the problem we all face with our tongues. Next, he dove into the problem of anger and its roots.

"Why do you fight and argue?" James began. "Isn't it because you want something but don't get it?"

Anger produces ...

A—Actions that are wrong

N—Neglect of doing what is right

G—Grief

E—Energy spent in selfish ways

R—Relationships that are damaged

James knew this was the root cause of anger, but he also knew it was only part of the problem. "You get angry because you don't have something you want, and you don't have what you want because you don't take it to God and ask Him," he wrote. It was far easier for the believers to fight for something, demanding their rights, than it was to humble themselves and take their desires and needs to God.

"Sometimes God doesn't answer your prayers and give you what you ask Him for because you have selfish motives. You're only asking for things you yourselves can enjoy," James wrote.

It's natural for us to want to win an argument for the sake of pride or to have something special happen so that others will notice. And when we don't get these things, we may get angry. But this is the result of wrong motives. Our natural temptation is to fight with words or anger to make something happen and try to get what we selfishly desire. That's the danger with the anger trap.

> *Ephesians 4:26–27 tells us not to let the sun go down while we're still angry, which allows Satan a foothold. When we stew over something, we often try to guess the other person's motives (usually incorrectly!), which results in even greater misunderstanding and bitterness.*

Anger comes from unmet needs or desires that we haven't taken to God. Often, anger is our own selfish reaction when we don't get our way. When this is the case, anger is sin.

Footwork

Check out James 4:1–2. What does it say? What do our desires cause us to do?

What should we start doing with our desires? (*Hint:* Look at the last part of verse 2.)

Fruit

Before you let off steam next time, examine your heart and ask yourself, "Am I looking out for my own interests, or am I looking out for the interests of others?"

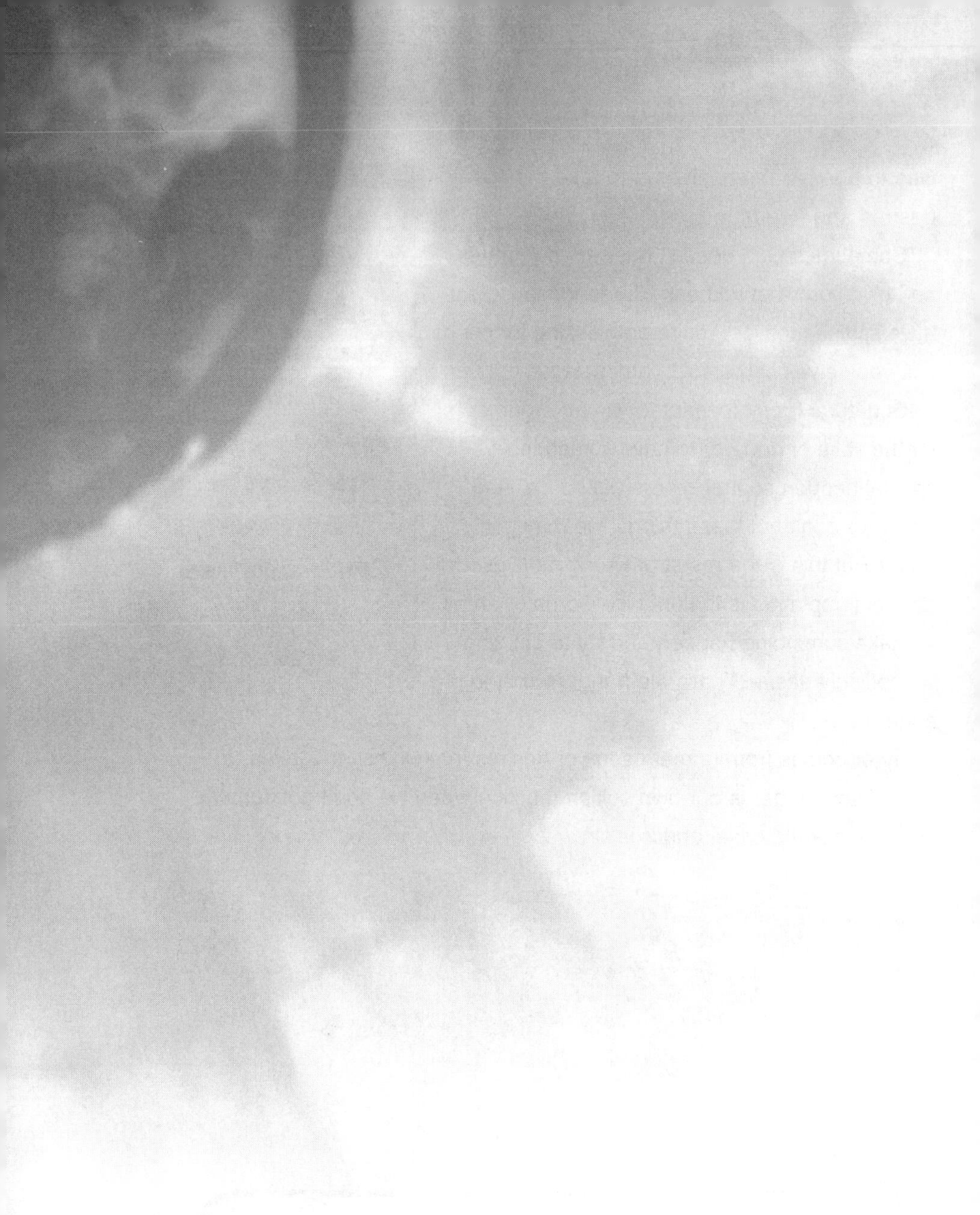

of Bithynia, writes Trajan with concern

1 Peter

The apostle Peter, who had been one of the Lord's disciples, wrote the book of 1 Peter. From the first twelve chapters of Acts, we learn that Peter became a strong and respected leader over the Jerusalem church. God did great things in and through Peter's life, just as Jesus had promised.

Because Peter identified himself by his Greek name (Peter) instead of his Jewish name (Simon) in this letter, we know that he was writing to Greek believers. Because of persecution, these believers had been scattered throughout the northern regions of Asia Minor—northern Pontus, Galatia, Cappadocia, Asia, and Bithynia.

Not knowing the Greek language very well, Peter enlisted the help of Silas to translate his message and write it down for him (1 Peter 5:12). As you may remember, Silas—also a Roman citizen—was Paul's coworker on his second missionary journey and was chosen to help deliver the decision of the Jerusalem council to the first Gentile church in Antioch (Acts 15:40–41).

Peter wrote this book to encourage the believers who were suffering terrible trials because of their faith in Jesus. In the past the Jewish religion and Christianity were closely linked. As a result, Rome had acted kindly toward Christians. (Roman soldiers even rescued Paul from angry Jews!) But over time Judaism and Christianity split apart, and the differences

about the spread of Christianity.

between the two became more noticeable. Because of this, Christians became easier to spot, and they eventually became targets for persecution. This set the stage for a madman Roman emperor named Nero.

In AD 64 when Nero attempted to burn down Rome so that he could rebuild it, his citizens became furious. Seeing this, Nero looked for someone else to pin the blame on and zeroed in on the Christians, stirring up hatred against them. As a result, cruel and illegal things were done to the believers, with Nero leading the way. At his command, Christians were rolled in pitch, then set on fire and used as torches to light his garden.

As you read through 1 Peter, notice what Peter told the believers to do in the midst of all their difficulties. What did he tell them about standing strong? What were they to stand strong in and why? ————————————————————————

A Lifetime Guarantee
Taken from 1 Peter 1—2

— Foundation —

Think about the things you treasure. Will any of these things last forever? Are they able to give you strength, direction, hope, and encouragement? Take a few minutes to thank God for His Word and for the fact that it will always stand firm, even when everything around you falls apart.

Focus

Has anyone ever said to you, "Oh yeah? Well, give me three good reasons why I should believe that your Bible is different and more special than any other holy book from any other religion?"

Peter knew that the believers needed encouragement, and they needed it now! They needed to focus their thoughts not on their trials and sufferings but on God and the blessing of salvation. Though Peter had many important things to say, he started his letter with praise.

"May God, the Father of our Lord Jesus Christ, be praised! In His loving mercy, He allows us to have a living hope in Jesus and a reward that will never die or fade away! You who are shielded by God's power through faith have this reward in heaven. Remember the hope you have because of Jesus and rejoice, even though for now you are suffering various trials," Peter said.

Peter explained to the believers that their suffering was a test of their faith. Much like fire proves how pure gold is, their fiery trials would prove how pure and true their faith was. Encouraging them to stand strong, he wrote, "So be self-controlled and be ready to act. Keep your minds and hearts set on the hope you have in Jesus and the grace He has given you. Don't return the evil desires you once had before you believed, but rather live a holy life, for God has commanded us to be holy because He is holy."

Next, Peter reminded his readers how they were saved from their empty way of life through the blood of Jesus and born again through the Word of God. "God's Word never becomes old or outdated. Even though it was written long ago, it applies to us here and now. It is living and will never die. Unlike grass that withers or flowers that fade away, God's Word will remain forever, for it is God's words, not man's."

The words Peter quoted in 1 Peter 1:24–25 come from Isaiah 40:6–8: "The grass withers and the flowers fall, but the word of our God stands forever." The words in both of these books were written to encourage God's people. Curious about what was going on in Isaiah's time? Find out for yourself in the Old Testament.

Peter knew that if the believers remembered this, they would be able to trust and stand on God's promises in the Scriptures. The Scriptures were special not just because they were God's Word but also because they had been proven, tried, tested, and found to be true. People will come and go, much like grass, but God's Word never changes.

"Knowing this," Peter wrote, "you should have a thirst and desire to know God's Word just like a baby who craves milk. God's Word helps you grow in your faith. You have already tasted and seen that God is good to you. Continue to stand firm by trusting His Word and all that He has given you," Peter wrote.

Footwork

Look up 1 Peter 1:24–25. What does it say? Now skip down to verse 2 of chapter 2. What are we instructed to do? What will this do for us?

God's Word is much greater than anything ever written, including holy books from other religions. His Word and His Word alone has been proven to be without fault, withstanding attacks over many generations.

Fruit

You may meet people who will try to prove that the Bible is wrong or full of mistakes. Don't worry. Over the ages no one has ever been able to do this, nor will anyone ever be able to. God's Word has stood and will continue to stand against the arguments of the smartest people. It is absolute truth. There is no other book like it. You have God's lifetime guarantee on that—both for this life and the one to come!

No Comment

Taken from 1 Peter 2

— Foundation —

Spend a few minutes thinking about the suffering Jesus endured before He died on the cross and how He handled that pain. Then praise God for what Jesus did for you and the example He set.

Focus

Have you ever been unfairly blamed for something you didn't do?

Peter had just reminded the believers to stand firm on God's Word. Now he went on to remind them of Jesus' example. "Jesus suffered for you. While He was suffering, He set an example so that you will know how to act when you are suffering."

Peter knew how Jesus had lived each day—he was an eyewitness to Jesus' life. He had seen the crowds press in on Jesus, everyone wanting something and hoping to be healed. He had heard the crowds cheer when Jesus entered a village. He had seen Jesus' love, kindness, patience, and wisdom. He had heard Jesus' teachings and knew that Jesus personally lived the very things He taught. Peter had been there when Jesus did miracles and when the crowds sang His praises. He had also been there when things took a turn for the worse.

Peter closed his eyes for a moment as the memories returned. He recalled the example Jesus had set while He suffered for something He didn't do. He remembered the look of love in Jesus' eyes as Jesus thought only of those He was suffering for and not about His own circumstances. Instead of claiming His rights as God, Jesus had held His power under control—willingly. All these things burned an image in Peter's mind.

"Jesus suffered for you and left an example for you to follow," Peter wrote to the believers. "Jesus Himself did nothing wrong—He was perfect, without sin. His words were never deceitful; He spoke only the truth. When others angrily insulted Him, He didn't return their insults. Though in pain, Jesus didn't make any threats. Instead, He put His life in the hands of God the Father, knowing that God judges justly and He has the last word."

> **Hurl *means "to throw with great force and violence." Those who hurled insults at Jesus did it to hurt Him. There was no mistake; Jesus was their target.***

Peter paused a moment then continued. "Jesus, who once was cheered as a hero, suffered the insult of being put to death as an outcast. He took our sins on Himself so that we might be set free from the power of sin and live in righteousness before God."

Peter sat back and thought about how Jesus never took His eyes off the One He served. Because He was God Himself, fully deserving of worship and praise, He suffered greater insult than any of us could ever suffer. And yet, Peter thought, love still controlled His every action and thought. Jesus set an incredible example for us to follow.

Footwork

Read 1 Peter 2:23. What three things did Jesus do while he suffered. Because Jesus knew that God's judgment would come in the end, He willingly entrusted Himself to His Father. God would set the record straight at the appropriate time.

Fruit

Based on Jesus' example, how will you try to respond this week if others pick on you, make fun of you, or wrongly blame you for something you didn't do?

Let Me Tell You
Taken from 1 Peter 3—5

Foundation

Take some time to talk with God before reading today's lesson. Ask Him to quiet your thoughts so you can learn from Him.

Focus

Do others treat you differently when they discover you're a Christian?

Peter knew that sooner or later the lives of the believers would change as they followed Jesus' example (even to the point of death). Observing this change, nonbelievers would likely ask questions. Though some might ask questions out of anger or frustration, others would undoubtedly be motivated by admiration and respect for the believer's courage.

"My friends, when painful trials come into your life, don't be surprised," Peter wrote. "Instead, look at them as opportunities to tell others about Jesus. In your hearts, keep Christ as Lord. Never lose sight of Him, and live for Him in every circumstance. When people see your strong example, they'll ask what makes you so different. They'll want to know why you have so much hope. Be ready at all times to answer anyone who asks about your faith, and live your life in such a way that it will cause people to ask questions!" Peter wrote. "But when they do ask," he cautioned, "be gentle and respectful when you answer, simply telling them about the Lord and what He has done for you personally."

Peter continued, giving specific challenges about living for God. "When some people see your life, they'll think you're strange for not joining them in their activities. Some may even give you a hard time. Don't worry about it; they'll have to answer to God for their own actions. Instead, you should keep a clear mind and be self-controlled so that you will be able to pray. Express a deep love for one another, for love bears with the sins and wrongs of others. Serve others in God's strength, using the gifts and abilities He has given you. When you live for God in this way, you'll bring glory and praise to Him," Peter wrote.

"If other people insult you because you're a believer, and you suffer for the name of Christ, consider it a compliment. It's obvious that people can see God's Spirit at work in your life."

With words of encouragement to stand strong and to turn to the Lord with all their fears and anxieties, Peter closed his letter to the believers. He knew that they were suffering, but he also knew that they were in good hands. Their suffering wasn't pointless but purposeful, and their God was ever present and powerful to help them.

> *As your life brings honor to God those around you will take notice. No matter how they respond to you, you'll always have an opportunity to share your faith because of this.*

> *The term Christians occurs only twice in the New Testament—once in Acts 11:26 and once in 1 Peter 4:16. It was a label first used by people who were hostile to Christianity.*

Footwork

Look up 1 Peter 3:15. What does it say? What are you challenged to do?

as a Roman city, Aelia Capitolina,

Fruit

Reread the first sentence of 1 Peter 3:15 in your Bible. How do you think this is accomplished? Our hearts are often referred to as the place where we feel emotion. In our hearts we feel fear, frustration, joy, and love. We often let our hearts rule out our heads, and our heads rule out our actions. Not good!

This verse in 1 Peter talks about setting apart Christ as Lord. Where? In our hearts! Take a few moments to think about how you respond to circumstances around you. If you tend to react from your emotions (gut response), then you haven't set apart Christ as Lord in your heart. And, chances are, your life isn't causing others to ask questions.

Take time to do some business with God. Tell Him you want Him to be Lord of your heart. Memorize 1 Peter 3:15 and use it as your daily goal. Write it on an index card, cut it out in the shape of a crown, and stick it on your bathroom mirror as a daily reminder.

and building a temple to Jupiter on the

once stood). • AD 122 - Hadrian's Wal

2 Peter

Faith facts

Peter wrote his second letter three years after his first letter. He wrote to the same group of believers, but the use of his Jewish name (Simon) tells us that he was writing to others too.

In his first letter Peter warned and encouraged the believers about the trials and suffering they would experience from nonbelievers. In this letter he wrote to warn them about the dangers from within the church. As he instructed them about false teachings, Peter challenged them to grow up in their faith.

Peter wrote this letter while he was in Rome facing certain death. Nero killed Peter in AD 67, around the same time Paul was killed. Peter died in the same manner as Jesus—by crucifixion. Tradition tells us that Peter asked to be crucified head downward because he felt unworthy to die as Jesus had.

Measure It Up
Taken from 2 Peter 1

--- Foundation ---

Spend a few minutes praying before you begin today's lesson. Ask the Lord to show you where you stand spiritually. Ask Him to show you how you've grown and where you still need to grow. Finally, ask Him to continue helping you grow spiritually and thank Him that He's a God who cares deeply for you.

Focus

Do you ever wish you had a yardstick to measure your spiritual growth so you could know how you were doing?

Peter knew he didn't have much longer to live, and his heart yearned for the believers to whom he wrote. If they were to stand strong against false teachings, they'd need to grow.

"Through Jesus' divine power we have everything we need to live life in a godly way. This divine power comes through knowing Jesus and growing in our walk with Him," Peter wrote.

Faith in Jesus provided the foundation for the believers to begin their walk with God. Now, however, they needed to grow and mature in their faith by putting it into action and allowing it to change their lives.

So Peter went on to encourage them to add other qualities to their faith. "With the help of the Holy Spirit, build upon the foundation of faith by living a life that shows goodness." The believers needed to act on the opportunities God provided and live the way He had designed for them to live. This was the first step.

"On top of goodness," Peter wrote, describing the process of building with bricks, "add knowledge." This knowledge was a personal knowledge of God and something that would help them walk worthy of the Lord.

"On top of knowledge, add self-control," he wrote. Self-control is the determination to do what Jesus would do. Peter knew that it was one thing to be called to live a holy life and to get to know the Lord better, but it was another for believers to let that knowledge change their actions and attitudes. This brought Peter to his next building block.

"Perseverance should be added to your self-control," he stated. Perseverance is continuing to do what's right, even when your old sinful nature tries to convince you to stop. Perseverance always keeps trying to do what it sets out to accomplish.

"Then add godliness to perseverance," Peter continued. Godliness is beneficial for this life as well as in heaven.

"And on top of godliness, add brotherly kindness." By being kind, tenderhearted and forgiving of others the way Jesus had forgiven them, they would show that they had grown spiritually.

"Finally," Peter wrote, "on top of brotherly kindness, add love." Love was the highest achievement of all, for walking in love meant imitating God. The believers would only be able to walk in God's kind of love by starting out their relationship with Him through faith, and then growing in goodness, knowledge, self-control, perseverance, and godliness. As their lives demonstrated godliness, they would be able to express kindness toward other believers, and finally they would be able to show love for all people, regardless of the circumstances. These building blocks would measure their growth in the Lord.

> *Self-control isn't sheer human willpower. Thinking it is will either set you up for failure or for a fall because of pride. Self-control is a decision you make to yield your life to the control of the Holy Spirit.*

Peter knew that if the believers grew in these areas and matured in their personal walk with God, they would stand strong not only in the midst of their trials but also against false teachings.

Footwork

Look up 2 Peter 1:3. What does it say? Who gives us the strength and ability to grow spiritually? Remember that the Holy Spirit is the One who battles within us to help us become spiritually mature. We must cooperate with Him by showing self-control and by never giving up the fight.

Fruit

Where do you stand spiritually right now? Are you growing in your relationship with God, or are you still back at the first building block?

Something's Wrong Here

Taken from 2 Peter 2—3

Foundation

Thank the Lord that His Word is truth. Thank Him for the Holy Spirit, who guides you in the ways of truth. Ask the Lord to protect you from false teachers, who teach wrong things about Him.

Focus

Have you ever wondered whether you would be able to recognize a false teacher (or false teachings)?

Peter knew that as the believers matured in their faith, they would be able to spot false teachers and wrong teachings. In the meantime, however, they needed to be warned that such people existed. Some were even in the church, pretending to be believers!

"Don't be surprised when false teachers come into your fellowship and try to teach wrong things. They lay their wrong teachings next to the truth for people to consider. But be careful! These false teachers aren't always easy to spot, because they wrap their wrong teachings in just enough truth to make them seem all right at first glance," Peter warned. "Many people will unknowingly be led astray by these people.

"These false teachers are controlled by their own desires and greed,"

The Greek word for "false" is the same word from which we get the English word plastic. False teachers took their teachings and molded them (like plastic is molded) to fit people's circumstances, hoping to attract them.

Peter continued. "Their words seem smooth and even desirable, yet they lead people further away from the Lord."

Peter also knew that some people would dare to mock God, saying, "Jesus isn't coming back! He promised to return, but just look how long it's been!" These false teachers purposefully stir up doubt about the Scriptures and God's promises by making people think that truth is whatever feels right for each person. They themselves are untaught and don't know the real truth.

Peter paused for a moment before closing his letter. He knew the seriousness of the matter and knew that the believers would pay careful attention to his warning. "Now that you've been warned about such people in advance," Peter wrote, "guard yourselves so that you won't be led astray by their false teachings. Concentrate your efforts on growing in grace and in your knowledge of Jesus Christ, our Lord and Savior. If you're growing in your walk with Him, you won't fall into the traps of these people."

Footwork

Look up 2 Peter 3:17–18. According to these verses, what two areas do we need to grow in to protect ourselves from false teachers (and false teachings)?

Fruit

Many false teachers and religions use Christian words but attach different meanings to them. Don't be fooled. Be on your guard and continue to grow in your walk with the Lord.

People who work in banks can spot counterfeit (false) money not because they study the different counterfeits but because they're very familiar with the real thing. Counterfeits will always come along; you can count on that! But those who know God's truth inside and out can easily spot anything false.

Judah lead a Jewish revolt due to

Hadrian's antiJewish persecutions.

1, 2, 3 John
(Selections from 1 John)

Of all the disciples, the apostle John—the writer of 1, 2, and 3 John—was closest to Jesus. He is believed to have been born in the city of Bethsaida, the hometown of Philip, Andrew, and Peter. John was also the author of the gospel of John and the book of Revelation.

Although John didn't clearly say who he was writing to, it's believed that he sent his letter to the church in Ephesus where he spent the last years of his life. In our reading through the New Testament, we will study only 1 John. You might want to read 2 and 3 John on your own—they contain some great treasures.

The purpose of 1 John is to give assurance to all believers. It seemed that some of the believers were fighting with one another while others were quietly doubting their own salvation. With love and tenderness, John wrote to encourage them and set the record straight.

As you read through 1 John, take your time. Notice the great sense of encouragement you gain as you study this book. ———————————————

D 135 — Jerusalem is destroyed.

Testing ... 1, 2, 3
Taken from 1 John 1—3

Foundation

Take time to prepare your heart before today's lesson, just as you've been doing throughout this devotional. Get real before God by coming honestly and humbly before Him.

Do you ever worry that you might not really be a Christian?

Guilt, guilt, and more guilt. Guilt over arguments, guilt over messing up and giving in to sin, guilt over a lack of love for others. The believers John was writing to were struggling with major guilt!

John knew those feelings well. With his strong personality, he had sometimes been unkind toward others. As a matter of fact, Jesus even nicknamed him and his brother, James, "the Sons of Thunder!" But in spite of John's personality trait, Jesus was able to change John's life for the better.

John knew that the believers to whom he was writing needed encouragement. They needed to be challenged to be honest before God. In so doing, they would improve not only their relationship with Him but also their relationships with one another. They would be able to stand their ground against Satan and the doubts he tried to place in their minds concerning their salvation.

John pulled out his parchment and set to writing. "What I'm writing to you concerns Jesus, who is the Word of Life. I have not only heard Him with my own ears and seen Him with my own eyes, but I've actually touched Him,

Rabbi Akiva is martyred. Jews are

personally experienced His friendship, and know Him to be true."

John was older now, and those to whom he wrote had never had the opportunity to see the things he had seen with his own eyes. Because he was an apostle and one of Jesus' original disciples, he could write about these things with authority.

"If we insist that we never sin, we're only fooling ourselves. But if we admit our sin to our faithful and just God, He will forgive us. Not only will He forgive us, but He will also cleanse our hearts and purify our lives from everything that isn't righteous and holy."

John had tried this promise and knew it to be true. He also knew that believing God and doing what He says shows what a person really believes and whether they really know Him. "If we follow His commands, we can be assured that we know Him," he wrote.

Then he went on to say that true believers aren't ruled by hate but instead are willing to confess their wrong attitudes and ask God to forgive them. They don't make a habit of sinning, although they may sin at times and make mistakes. They don't love the world or live for its treasures, but instead they love Jesus and aren't ashamed to tell others about Him. A perfect life isn't an indicator of a true believer, for no one can be perfect. Rather, the true evidence that a person belongs to God's family is a life that seeks God and desires to live for Him.

John paused a moment as he thought about God's amazing love. Then he continued writing, hoping that his words would sink deeply into the

> *According to 1 John 1:9, "God is faithful and just." That means we can be assured He will forgive our sins (because He is faithful) and that doing so doesn't compromise His holiness (because He is just). All that's left for us to do is confess our sins.*

> **Confess** *simply means "to agree with God." When you confess your sins, you agree with God (who knows exactly what you've done) that you did something wrong. You can then ask His forgiveness.*

believers' hearts. "Think about it! God has heaped His incredible love upon us and calls us His children! The Father sent the Son to be the Savior of the world. We can stand confident in this and know that we live in Him and that He lives in us. We know this because God has given us His Spirit."

Footwork

Look up 1 John 2:6 in your Bible. What does this verse tell you? This is where the rubber meets the road!

Fruit

As we strive to walk as Jesus did, we'll mess up and do wrong things—much like John did. When we fail, we often feel guilty and begin to hide from God (just like Adam and Eve did!). Much to Satan's pleasure, we also begin to doubt our salvation. The more Satan accuses us, the guiltier we feel, and the guiltier we feel, the more we doubt—and the more we hide from God.

The way to avoid falling into this trap is to stand firm on God's promises. Look up 1 John 1:9 and read it for yourself. Mark this verse. Now read it aloud and say your name in the place of the words *we* and *us*.

Do you need to confess anything to God right now? Take time right now to do it. Also, commit this verse to memory and use it whenever Satan tries to lay a guilt trip on you or get you to doubt your salvation.

All This Is Mine?
Taken from 1 John 4—5

Foundation

As you finish 1 John, ask the Lord to help you become more assured of your salvation. Ask Him to work in your life so that you'll be able to reflect His love to others.

Focus

Do you ever wonder why loving others is so important to God?

John sat staring at the parchment, his heart full of love for the believers he was writing to. He had already encouraged those who doubted their salvation. Now he would go a step further and reassure them of all the treasures they had because of God's love. Once they understood this, they could return that love to God by loving one another.

Putting his pen to the parchment, John described for the believers what God's love is like. "We don't understand love because we love God," he wrote. "No, God showed us real, true love by sending His Son as a sacrifice for our sins to make us 'at one' with Him." God's love didn't depend on what others did. It was a love of action and giving to those who didn't deserve it. God gave the very best He had for the very worst of us.

John continued writing, "God's love casts away all our fears and allows us to grow. His love helps change our desires so that we don't make a habit of sinning. Because of God's love, we're able to ask Him anything in prayer and know that He hears us. His love keeps us safe so the Evil One

excommunicated in Rome for heretical

359

> *Love isn't a feeling; it's an action. It's looking out for the highest interests of others. That's what God does for us. And that's what He expects us to do for others.*
>
> ---
>
> *In the Old Testament the Jewish people knew that loving God meant obeying Him. The two went hand in hand.*

(Satan) can't harm us. The world is under Satan's power, but we are children of God and belong to His family. This is all because of God's love and what He did for us through Jesus."

The believers were familiar with this, yet John knew they needed to be reminded. Knowing and acting are two different things. "Dear friends," John wrote, "let us love one another for love comes from God. Whoever fails to love must not know God, because the very nature of God is love. Since God (who is so mighty) loved us (who are so sinful), we have little choice but to love one another. In so doing, we obey His commands and express love back to Him. Real love is to obey His commands."

The believers who didn't express God's love were in danger of drifting away from Him. Perhaps they were too busy or too tired to love one another. Or perhaps God's love had met their needs, so they didn't think to look beyond themselves and their own wants to the needs and interests of others.

John closed his letter with a simple sentence that would stand as a challenge for all believers throughout time: "My dear children," John warned, "don't turn to idols or to anything that would keep you from returning God's love."

Footwork

Turn to 1 John 4:19–21 in your Bible. According to this verse, why do we love? Why is loving others so important? (*Hint:* There are two reasons—one is found in verse 20, and one is in verse 21.)

Fruit

An idol isn't just a statue that sits on a shelf. It is anything that takes the place of God or what He commands you to do. Idol worship involves loving things more than you love God. At times you'll be tempted to trade all the treasures you have in God's love for things that can't satisfy—or that even come close. Although these other things may seem promising, they only lead to emptiness. Don't give in. Guard your heart and respond to God's love with love for Him. Show Him love by doing what He commands.

jude

Jude was written eighteen years after the book of James and almost twenty-seven years before the books of 1, 2, and 3 John. In our Bibles, however, we find it coming after 1, 2, and 3 John. (Remember, the New Testament isn't put together in the order it was written.)

Jude, like James, was a half-brother of Jesus. Since Jesus was born of the Holy Spirit, He only had his mother (Mary) in common with His brothers, who were also born of Mary but had an earthly father, Joseph. Like James, Jude didn't believe in Jesus as the Savior when Jesus was still alive. Not until after the resurrection did Jude come to realize that the words Jesus had said about Himself were true. At that point, Jude became a believer in Christ.

Although this book applies to all believers, Jude addressed his letter to Jewish Christians. In it, he warned against those who come into the church and try to lead believers away from their faith in Jesus.

As you read this book, notice what Jude had to say about false believers. Also, be encouraged by the final note of victory all believers share in Jesus.

Watch It!
Taken from Jude v. 1–23

Foundation

Spend time thanking God for His truth and for giving you the ability to know Him. Ask Him to protect you from the influence of those who might try to pull you away from Him.

Focus

Do you ever wonder how some people get pulled into false religions and cults?

As much as Jude wanted to write a joyful letter celebrating salvation, God had burdened him with a different message. He knew he must write what God had placed on his heart.

"Dear friends," Jude began, "I wanted very much to write about the salvation we all share, but God impressed something else on my heart. I felt that I needed to give you a word of warning about certain impostors who have slipped into your fellowship."

The impostors Jude described were men who had joined up with the believers, pretending to be one of them when actually they were enemies. "These godless men distort the meaning of God's grace by making it into an opportunity to sin. Not only that, they deny Jesus Christ our Lord."

Jude continued, describing how these people behave and the judgment they will one day face. He also compared their actions to those of three men in the Old Testament. "May they be cursed, because they have created their own ways of worship, and they hate those who are righteous, much like Cain hated his brother, Abel. They pretend to serve God while encouraging others to sin so they might gain from it, much like Balaam. They rebel against God's authority by standing against those God puts in charge, much like Korah led a revolt against God's chosen leaders, Moses and Aaron. Their only end is destruction."

Jude described these impostors as "clouds without rain"—they made all kinds of promises but didn't deliver and were soon gone, just like a cloud driven by the wind. Such people were like uprooted autumn trees that bore no fruit. With no spiritual foundation, they bore no spiritual fruit. Without a foundation or fruit, they were as good as dead!

Jude then turned from a warning to a challenge for the believers to resist being taken in by such impostors. "Dear friends, build yourselves up by growing in your knowledge of the faith." By "the faith," Jude meant the true teachings the believers had received from the apostles, which were now recorded in Scripture. The more they built themselves up in Scripture, the better able they would be to stand against falsehood. "Keep on praying as you are directed by God's Holy Spirit, and stay in God's love," he instructed. This meant that they were to continue depending on the Holy Spirit in all areas of their spiritual lives and to grow even more in their love for God. The believers were to keep their eyes focused on Jesus who was their hope.

Jude's final words summed up everything he

Jude also compared impostors to shooting stars that gave little light and had no direction. Unlike the fixed stars by which sailors navigated their boats, those who plotted their course by shooting stars would only be led astray and lost.

In Acts 20:29–31 Paul compared false teachers to savage wolves who distort the truth, lead believers astray, and destroy their faith in the Lord. Peter also gave a strong warning about false teachers in 2 Peter 2:1–3. Jude's words both summarize the unseen dangers of false teaching and remind believers to be on their guard against it.

Marcus Aurelius rules Rome. While on a

365

had written: "Stand and fight for the faith," he wrote. By living and fighting for the truth, the believers would be fighting against impostors and false teachings.

Footwork

Find Jude v. 3 in your Bible. (Note: Since Jude is only one chapter long, this number refers to the verse.) The word *contend* means "to do battle for, to defend." Now skip down to verses 17, 20, and 21. According to these verses, how do we contend for our faith?

Fruit

Enemies of the gospel don't wear big signs stating that fact. Rather, they work undercover, trying to win the favor of others and then leading them astray. Jesus warned about such people. Today we have a term for groups of people who do this: *cults.* Cults usually have a leader who is likeable and thought of as great or wise. Some may claim to have a word from God or have special abilities. They often try to separate you from your family, or they may have peculiar rules to follow. Watch out for cults. Take the steps Jude instructed believers to take to protect themselves from false teachers: build up your faith, pray, keeping yourself in God's love, and look to Jesus. These will keep your focus and head in the right place.

Victory! Yesss!
Taken from v. Jude 20–25

Foundation

Spend a few minutes praising God for His power and strength.

Thank Him that He is in control and sees and knows everything.

Thank Him that He has the final word on things.

Focus

Have you ever been in a situation where all you could do was try your best and hope that everything would work out?

"Keep growing in faith, keep praying as you are directed by God's Holy Spirit, stay in God's love, and wait on His mercy." Jude knew all these were important things to do when watching out for false teachers and impostors. Believers needed to do these things for themselves.

With a sigh of relief, Jude's thoughts soared upward as he recalled the One who really gives the victory. This victory isn't just protection against impostors; it also applies to every area of a believer's life!

"Praise be to Jesus, the One who keeps us from falling." Jude's pen seemed to explode across the page in a final note of triumph. He knew that believers would stumble and fall. They would make mistakes

> *Closing a letter with praise was something typically done at the end of a synagogue service. It also fulfilled Jude's original desire to write in joyful terms to the Jewish believers (verse 3).*

and mess up, but God was still in control. Jesus was faithful and more than able to keep the souls of believers and protect those who had given their lives to Him.

"Not only will Jesus keep you from falling," Jude wrote, "but when He presents you to the Father in all His glory and splendor, you will stand before Him with overwhelming joy because you are spotless and blameless in Christ." There were no greater words of encouragement and confidence that Jude could have given to believers. Victory and success did not rest on the shoulders of each believer like something they were responsible for; they rested in the hands of Jesus. Believers didn't have to just hope everything would work out; they could know it would.

Jude then ended his letter on a note of celebration and victory: "There's only One worthy of eternal glory, majesty, power, and authority that comes through the Lord Jesus Christ: God our Savior! Amen."

Footwork

Find Jude v. 24–25 in your Bible. What do these verses tell you? What is the result of Jesus' keeping us from falling? (See verse 25.)

Fruit

Jude v. 24 is another great verse to put in your memory bank. It's a reminder that we have victory through Someone who is far greater than we are—Jesus!

Take a piece of paper or an index card and copy down this verse. On the back of the card, draw a picture of the things that cause you to fall (your attitudes, your relationships with others, and so on). Spend a few minutes giving these things over to God. Then place this verse where you'll see it every morning. For the next five days read it while you're dressing and remind yourself of the victory you have in Christ. Then, as you face your day and stumble into the things that tend to make you fall, remember the victory you have in Jesus and act accordingly.

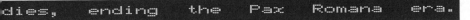

dies, ending the Pax Romana era.

From this point the Roman Empire begins

Revelation

The Greek word for "revelation" is apokalupsis, which means "unveiling, unwrapping, uncovering something that was hidden." The book of Revelation centers on one thing alone: Jesus Christ. It not only reveals details about Jesus (such as the fact that He is Judge, Redeemer, and triumphant King) but also describes future events (such as the judgment of people, nations, and sin).

The apostle John, who wrote the gospel of John and 1, 2, and 3 John, also wrote Revelation. As you may remember, John lived in Ephesus at the end of his life and was one of the last apostles who were still alive.

When John wrote the book of Revelation, however, he was living in exile on the island of Patmos (a type of prison island) where he'd been sent by the Roman emperor Domitian. Domitian insisted that all people worship him and demanded to be called "lord" and "god." Those who refused to do so were punished or put to death. John was on the island of Patmos because he refused to worship the emperor.

As you read through the book of Revelation, hang in there. Some parts of this book are difficult to understand. Some parts we may not fully understand until we get to heaven. Keep your mind on Jesus who is the center and focus of this book. Don't get distracted by the little stuff like when certain things might happen. All you really need to know is that if God said they'll happen, they will!

If we were to tackle the entire book of Revelation, we'd need a separate devotional dedicated solely to this book. Instead, we'll read through portions of Revelation just to get a taste and feel for what it's all about. ——

to decline. . . . .

That Hits Close to Home
Taken from Revelation 1—3

Foundation

Before you read today's lesson, stop and ask the Lord to speak to your heart through His Word. Ask Him to help you get a better picture of who He is and who you are.

Focus

Has someone ever corrected you for something you were doing wrong but didn't show you how to do it right? Jesus doesn't deal with us that way.

John wrote his letter of the Revelation to seven churches in the province of Asia that were on a mail route. If you look at a Bible map, you'll find Ephesus, the first city on the route, on the coastline of Asia not far from the island of Patmos. Then going north, you'll find Smyrna, then Pergamum. Then the route turns east and heads south. The rest of the cities followed: Thyatira, Sardis, Philadelphia, and Laodicea.

These seven cities each had a church to which John addressed a special part of his letter. As John's letter was passed along the mail route, members of each church read the whole letter and gave special attention to the section specifically directed to them.

John began his letter of the Revelation by focusing his readers on the person of Jesus. "To him who loves us and has freed us from our sins by his blood … to him be glory and power for ever and ever!"

Next, John described how he was on the island of Patmos when God gave him this vision and told him what to write. John began with the words Jesus said about Himself: "I am the beginning and ending of everything. I am the eternal Almighty—Alpha and Omega." Then John tried to describe all that Jesus allowed him to see in his vision.

As John wrote to each church the things Jesus told him, he noticed that each description Jesus gave about Himself fit a specific need that particular church had.

The first church was in Ephesus. According to the Lord, Ephesus had one problem: The believers had abandoned their "first love" (who was Jesus). They hadn't lost their love; they had just left it. Jesus described Himself to them as the One who empowers the church and makes His dwelling among believers. He is the powerful One, their Protector and Provider. They needed to remember this, repent of their wrongdoing, and rekindle their love for Him.

The next church was in Smyrna. In this city, emperor worship was required. Those who chose not to worship him faced great persecution. To this church Jesus had nothing bad to say; instead, he encouraged them to endure persecution even if it led to death. He reassured them that He is the Alpha and the Omega and the Conqueror of death. (This church still exists today in the city of Izmir, Turkey.)

The church of Pergamum, on the other hand, didn't receive a good report. Although Jesus at first praised these believers for remaining true to their faith, they hadn't grown. They also tolerated false teachers. Jesus described Himself as the Judge who would judge their actions with a two-edged sword (the Word of God) coming from His mouth.

Alpha is the very first letter of the Greek alphabet; Omega is the very last letter. Jesus' comparison of Himself to those letters signifies that He is both the beginning and the end of all that matters in life.

The name Smyrna comes from the Greek word myrrh and is a picture of suffering. The believers in Smyrna suffered great persecution. Interestingly, this church is one of the few that still exist today!

Jesus said the church at Thyatira was improving but still tolerated sin. He described Himself to them as the holy Son of God, full of purity—looking at them with laser-beam eyes to see what was inside. Instead of the danger coming from outside sources, the church of Thyatira was rotting from the inside! By the end of the second century, this church had vanished.

The next church, Sardis, was accused of being dead. Once it was a great church but no more. Little by little these believers began to change until, finally, all that remained was a group of people playing church. They didn't have God's Spirit living in them. Jesus described Himself as the One who has and gives the Holy Spirit and who gives power and life.

The church in Philadelphia was the next church mentioned. Of this church Jesus said only good things. Philadelphia was a missionary church and a gateway to spreading the gospel in the East. Jesus said that even though they had little strength, they kept His word and hadn't denied Him. Although it wasn't a perfect church, the believers there pleased God. Jesus described Himself as the One who is holy (set apart) and true—the One who has the keys and rewards of heaven.

The last city on the mail route, Laodicea, had its water piped in from a nearby city. By the time the water reached them, it was lukewarm and unappetizing to drink. Jesus used a description these believers would fully understand. Accusing them of being lukewarm, Jesus stated that He would spit them out of His mouth. These believers felt they needed nothing and were doing fine when actually they were spiritually poor, blind, and naked in the Lord's eyes. To them, Jesus described Himself as being "the faithful and true witness—the Amen." Everything He says is always true, including His description of this church, what He desires, and what He provides.

Footwork

Read Revelation 1:3. What does this verse say? How should you respond to the words of the Revelation?

Fruit

Take a moment to review Jesus' descriptions of each of the churches. Which description would you say best describes your walk with Jesus? When you find one that seems to describe you best, read what Jesus has to say about Himself and His character—and what He promises to provide for you. Take Him up on His promise; make a change if needed. Live your life in such a way that will honor Him. Then enjoy being honored by Him when he says, "Well done, good and faithful servant!" (Matthew 25:21).

The Reason
Taken from Revelation 4—7

— Foundation —

Spend some time in prayer, asking God to help you gain a better understanding of Jesus' glory and the worship that's due Him. Ask Him to help you appreciate all the more who He is and what He has done.

Focus

Do you ever wonder why Jesus is waiting so long to come back?

John saw a magnificent scene in heaven, a glimpse of Jesus' glory and all the amazing things that are to come. Because our minds and eyes have never envisioned something so awesome, we have a hard time understanding the things John saw.

John began by describing a throne in heaven. The One sitting on the throne looked like precious stones—jasper, much like a brilliant diamond, and a carnelian (a red ruby). Beautiful beyond all comparison, the throne was circled by an emerald-colored rainbow.

Around the main throne, twenty-four elders sat on twenty-four lesser thrones. Their crowns weren't like that of a king but rather like those rewarded to runners who finished as winners in the Greek games. It isn't clear whether these elders represent believers who have been rewarded in heaven or angels who have been given great responsibilities. But either way, the point is that they were worshipping God, the One sitting on the throne. John also saw lightning and heard thunder coming from the throne. Standing in front of the throne were seven lamps that symbolized the Holy Spirit. John also saw in front of the throne a sea of glass that was as clear as crystal. And around the throne were four living beings, which John compared to a lion, an ox, a man, and a flying eagle. Each being had eyes covering it and six wings. We don't fully understand the significance of these beings, but some suggest that they represent God's character. He is all-knowing and all-present (the eyes and wings). The lion represents His power and majesty. The ox shows His faithful work and patience. The man represents intelligence, and the eagle represents God's supreme rule and authority.

The important thing to note is not what these beings were but rather what they did, which was worship God as the Creator of the universe. The elders worshipped God by laying their crowns before His throne, which set the stage for Jesus.

Next, John saw Jesus as the Lamb of God and heard those who were worshipping say, "Worthy is Jesus, for He was slain, and He purchased with His blood people from every tribe, people group, and nation on earth, and from every language.... Praise, glory, power, and honor belong to the One who sits on the throne and to Jesus, the Lamb!"

After this, John looked up and saw a great number of people that couldn't be counted—believers from every tribe, people group, nation, and language standing before Jesus in white robes. Then he told of the judgment that would come upon the world in God's perfect timing.

When we reach that perfect time, Jesus will come back as He promised—suddenly and with great victory. Until that time His Word must be preached around the world so that people from every tribe, every language, and every nation will have a chance to be included with those who worship around God's throne.

Interestingly, the jasper and carnelian stones were the first and the last of the twelve gemstones worn across the High Priest's robe.

Daniel, a book in the Old Testament, also has much to say about the end times.

Footwork

Turn to Revelation 7:10 in your Bible and notice what it says about salvation. Now look at verse 9. Who is singing this praise?

Fruit

Will some people be in heaven because they heard about Jesus from you? Your faithfulness to share the gospel and live a God-honoring life has an impact on people that's far greater than you can ever know. Live for God until Jesus returns.

Journey Onward!
Taken from Revelation 19—22

Foundation

As you finish the book of Revelation, notice Jesus in all His glory, might, honor and power. He is the Victor. He will come back again as He promised; with each day His return draws nearer.

Focus

Do you ever wonder what heaven will be like—and whether it will be boring?

"I saw heaven opened," John described, "and a white horse with One sitting upon it who is called Faithful and True. In righteousness He will judge and wage war. His eyes are like flames of fire, and He wears many crowns upon His head. He is clothed with a robe dipped in blood and He comes for final judgment and victory. His name is called the Word of God. All the armies of heaven were clothed in fine white robes and were following Him upon white horses. And on His robe and His thigh He bore this name: king of kings and lord of lords."

John went on to describe Jesus' return to earth, writing about the great judgments that would come and how Satan would be cast into the lake of fire. The earth as we know it will pass away, but a new heaven and earth will be created—much different and far better. We don't know what it will look like, except that it will have no sea. John then went on to describe the New Jerusalem that came down to earth from heaven.

"Then a new Jerusalem (the city where God lives) came down from heaven to earth," John wrote, "and a loud voice from the great white throne said, 'Look! God has come down from heaven to live with His people forever. They belong to Him, and He is their God. He will dry all their tears and will take away all pain and mourning and death, for the old world and life no longer exist.' Then the voice said, 'I am doing a brand-new thing!'"

> *In his gospel, John recorded Jesus' words about heaven: "I am going there to prepare a place for you. And ... I will come back and take you to be with me that you also may be where I am" (John 14:2–3). This very well may describe the New Jerusalem.*

Then an angel took John on a tour of the New Jerusalem, which was filled with God's glory. Gleaming like precious gemstones, it was surrounded by four high walls with three pearl gates on each side. As for size, the city measured 1,400 miles in length, width, and height, and the wall surrounding it was 216 feet thick! The city looked like gold but was clear like glass. The city wall had twelve foundation stones, and on each of them the names of the twelve apostles were written.

John noticed that there was no temple in the New Jerusalem. This was because the Lord God (the Almighty) and the Lamb (Jesus) were its temple. The city also had no sun or moon to shine upon it because the glory of the Lord supplied it with blazing light.

When this new heavenly Jerusalem comes down to the new earth, the curse of Adam and Eve will end. No healing will be necessary. God and the Lamb will live forever in the new city, and God's throne will also be in it. Our highest joy and privilege will be to serve our Lord for eternity and rule with Him. We will see Him face-to-face, and His name will be written on our foreheads, showing that we belong to Him!

As John finished his letter, he stated that everything he had written about was true. Then he gave a warning: "If anyone adds to these words, God will pour out on him the judgments written in this book. And anyone who leaves out any words of this prophecy will lose the inheritance written about in this book."

Then John heard the final words of Jesus. "In a very short time I will be coming back."

As John pondered the awesome things he had seen in the future, he knew that eternal life with God would be far from boring! Then in closing John breathed a prayer that expressed the longing of every believer: "Yes! Come back soon, Lord Jesus!"

Footwork

In your Bible, look up Revelation 22:7. What does Jesus say to us? Who will be blessed?

Fruit

Your relationship with God begins here on earth and continues in heaven (the New Jerusalem). Continue on your journey with God and keep growing in your relationship with Jesus. Even though you've arrived at the end of this book, much ground still waits to be covered. Look up Revelation 22:21. Never forget that we live by the grace of the Lord Jesus Christ. Keep your focus ever on Him.

Faith facts

A Special Message Just for You!

The most important decision you will ever make in your life is the choice to either accept or reject Jesus. Some people think they can get by without making this decision, but that isn't true. Jesus said that if you don't choose to follow Him, you're actually choosing to reject Him!

In the Bible we learn these facts about ourselves and God's gift of salvation:

- We're all sinners (Romans 3:23), and we aren't able to live up to God's standards of holiness. *Sin* means "to miss the mark or target." No matter how hard we try, we'll always fall short of God's standards. This creates a big problem because it means that no human can ever get to heaven by trying to live a good life. And this creates another problem because God is righteous and He must punish sin.

- The consequences of sin is death (Romans 6:23). This death is not only physical but spiritual. Just as physical death separates us from our loved ones, spiritual death separates us from the love of God. Those who have sin in their lives can't enter heaven where God is.

- "The gift of God is eternal life" (Romans 6:23). Because of God's great love and mercy (John 3:16), He sent His Son, Jesus, to die on a cross and pay the penalty for our sins. We didn't earn this gift and don't deserve it.

- We must receive this gift from God (John 1:12). Just as a gift isn't ours until we accept it, we must choose to accept God's gift of eternal life in Jesus.

In John 14:6, we learn that there is only one way to have our sins forgiven so we can experience a right relationship with God and then go to heaven to be with Him when we die. Jesus said, "I am the way and the truth and the life. No one comes to the Father except through me."

You can receive this gift by believing upon the Lord Jesus Christ. When you do this, you become a child of God and belong to God's forever family. Eternal life doesn't begin when you die; it's a relationship that begins right here and now—the moment you receive Jesus Christ as your Savior—and then simply continues on in heaven when your days on earth have ended.

How can you begin this relationship? You can simply pray to God and tell Him that you want a relationship with Him. There's no special formula or words. God offers you the gift of salvation and is waiting for you to accept it.

Tell God you're sorry for your sins. (Sins are any wrong things you do or wrong attitudes you have, such as anger, pride, selfishness, and so on.) Ask God to forgive you. Tell Him you want to become a part of His forever family.

Thank Jesus for dying on the cross for your sins and for taking your punishment. Ask Him to come into your life and make you the kind of person He wants you to be. Jesus said that He will give eternal life to anyone who comes to Him.

Now that you've asked Jesus to come into your life, you've begun your walk with God. Just like newborn babies need to grow, you need to grow too. You do this by reading your Bible, praying, going to church, and seeking to live the kind of life that pleases God.

Congratulations! You've just begun an exciting and life-changing journey!

Bibliography

Anthony, Michael J., and Warren S. Benson. *Exploring the History & Philosophy of Christian Education*. Grand Rapids: Kregel, 2003.

Walvoord, John F., and Roy B. Zuck. *The Bible Knowledge Commentary, New Testament*. Colorado Springs: Scripture Press, 1983.

Walvoord, John F., and Roy B. Zuck. *The Bible Knowledge Commentary, Old Testament*. Colorado Springs: Scripture Press, 1985.

Bruce, F.F. *Paul: Apostle of the Heart Set Free*. Grand Rapids: Eerdmans, 1977.

Keener, Craig S. *The IVP Bible Background Commentary, New Testament*. Downer's Grove, IL: InterVarsity Press, 1993.

Walton, John H., Victor H. Matthews, and Mark W. Chavalas. *The IVP Bible Background Commentary, Old Testament*. Downer's Grove, IL: InterVarsity Press, 2000.

Johnson, Joni A. *World History & Literature*. Dayton, OH: Blue Earth Publishing, 1997.

Life Application Study Bible. Wheaton, IL: Tyndale, 1996.

Master Study Bible, NASB. Nashville: Broadman & Holman Bible Publishers, 1981.

NASB Open Bible, Expanded Edition. Nashville: Thomas Nelson, 1985.

NIV Study Bible. Grand Rapids: Zondervan, 1995.

Hyndman, Rob J. *The Times: A Chronology of the Bible,* Rob J. Hyndman (online PDF material) www-personal.buseco.monash.edu.au/~hyndman/bible/times/contents.htm.

Gundry, Robert. *A Survey of the New Testament,* 3rd ed. Grand Rapids: Zondervan, 1994.

Stanton, Mary, and Albert Hyma. *Streams of Civilization, Vol. 1*. Arlington Heights, IL: Christian Liberty Press, 1992.

Chisholm, Jane. *Usborne Book of the Ancient World*. Tulsa, OK: EDC Publishing, 1991.

Word Sight, "Bible Time-line," Word Sight, http://www.wordsight.org/btl/000_btl-fp.htm.